IRISH TRAMS

James Kilroy

COLOURPOINT

For Helen, Claire and Mia

The Colourpoint Logo
The Colourpoint is one of the most beautiful of all the long-haired cat breeds. Persian in temperament and shape, it has the coloured points of the Siamese on the face, ears, paws and tail. The Colourpoint logo depicts a real blue-cream point kitten, Lady Jane Grey, and was drawn by Rhoda McClure, a fifth form art student at Omagh Academy, Co Tyrone.

© J. Kilroy
Dublin
1996

ISBN 1 898392 02 1

Cover design: Norman & Sheila Johnston
Layout and design: Norman Johnston
Edited by: Norman Johnston
Typeset by: Colourpoint Press
Film output: Typeform Repro
Printed by: ColourBooks

NOTE: In writing this book it was difficult at times to distinguish between *railways* and *tramways*. All systems using horse or electric traction have been included, but with steam trams there is a grey area between tramways and light railways. To qualify for inclusion in this book I have taken the view that steam tramways must at some stage have used tramway type locomotives and must, even in part, run through the streets of a town or city. Some systems which by Act of Parliament were legally *tramways*, have therefore been excluded.

Colourpoint Press
Omagh Business Complex
Gortrush
OMAGH
Co. Tyrone
BT78 5LS

Tel: 01662 249494
Fax: 01662 249451

Title page: **Open-top Dublin electric tram No 11 in original condition. This tram was built for the Dublin Southern Districts Tramways, as an electric car, by Milnes in 1896. She was a 53 seater on a Peckham truck. After takeover by the DUTC, she was put on the Clonsilla and Dartry lines until 1910. In 1915 or 1916 she was given a vestibule and then operated on the Kingsbridge line. She was replaced in 1925 by a new 'Standard' tram. The photograph was taken outside Monkstown church around the time of the opening of the line in 1896. A colour drawing of this type of car can be seen on page 88.**

W Lawrence, author's collection

CONTENTS

ACKNOWLEDGEMENTS

When it comes to gathering and assimilating material, an author is very dependant on the advice and direction of knowledgeable people. My name may be on the cover as author but my task could not have been accomplished alone. It was necessary for me to approach many people in my endeavour to collect and collate and, without their help, this book would not have entered print. To begin with, I would like to thank Norman Johnston for coercing me to accomplish the task; and, together with his wife Sheila, for their constant kind words of encouragement along the way. My deepest gratitude goes to my wife Helen for typing and re-typing the text many times, and for her countless corrections of my grammatical errors. Charles Friel did a valuable and painstaking proof read of the final manuscript.

My good friend Michael Corcoran, President of the Transport Museum Society deserves thanks for permitting me a preview of his forthcoming book on Dublin trams, *Through Streets Broad and Narrow*, and for his observations and indeed corrections, especially of the Dublin material. Similarly, my gratitude to Walter McGrath for his invaluable assistance concerning the Cork trams and some of the smaller systems. The same expression of gratitude goes to Cecil Slator, and the late Reg Ludgate (who sadly passed away while this book was in preparation) for their expert help with the Belfast chapters. Michael Pollard, and Alfred Montgomery (Assistant Keeper of Industrial Archeology at the Ulster Museum) gave considerable guidance with the other Northern material. In drawing the maps for this book I have relied heavily upon the painstaking work of JC Gillham, whose hand-drawn maps are second to none.

I am very grateful for those who made their photographic collections available to me. These included many of those mentioned above, but also a special thanks to John Kennedy, Charles Friel, Barry Carse, Jim Tinneny, Mike Maybin, Ron White and also the Irish Railway Record Society. I was very dependant on artwork to provide colour of most tramway systems apart from Belfast and the GNR lines. In this regard I am very thankful to An Post for making available Charles Roycroft's excellent drawings for the 1986 set of stamps, and to the Lord O'Neill for permission to use the painting by Sean Bolan of the Blessington tram.

Where tramway matters were concerned, thanks to Bill Garrioch for permitting me to browse through his vast collection of material. I enjoyed the many hours with Bert (Harold) Brown, listening to his fascinating stories about Dublin trams. I recall my chats with Sam Twaddle concerning the Causeway Tram. Tom Redmond and the late Dick McGlue also deserve my gratitude for their information on the Hill of Howth trams. I acknowledge the patience shown to me by fellow Museum members Pat Kirwan, Jack Kinane, Liam Kelly, Marcus Cashen, Jim Crosland, Bob Dawson and especially John Kelleher and John Wheatley. A special thanks to Julie Fegan and Colm O'Mahony for commenting on the many route maps. A 'thank you' to my friend David Dunne for the care he took in developing many of the black and white photographs.

I also want to take the opportunity to express my sincere gratitude to Captain Christopher Gaisford St Lawrence, the owner of Howth Castle, for providing the facilities for the Transport Museum at the castle, which have enabled the continued restoration of Irish trams.

Most people are well capable of writing a book, but without the support and encouragement of knowledgeable people and friends, their dreams perish. I have been very fortunate indeed.

Finally I would like to thank my readers for buying this book. I hope you enjoy reading it as much as I enjoyed writing it.

Jim Kilroy

January 1996

ABBREVIATIONS USED IN THIS BOOK

AEC	Associated Electrical Company	DK1	Dick Kerr bogied rebuild of a Belfast Standard Red
BBCPJR	Ballymena, Ballymoney, Coleraine and Portrush Junction Railway	DLER	Dublin and Lucan Electric Railway
BCDR	Belfast and County Down Railway	DL&LST	Dublin, Lucan and Leixlip Steam Tramway
BCR	Belfast Central Railway	DNGR	Dundalk, Newry and Greenore Railway
BKT	Blackrock and Kingstown Tramway	DSDT	Dublin Southern Districts Tramways
BNCR	Belfast and Northern Counties Railway	DSER	Dublin South Eastern Railway
BNT	Bessbrook and Newry Tramway	DSPCA	Dublin Society for the Prevention of Cruelty to Animals
BST	Belfast Street Tramways	DTC	Dublin Tramways Company
BTH	British Thompson Houston	DWWR	Dublin, Wicklow and Wexford Railway
CBPR	Cork, Blackrock and Passage Railway	DUTC	Dublin United Tramways Company
CBR	Cork and Bandon Railway	GNRI	Great Northern Railway of Ireland
CBSCR	Cork, Bandon and South Coast Railway	GPO	General Post Office
CCR	Cork City Railway	GSR	Great Southern Railways
CDR	County Donegal Railways	GSWR	Great Southern and Western Railway
CDT	City of Dublin Tramways	IRRS	Irish Railway Record Society
CHHT	Clontarf and Hill of Howth Tramway	LLSR	Londonderry and Lough Swilly Railway
CIE	Córas Iompair Éireann	LMS	London, Midland and Scottish Railway (owned NCC)
CMDR	Cork and Macroom Direct Railway	LUAS	Irish for 'speed'
CMLR	Cork and Muskerry Light Railway	MGWR	Midland Great Western Railway
CVBT	Castlederg and Victoria Bridge Tramway	NCC	Northern Counties Committee (successor to the BNCR)
CVR	Clogher Valley Railway	NDST	North Dublin Street Tramways
CWT	Cavehill and Whitewell Tramway	NIRTB	Northern Ireland Road Transport Board
CYR	Cork and Youghal Railway	NWRR	Newry, Warrenpoint and Rostrevor Railway
DART	Dublin Area Rapid Transit	PT	Portstewart Tramway
DBST	Dublin and Blessington Steam Tramway	RIC	Royal Irish Constabulary
DCT	Dublin Central Tramways	RPSI	Railway Preservation Society of Ireland
DDR	Dublin and Drogheda Railway	TMSI	Transport Museum Society of Ireland

PREFACE

I was born in Dublin during the war years and remember well the ration books, the green smelly turf fires, the blackouts, etc. I can recall the bomb damage in the North Strand, the mounds of rubble and the BBC news bulletins. It was some years later, after the war, that I had my first taste of a banana or an orange.

We lived at the time in the quiet little village of Artane in north Co Dublin, set on a hill outside the city and it was downhill all the way as far as Fairview. The village shop was run by the two elderly Carroll sisters and provided the day to day requirements. I fetched milk in a jug from the nearby Bedford farm. Items such as household goods, clothes and shoes necessitated a journey into town on a No 42 bus and it was on these visits that I first became acquainted with the electric trams.

A nostalgic scene in the centre of Dublin. Nelson's Pillar in O'Connell Street was the terminal point for many of Dublin's trams. In this view we see Standards Nos 111 and 21, Luxury car No 43 with Balcony car No 189 just visible to the right.

Author's collection

The electric trams gathered around Nelson's Pillar in O'Connell Street and my first awareness was that they looked more awesome and impressive than their frail cousins, the motor buses. Somehow I knew that their days were numbered and that their frail cousins would eventually replace them and reign supreme on the streets of Dublin. It was not, however, until much more recent years, with the advent of the massive Atlantean bus, that buses increased sufficiently in size to equal the City trams in terms of grandeur and capacity.

I was quick to realise that the trams ran on rails and that the front and the rear looked exactly the same. The humming of the motors, clanking of the bogies and vibration of their movement through the cobbles, set them apart from the buses. The swishing trolley, the swaying from side to side and the lurching fore and aft all had a character of their own. The

trolley wheel running along the overhead power cable made a sound like sausages sizzling in the pan and often sent off a shower of sparks. I can clearly recall the sounds of the clanging of the gong and the clicking of the ratchet swan's-neck brake handle. The motor man stood with his legs apart and arms outstretched, his left hand on the controller handle, his right on the brake. This stance looked most impressive and many of the drivers swayed from side to side in rhythm with the motion of their trundling fortresses. In his smart black uniform and cap he had a formidable appearance, rather like a captain at the helm of his ship. He stood proudly in full view of his passengers and public alike, quite unlike his bus counterpart who was encased almost invisibly in his miniature cabin and quite aloof from his passengers. In some of the smaller trams, the richly varnished seats, much darkened over the years, sat longitudinally along the sides and the passengers faced those on the opposite side. My short legs could not reach the floor and swung from side to side with the motion of the tramcar. I enjoyed this position as I was free to observe the expressions of the multitudes across the gangway as they came and went. With transverse seating, typical on all buses, I usually felt imprisoned by a parent on the outer side while I was left to contemplate the boils on the red neck of the gentleman one seat ahead.

The Dublin tramway system survived in part until 1949. No doubt the war years and shortage of fuel prolonged the running of the electric tramcars for many years after their planned demise. It is an ill wind that doesn't blow some good. At the time of writing, new proposals are on the desks of the city planners to reintroduce electric trams back into the City of Dublin. Perhaps some day I will again experience the pleasure of a tram ride across my city streets, not in old double deck stock, but in their sleek articulated continental cousins. Although they will be referred to as *light railways*, they are essentially trams. What's in a name?

With the passing of the Dublin trams, a legacy of their extensive routeways and electric paraphernalia survived for many years. I can recall the bruised knees I received when, riding my bicycle into town, I caught the front wheel in the grooved tram rail. When the rails turned away from my direction of travel my bike would follow the rails and run out from under me, leaving me sitting bewildered in the middle of the road. One quickly learned to raise the front wheel out of the groove by rearing the bike horse-like and all cyclists of the forties and fifties will recall the need to do this. I remember hearing a story about a youngster who would cycle after the trams, sucked along by their motion. In this manner he felt that the tram protected him not only from the weather but from the onslaught of other road users. What he was not aware of was that some road works were under construction between the tracks ahead and that workers chose to remain in the hole while the trams passed overhead. I can imagine their surprise when this youngster fell amongst them, bike and all. Certainly this would never have happened behind a bus.

After the closure of the Dublin City trams, the Hill of Howth trams survived for a further ten years, in spite of many threats. I came to Howth almost every week to climb her hills, stalk her woods, and swim and fish in her seas. No matter where one went, one was in sight or sound of the electric trams as they slowly climbed her majestic gorse clad hills and descended the other side. They were rather like the famous Duke of York's army who were marched to the top of the hill and then marched down again. I travelled on them on and off and developed an affection for them over the years. I was at boarding school when the system finally succumbed. Unaware of this, I cycled to Howth on my bicycle some days after the closure. I waited at Sutton Cross expecting to see one of these splendid blue and cream trams clanking her gong as she made her way cautiously through the Cross, with the customary shower of sparks from the overhead cable when crossing the dead section where the City trams once crossed over the Hill tram route. But no tram came. As the stark reality of the situation dawned on me I felt deep sadness. It was like the passing of an old friend.

With time, I forgot about the trams, went about my studies, qualified as an architect, married and went to live and work in London.

I returned to Dublin in the early 1970s and set up home in Howth, not far from the old Dungriffin halt. At this stage, as far as I was concerned the trams were a thing of the past and I never paid them a thought. That is, until one September evening when bringing my eldest daughter Claire for a walk around Howth summit, I tripped over something in the long grass, and stooping down and parting the grass, I discovered the remnants of one of the tram poles. Later that evening I returned with a hack saw and cut off part, with the intention of making an ornament out of the heavily corroded section, moulded as it were by the effects of time. This section of pole sat in my study and became a ghost of the past. Then I began wondering about the Hill trams. What had happened to them? Had any survived?

Gradually the memories of their glorious past, the seemingly endless warm summers, the carefree climbing of the hills of Howth and tireless watching of the blue and cream trams slowly creeping through the gorse and heather, generated a reaction in me and I had to find out what had become of them.

In June 1976, I discovered that No 9 from the Hill of Howth fleet had survived, and was at Castleruddery, Co Wicklow. One Saturday morning shortly after, I set out with my daughter Claire to see No 9, now in the possession of the Transport Museum Society of Ireland. I found a battered hulk, rather than a preserved tram, in a state of severe decay after years of vandalism, stripping and weathering. I joined the TMSI and persuaded them to let me undertake her restoration. Now she is fully restored and on display in the Transport Museum at Howth Castle. In 1993 when I was approached by Colourpoint Press to write this book, I knew that it would give me an opportunity to indulge some of my loveliest childhood memories and at the same time answer a challenge.

Trams, of course, were not confined to the Dublin area. As with many good Dublin men, my mother was from Cork and, like all Cork people, she was fiercely proud of that fact. Normally she was a quietly spoken woman, but if she received a telephone call from a fellow Corkonian the full strength and volume of her Cork accent returned. I was sent to the little village of Glanworth, not far from Fermoy, quite frequently and trips to Cork City were eagerly awaited. My mother was a nurse in the North Infirmary and she would often have travelled on the trams. Indeed, I often heard her mention them. Every Christmas, the 'parcel' arrived from Cork with the usual goose, plum pudding and other goodies and inevitably several issues of Cork journals were used for the packaging. As a young lad, I recall that one of these, the Holly Bough, carried an article about Cork trams, with excellent photographs, written by Walter McGrath. I can recall studying these in detail. Years later, I was asked to give talks on behalf of the Transport Museum, concerning our tram restoration programme, to the Cork branch of the Irish Railway Record Society. I was always very courteously treated and well dined at the Metropole Hotel. It was on one of these visits that I met Walter who had just brought out a book on the Cork trams, titled *Tram Tracks Through Cork*, and an excellent read it was too. Walter had a deep passion for the old Cork trams and, as he admits himself, more from the romantic than the technical point of view. Anyone who reads his book will know exactly what I mean. It would not have been possible for me to write about the trams of Cork without having met Walter or read his book.

Although I am informed that the name *Kilroy* can be traced back to the Kings of Ulster, I have no relations in that part of the island and all my family contacts were either from Cork or the Midlands. As a child, I had no reason or plans to visit Belfast — that is until fate lent a hand. The year was 1957 and I had been on an education course in Donegal when my unscheduled visit came about. It was also my first acquaintance with one of the narrow gauge railways for which Donegal was so famous. For my return journey to Dublin, I was put on such a narrow gauge train at Letterkenny by one of the administrators of the course, and given strict instructions to change to broad gauge at Strabane. I was to make a further change at Portadown for the Dublin train. I slept most of the journey and missed my change, and instead arrived in Belfast, totally unaware that I was not back home in Dublin, and looking forward to my parents' embrace. I disembarked from the train, quite oblivious to my predicament, until I realised that I was the only one with a strange accent. The pillar boxes were red and no parents eagerly awaited.

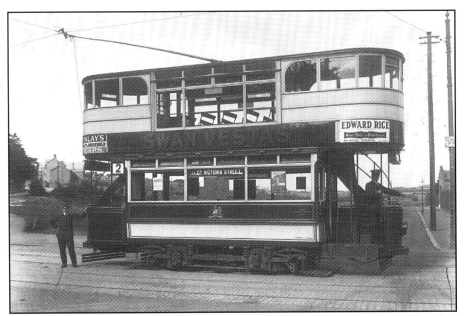

Belfast Corporation Tramways No 89, built 1905, as rebuilt in 1923 with enclosed upper deck, but retaining an open lower deck, the only car to be so treated. *AR Hogg, Ulster Museum*

Knowing nothing of life in Northern Ireland, I started off by asking the way to the nearest 'Garda' station! A kind passer by directed me to a police station and having explained my penniless predicament to the RUC, I was delivered into the hands of a Mrs McLarnan who ran a guest house. My parents were notified of my whereabouts and thus began one of the best adventures of my life. My surroundings were completely different from what I had been used to. It was mid July and the streets were ablaze with bunting and flags. It was my first sight of the Union Jack and instead of green buses they were red and cream. Enthralled by my new surroundings and sense of festivity, I wandered aimlessly about and became quite lost. I was taken in by a family, given a lovely tea and, afterwards, I was escorted right to the steps of Mrs McLarnan's guest house. I had never been treated in so friendly and helpful a manner and my first impression of Belfast was that of a colourful vibrant city, inhabited by a most warm and considerate populous, and I am glad to say that I still cherish these sentiments after many further visits.

The trams had just gone and in their place I encountered the trolley bus for the first time. I noticed that they were more streamlined and, in my opinion, were more handsome than the normal half-cab bus. What struck me most was their silent and fumeless motion. I was struck also by their trolley arms and was not sure if they were trams without tracks or buses without engines. Either way, I was very impressed by them.

When I later developed an interest in trams, the Belfast Transport Museum at Witham Street became the mecca of the tram restoration team and I became a frequent visitor, not only to study No 4 from the Hill of Howth tramway but the many other interesting exhibits. I usually wrote to the museum authorities in advance of our visits to procure permission to board the trams, and once more the courtesy that I had learned to expect was afforded me and my team on all occasions. I remember being told by the staff that they had never witnessed such enthusiasm by any visitors, as that of the Dublin group and that we were certainly the only visitors who spent more time crawling under the exhibits than on them. This was something of a joke between us. I was permitted to film the exhibits and use the material in fundraising talks not only elsewhere in Ireland and England but also with Northern preservation groups.

I was greatly impressed with the Belfast trams on exhibition in the old museum at Witham Street. They had a great sense of presence about them and were constructed to the highest standards. Their highly ornate varnished interiors, attention to detail and the unusual names of the trucks and controllers made them very different from anything I had seen in Dublin. They were also the first 'complete' trams that I had seen, apart from my childhood memories of Dublin trams before the closure. They certainly emphasised to me that a tram was a tram, no matter from where. The magic about them was just as evident in Belfast as it was in Dublin. When it came to intricate detail and gadgetry the Belfast tram surpassed anything I had ever seen. My great regret was that none of the fine McCreary cars survived. They were certainly the equal of any of the Dublin Luxury cars in terms of finish and appearance. Indeed, with their enclosing platform doors they looked in many ways more streamlined. The Belfast trams had a distinctiveness of their own and were unmistakably Belfast. Perhaps it is the way in which almost every city can be identified by its individual tram designs that makes their study so rich and exciting.

Over the years of restoration I met many very knowledgeable people deeply involved with tram lore. This book will try to avoid too much technical detail and is directed to those who either remember the old trams and wish to relive some fond memories, or to those too young to remember but who are either curious or enthusiastic where matters of transport and machines are concerned.

As I spend so much of my time away from my family, in pursuit of my hobby of tram restoration, I have decided to name the trams in the Howth Museum after my wife and daughters. This follows the time-honoured tradition of naming ships and railway locomotives. The plates bearing the names will be removable, should the trams be required for film work. Hill of Howth No 9 will be named *Helen of Howth* after my wife; the Dublin open front car, No 224, will be *Claire*; and last but not least, Giant's Causeway No 9 will be called *Mia* after my youngest.

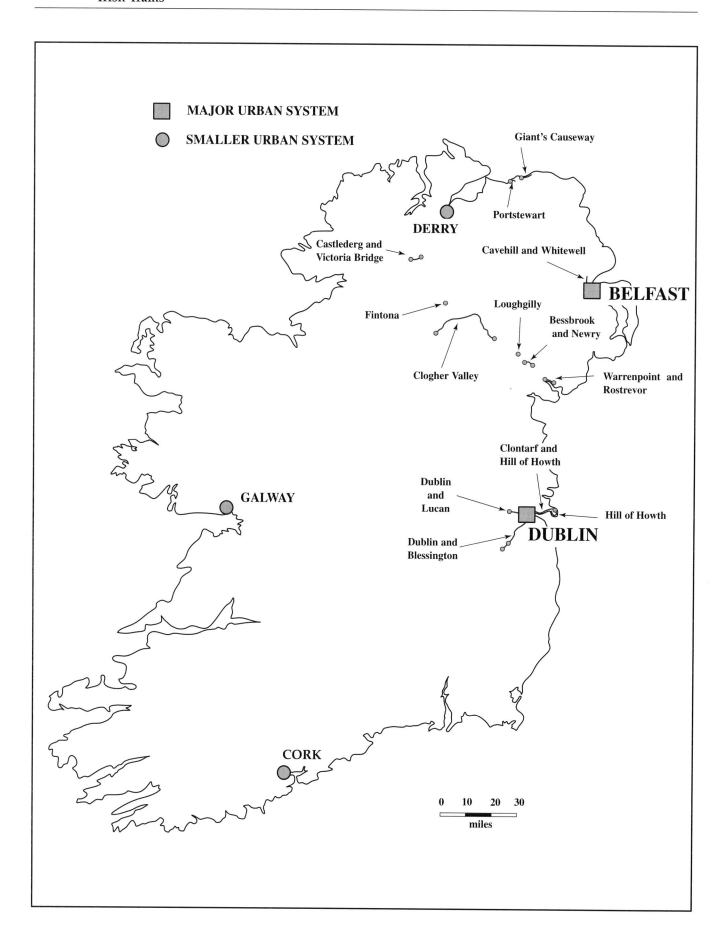

INTRODUCTION

The origin of the tram can be traced back to the 16th century when the produce of mining was mule-hauled, man-hauled or winch-hauled along rudely laid stone chip roads.

As one pit was exhausted, there was a need to lay further roadways and soon a network of chipped tracks covered the mining area. The matter was greatly exacerbated, in the case of underground workings, by soft conditions and inclement weather. Many of the carts had wheel spacing based on the old Roman roads of Europe and this approximated to the future English railway gauge of 4'8½". The constant laying of stone based roads was slow and expensive. To counteract this, heavy balks of timber were laid end to end, and secured with hardwood pegs. These balks of timber were laid on transverse timber sleepers and later had timber upstands running continuously along their outer edges. This arrangement could be re-used many times and could be relaid with speed. Later on, iron replaced the timber upstands. The upstands were to prevent the wheels from slipping off the edge of the plank.

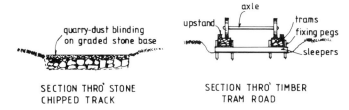

SECTION THRO' STONE CHIPPED TRACK

SECTION THRO' TIMBER TRAM ROAD

A great many of the mining navvies were Scottish and spoke in their Gaelic dialect. It has been said that they called these heavy balks of timber tracking *trams*, derived from the Scots Gaelic word *trom*, meaning a heavy lintel or threshold or beam, and that is how the word entered the railway vernacular of the day. The Scandinavian word for a heavy beam is *tromm*, a name also given to the heavily built carts used to transport the produce of mining.

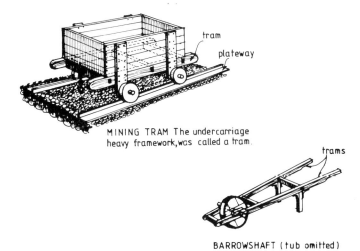

MINING TRAM The undercarriage heavy framework, was called a tram.

BARROWSHAFT (tub omitted)

On account of the strong Scandinavian connection with Scotland, perhaps the word is of shared origin, so it may not be too untrue to say that the word *tram* is of Scandinavian/ Gaelic origin. The *Oxford Dictionary* states that the name originates from the word *traam* or *traem* which is low German for a 'balk, beam or barrowshaft' and that this word is also Middle Dutch and Middle Low German in origin.

The same meaning is found with the East Frisian word *trame* or *treme* and is similar to West Flemish. In the *Brewer's Dictionary of Phrase and Fable*, these early plank roads were called *dram* roads from the Greek word *Dram-ein*, meaning 'to run', and the wagons using them were originally called *drams*. Some authorities believe therefore that *tram* is a misspelling of *dram*. Eventually the timber tram tracks were replaced by iron flats with upstands and often sleepers were dispensed with and replaced by heavy blocks of stone with oak plugs into which the iron plates were fixed.

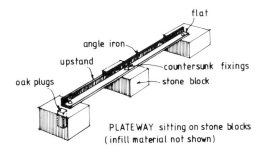

PLATEWAY sitting on stone blocks (infill material not shown)

Several of these plateways, sometimes called *gangeways*, were laid by a man called Benjamin Ou<u>tram</u> and it has also been suggested that his plateways were called *tram-tracks* after him. William Jessop had the brain wave of removing the upstand from the plateway, fixing it to the wheel and calling it a flange. The iron rail was now cast with a recess, or groove, to receive the flange (see overleaf). It is amazing that such an obvious idea took so long to discover. Thus, the tram track entered the scene.

Until the beginning of the 19th century, the sole use of these tram wagons was for mining. However, navvies used these carts for transport to and from the workings. In 1807, a Mr Benjamin French hired out a section of such a plateway which ran from Swansea to Oystermouth, in South Wales. He then converted a stagecoach and commenced the first passenger carrying service in the world. A horse-drawn tram ran in Vienna (Austria) at an exhibition in 1840. In 1854, a vehicle, with outside iron ladders and sidewalks giving access to the roof of the carriage, was introduced to run between Fintona Junction and the town of Fintona in Co Tyrone, on what later became part of the GNRI. This was one of the first such ventures in Europe and the Fintona branch, at the time of its demise in 1957, was the longest running horse tramway in the world. The earlier carriage, known locally as the *van*, was replaced with a more orthodox tram-type vehicle in 1883. Fortunately this has survived at the Ulster Folk and Transport Museum at Cultra, Co Down.

The first street tramway in the world was introduced by an Irishman, John Stephenson, to the streets of New York in 1832. He gathered funds and support from fellow expatriates and called the first such tram, or street car, *John Mason*, after the president of the company. This vehicle ran from Prince Street to 14th Street and resembled an early railway carriage. It weighed 2½ tons and carried 30 passengers. It provided a 15 minute interval service over a 4 mile route. Later on, Stephenson established a large tram construction business, creating the general appearance and principles of layout for all trams to follow. It would be true to say that the tram design, which prevailed throughout the early years of the establishment of trams all over the world, was introduced by an Irishman. One of his staff, Mr George Francis Train, came to Birkenhead, near Liverpool, to introduce what was then called the 'American Streetcar' and such a line was constructed in 1860. Stephenson used a 'step rail' form of track, as shown below, and this type of rail was copied by Train. There is more information about this type of rail in the Dublin chapter, page 18.

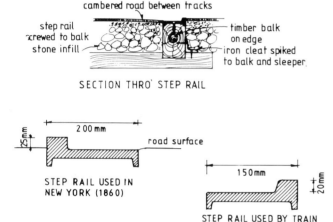

SECTION THRO' STEP RAIL

STEP RAIL USED IN
NEW YORK (1860)

STEP RAIL USED BY TRAIN

It is due to the successful efforts of Mr Train, that the street horse tramway spread across Europe. In the early years of expansion, a considerable amount of tram stock came from the Stephenson works. The 'Irish' tram was spreading worldwide.

Nowhere can the Irish be more proud where the tram is concerned than with the Giant's Causeway electric tramway. When it opened in 1883, it was the world's first full scale electric tramway and the first operated by hydro-electric power. In Berlin Werner Von Siemens had experimented with electric trams at Grosslichterfelde (1881) and Charlottenberg (1882). No one took up the system until the brother of the then Provost of Trinity College, Dublin, Mr William Traill, invited him over to examine the setting up of his experiment along a scenic stretch of Northern coastline in 1882. It is true that the Volks Electric Railway in Brighton had its *official* opening some months ahead of the Giant's Causeway electric tramway. However, the Brighton line was more of a scenic miniature railway and this delightful line is still running today. There is no doubt that the Causeway tram had been in service many months ahead of the Volks.

It is a source of great amazement to many transport historians to learn that the birth pangs of the electric traction era took place, not in any of the proud and noble cities of mainland

Europe, but along a deserted stretch of Irish coastline lashed by the Atlantic gales. The National Transport Museum at Howth Castle, Co Dublin, has rescued what is believed by a growing number of people to be the oldest surviving electric tram in the world — No 9 from the Giant's Causeway — one of the pioneers from the dawn of electric traction, dating from 1883.

Where trams are concerned, Ireland had many firsts. Jenny Richardson was the first woman to operate an electric tram, on the occasion of the opening of the Causeway. This tram was also the first to be operated by hydro-electric power. The Bessbrook and Newry tram was the first to use bogies and a bow-collector and to haul flangeless wagons. Dublin was the first city to provide a windscreen to protect the driver and, in 1903, the first to change points automatically. It was the first to operate the now worldwide Quaney safety link to prevent the overhead power cable from falling on the roadway. In the 1930s, Dublin was considered to have the finest and most efficient tramway system in Europe and the seventh largest, where fleet numbers and route mileage were concerned.

HORSE TRAMS

As this book is divided into sections dealing with horse, steam and electric traction, I want to say a few words about each of these in general before looking at specific systems. It is a cause of great surprise to me how long it took the idea of a tramway to become established, especially when the means and the knowledge had been around for such a long time. John Stephenson's passenger carrying service in New York in 1832 was the first real effort to set up a rail-based urban transportation system; yet several decades were to follow before the new system caught on and began to spread. When at last it arrived in Europe, its early European origins were not recognised and it became know variously as the 'American Street Railway', 'Amerikanische Eisenbahn', and the 'Chemins de Fer Americains'. There was an exhibition at Vienna in 1840 and another in Brussels in 1854, but nothing came of these.

The first permanent street railway in Europe was in Paris, introduced in 1853, by Alphonse Loubat, who had worked for John Stephenson in New York. He used an early form of grooved tram rail, as shown below. His tram was called a *hippomobile* and provided a regular service from 1855. The Fintona horse tram, although not a street tram, was already one year in service at this time.

SECTION THRO' EARLY GROOVED TRAMRAIL
USED BY ALPHONSE LOUBAT IN PARIS

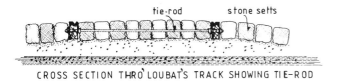

CROSS SECTION THRO' LOUBAT'S TRACK SHOWING TIE-ROD

The first serious horse tramway attempt in England was introduced by an Englishman, William Curtis, who obtained permission from the Liverpool Docks Company to run a passenger service along the docks in 1859. Whilst it did not succeed, it laid the way for the above mentioned George Francis Train, to lay a second line in Liverpool in 1860, on the banks of the Mersey between Woodside Ferry and Birkenhead Park.

It could be said that the first successful *tram* in England was produced by a *Train*! This event began the real public awakening and with the determined and relentless energies of George Train, the horse tramways of England finally became established and spread like wild fire. It took a long time to succeed, but when it did, it certainly made up for lost time. The introduction of tramways spread like a virus throughout the cities of Great Britain and the European mainland.

When one thinks of the great advantages of rail vehicles over road, it is not at all surprising that their popularity grew so rapidly. The ride over rails was very much smoother, swifter and quieter than the horse drawn omnibuses of the day. This is more easily understood when one considers that other road vehicles had iron tyres that clattered noisily as they rumbled along over rough cobble stones and gritty roads. A horse that with difficulty pulled 17 cwt, could now, with relative ease, increase the load to 40 cwt, making rail haulage more economical after the initial cost of laying the track.

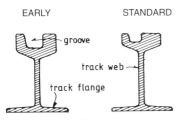

SECTIONS THRO' TYPICAL TRAM RAIL
Early rail had deeper and wider grooves
to suit railway type wheel flanges
Tram wheel flanges were smaller.

One of the most important features of the horse tram over the horse omnibus was safety. The omnibus depended on the stopping power of the horses and a light hand brake, whereas the horse tram had a very effective braking system and could hold the vehicle back, even if the animals tried to bolt. This was not so with the omnibus.

There was one horrific instance of this when a Dublin horse bus, with a full load, was passing over the Grand Canal on one of the steep hump backed bridges. The horses could not pull the load on the icy road surface and the hand brake could not hold the bus. As it slithered out of control the bus reversed off the road towards the canal. For a moment, it sat precariously

on the edge of the lock wall, but the poor horses could not hold the bus and over she went into the lock.

The lock was empty at the time and the lock keeper looked aghast at the bus and thrashing horses. He came to the unfortunate decision that if he were to flood the lock, the bus and horses would float to the top and facilitate a rescue. Onlookers watched in horror as the bus filled with water and vanished from sight and the thrashing of the terrified horses gradually ceased. Once the flooding commenced it could not be reversed until the lock was filled and the release gates opened. The full impact of this early morning tragedy was gradually revealed as the waters ebbed away. None of this would have happened with an effective braking system, or if the vehicle had been on rails.

The running of a horse tramway also had its complications. There was the matter of keeping the streets clean from horse dung which tended to accumulate at halts. After a shower, this became a slush and was usually pushed to the roadside by other vehicles. A passing bus inevitably obliged by spraying the bus queue with this slush when pulling in. Several of the early buses carried brushes against their wheels to prevent this, but the smell, particularly on hot summer days, was an additional problem.

Ideally each horse tram required eleven horses, though this was not always achieved. Each pair pulled the tram for a two hour period, or approximately six miles, and were then replaced by fresh horses. It was inevitable that one of the horses would either lose a shoe or become lame during a working week and the eleventh horse was a stand by. To provide proper accommodation for these animals a great deal of stabling was necessary with exercise yards, blacksmithy, harness sheds, massive granary, hay sheds, fodder stores and compost bays. Apart from the drivers and conductors, there were stable boys, resident vets and farriers, harness makers, night watchmen and attendants to keep the horses and the tram fleet in good repair. There was often a trainer to bring young horses along and generally show them the ropes. An inexperienced animal was usually placed with a well tried animal on a less busy route to help learn the trade. No stallions were used and, as a rule, all colts were gelded before their training commenced.

It was not unusual to provide cottages for the tramway staff close at hand. The work for the tramway personnel was tough and the hours long. Standing for lengthy periods open to the elements, often in dreadful conditions, was not conducive to good health and a bad chest was the usual price to pay. The wages were poor too. A driver's pay was around twenty two shillings (£1.10) a week for the first year, rising to twenty four shillings thereafter. The conductor was paid slightly more. The men worked an average of fourteen and a half hours per day, with an hour off for breakfast and dinner and some companies insisted that lunch was taken on the tram.

For the horses too, the work was hard. A willing horse was his own worst enemy and he would put his full energies eagerly forward to please his master. After about two or three years, their spirits were often completely broken. If not sold off for meat they were sold to cabbies and delivery men where the work was easier. A good ex-tram horse was eagerly sought. A wiser animal would take the strain more calmly and sometimes after some months out on grass would be returned to another period in harness. Several animals died on duty. Driver and horse developed a respect for one another and a good driver could prolong the usefulness of those animals entrusted to his care. Both shared a hard burden and a mutual sympathy grew. An uncaring master might let an animal walk unchecked for miles with perhaps some stone trapped in its hoof. This could render the animal lame for weeks and in extreme cases the animal would have to be destroyed. Flogging a horse was strictly forbidden unless for reasons of safety, or to avoid some danger. Not all systems were so hard. A horse tramway at a seaside resort, where the timetable was not so strict, could provide quite a good life for horses and tram staff alike and many horses survived in harness until a ripe old age. A city with hills was quite a different matter. The poem below looks at the work from the horse's point of view.

Oh let me like a tram horse fall, with cobbles at my feet
A martyr to stern duties call, on a noble Dublin street
The gongs loud tones, my weary bones, would wake with life
anew,
And I long to show before I go, what tramway steeds can do.
For years I've hauled my heavy load, from the city to Blackrock.
The butt of boys along the road, and cabbies on the block.
I'd hear them cry, there sure that I, must fall upon the way.
Till ladies old, had gone and told, the DSPCA.
Though some may pale, beneath the driver's flail, 'Twould be to
me relief
To end my life in mortal strife, and not as fluid beef.

Adapted from an anonymous poem c1902

STEAM TRACTION

The advantages of steam traction for hauling wagons of mining produce, coal and raw material was quickly recognised. These splendid machines roamed the countryside, belching out fumes, hissing like metallic dragons and clanking furiously along under the strain. It was not too long before their benefits to passenger transportation were realised and soon steam locomotives were ferrying a more precious commodity from town to town, much to the dismay and apprehension of many who observed them. Some believed that the speed of the engines would exhaust their air supply within the carriages and wagon loads of corpses would be delivered to their destinations — on time.

But initial fears were allayed and soon the steam locomotive won respect and approval. Town after town pressurised the railway entrepreneurs of the day to connect their town to the ever growing network. To be left out was certain economic suicide. However, to reduce construction costs, stations were usually built on the perimeter of towns, so steam engines rarely intruded into the centre. For many years the use of steam engines on roads was strongly discouraged, because of

the likely effect on horses. Laws to prohibit them within the town without substantial segregation from the public were rapidly drawn up. This prohibition meant that, in the British Isles, steam trams did not appear until the 1870s.

The distinction between a steam tram and a steam train was never very clear. If the passage of the vehicle was along the streets within the town and the passengers picked up at street level, then it was considered a tram. It was also necessary to reduce speed to perhaps 8 or 10 mph and generally avoid the nuisance of sound or steam emissions. Trains, on the other hand, attempted to achieve speed and usually picked up passengers along a platform. They were not, so to speak, street friendly.

When John Stephenson set up his horse tramway in New York in 1832, he initially used steam locomotives for part of the working. This was quickly prohibited by the authorities. It was necessary therefore, to make substantial adaptations to steam locomotives to make them more street friendly. To achieve this, locomotives were made considerably smaller in size, using vertical rather than a horizontal boilers to be compact. To avoid visible steam emission, the steam was often superheated and tall chimneys delivered the smoke emission well above roof level. To deaden the sound, baffles were used. It was more common, however, to turn the steam back into water by passing it through tubes located on the roof to cool it. This system was called condensing.

To limit speed, the engines were fitted with an automatic governor which applied the brake when the permitted speed was exceeded. Steam trams were amongst the first users of smokeless fuel. As no great speed was required, the wheels were usually quite small and it was often mandatory to have them covered from view by side skirtings. This was to keep running parts away from the public for safety reasons but it also prevented splashing, and to some extent it deadened track noise.

Apart from early experiments, the first recorded instance of a steam power on a street tramway was on the Frankford and Southwark Railway in Philadelphia, USA, which used a composite car (engine on the same chassis as the tram) between 1859 and 1893. The first steam tram to operate in England was also a combined engine and carriage built by John Grantham. This was tested unsuccessfully in London in 1873, but eventually ended up providing a service on the Wantage Tramway.

Composite cars were not really successful and passengers understandably felt uncomfortable sitting beside a pressurised boiler with a fear of explosion and the shudder and rattling of moving parts vibrating through the seats. The designers were quick to realise this and eventually designed a separate engine which hauled a passenger carrying trailer, usually two storey, with top deck screening to protect upper deck passengers from smoke and smuts. As a rule, these locomotives were designed to resemble carriages and make them less offensive to the general public and more acceptable to the equine fraternity who, by now, were growing more accustomed to the intruder into their domain of haulage. These were called *dummies* and the earliest tramway to use such dummies is believed to be the Market Street Railway Company in San Francisco which opened in July 1860.

This book will deal with those lines which operated within the city streets of Belfast, and Dublin, along with some of the more rural routes. Some were eventually replaced by electric traction and the rest struggled on until the 1920s and 1930s to be replaced by the petrol motor bus.

ELECTRIC TRACTION

If I told you that railed electric traction operated before horse trams, you would find this hard to credit. If I further told you that the first railed electric vehicles were run by a *blacksmith*, a *Farmer*, a *Page* and someone *Daft*, I doubt if I would be believed. Yet, what I am saying is quite true.

The first recorded running of a battery-powered electric vehicle, a model tramway, was by an American *blacksmith* from Vermont, named Thomas Davenport. This was at an exhibition in 1835, some thirty years before horse tramways appeared in Europe. Another American, Professor *Farmer* connected the battery to the rails rather than the locomotive.

Apparently a full scale electric vehicle was built in Scotland in 1836 by a Robert Davidson, but the machine was broken up by an angry group of railway men, who feared that the new contraption would be a threat to their livelihoods. A Professor Charles *Page* propelled an electrically powered vehicle on a test run in Washington in 1851 and reached the astonishing speed of almost 20 mph.

However battery power could never provide enough energy to operate a full scale tramcar, so electric traction was unable to progress until the discovery of the dynamo for generating electricity. In 1872 the Belgan-born ZT Gramme discovered that if a dynamo was fed electricity, it acted as a motor. The first successful electric locomotives were powered with these reversed dynamos.

The first such locomotive was built by Verner Von Siemens in 1879. It was powered by a 2 hp dynamo, and was demonstrated at the Berlin Industrial Exhibition, with the current being picked up from a third 'live' rail. A year later, Thomas Edison was experimenting with a similar locomotive at Menlo Park in the USA. It was also in the USA that an expatriate Englishman, by the name of Leo *Daft*, built a very successful locomotive called *Ampere* in 1883. Mr Daft played a very important role in the development of the electric tram in America.

Meanwhile, in Europe, Von Siemens was exhibiting his electric locomotive in various cities, including the International Electric Exhibition held at the Crystal Palace, London in 1881-82. He also exhibited in Vienna, Brussels, Paris, Prague and other cities, but it would appear that at this time no one recognised the importance of his invention.

Eventually, as mentioned earlier, he built his experimental line at Berlin, which became the world's first passenger carrying electric tramway in 1881. Whilst it was experimental in essence, it helped iron out many of the teething troubles of electric traction and showed the world that this new system of locomotion had considerable potential for the future.

In Britain the first experiment with an electric locomotive-hauled tram was at the Forestry Exhibition in Edinburgh in 1882. It had the honour of carrying the Prince and Princess of Wales, and the Prime Minister of the day, Mr Gladstone and his wife. This was possibly the first time that royalty and a senior politician were carried on the new system.

As mentioned earlier, the Giant's Causeway line in Ireland became the first tramway to commit itself to electric traction. Learning of Von Siemens' experiments, the Traill brothers, from Bushmills in Co Antrim, invited him to inspect the potential of introducing an electric tram line between Bushmills and Portrush. This was the first serious enquiry Von Siemens received and he grabbed at the opportunity and challenge.

He accepted a directorship in the Company, gave a £3,000 contribution, and the first true tramway system was set up with cars specifically constructed for the purpose. As faults, particularly with the problems of current leakage and the motors, were eliminated and the system freed itself from trial and error, the world looked on. It was not long before cities throughout the British Isles and Europe were asking questions about the new mode of transport and several authorities came to see for themselves. It was not until 1896 that the first electric tram travelled the streets of Dublin, and it took another decade before all major cities could boast an electric tramway system.

OTHER FORMS OF TRACTION

From time to time experiments were made with other forms of traction for tramcars. These have included such unlikely sources as ammonia gas (USA 1871), town gas (Britain, at three locations, one operating until 1920), and even clockwork! There were also some experiments with trams powered by fireless steam engines and compressed air.

One very successful means of traction was the cable car, used right up to today in San Francisco. A steam or electric operated power house kept a cable in continuous motion, out of sight under the street, using a series of wheels and pulleys to round corners, etc. The tram, or street car, could connect with the running cable by means of a gripping device which could draw the vehicle along and the vehicle could be released at will. It was a very safe and efficient means of transport, comfortable and pollution free, but it was very expensive to install, and was never used in Ireland. However cable cars did operate at Douglas, in the Isle of Man, and in Glasgow. In the chapter on the Blessington tram, the reader will find mention of another method of propulsion — the internal combustion engine — also used on the Clogher Valley and Castlederg and Victoria Bridge trams.

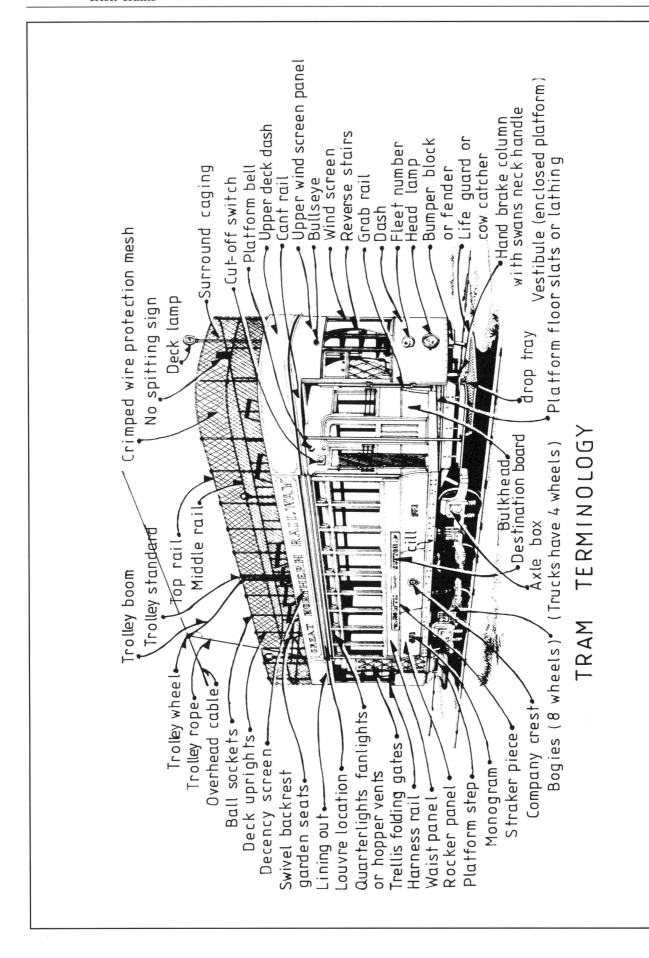

TRAM TERMINOLOGY

Trolley boom
Trolley standard
Top rail
Middle rail
Surround caging
Cut-off switch
Platform bell
Upper deck dash
Cant rail
Upper wind screen panel
Bullseye
Wind screen
Reverse stairs
Grab rail
Dash
Fleet number
Head lamp
Bumper block or fender
Life guard or cow catcher
Hand brake column with swans neck handle
Vestibule (enclosed platform)
Platform floor slats or lathing
drop tray

Crimped wire protection mesh
No spitting sign
Deck lamp

Trolley wheel
Trolley rope
Overhead cable
Ball sockets
Deck uprights
Decency screen
Swivel backrest garden seats
Lining out
Louvre location
Quarterlights fanlights or hopper vents
Trellis folding gates
Harness rail
Waist panel
Rocker panel
Platform step
Monogram
Straker piece
Company crest
Bogies (8 wheels)   (Trucks have 4 wheels)
Axle box
Destination board
Bulkhead
cill

GREAT NORTHERN RAILWAY

TRAM TERMINOLOGY

From time to time the text may refer to parts of the tram. Trams, like all other forms of transport, have their own terminology, and, among tram enthusiasts, any misuse is frowned upon. Most body part names have derived from carriage construction terminology and some of the terminology is shared with railway carriages.

For example, horse drawn carriages usually had large wheels carried on axles and were located outside the body of the carriage. To avoid projecting the wheels too far outwards, with a danger to the public, the body of most carriages had an inward sweep to reduce its width. This was known as a *tumblehome*. Most early horse and electric trams had their lower or *rocker* panels constructed with such tumblehomes.

The tram saloon body 'gable' structure was known as the *bulkhead* (usually with a sliding door). Where the upper deck rail projected beyond this, it was referred to as a *cant* rail, because it *cantilevered* over the platform. If the platform was enclosed with a windscreen the enclosed space was referred to as the *vestibule*. The projecting strip (usually covered with half round steel moulding) between the waist and rocker panels was called a *straker piece*, or *rubbing strake*, from the verb "to strike".

Whilst the derivation of the words usually makes sense, the meaning of some words is more obscure. For example, the upper deck surround panel was called a *decency board*, or *screen*, as its purpose was to hide ladies' ankles from view to street level. The *Director's Tram* at the National Transport Museum in Howth never had such decency panels as all the directors were gentlemen (which, in today's society, would be considered sexist) and there was no need to hide their ankles.

When trams first appeared, it was virtually impossible for ladies of fashion with hoops and bustles to climb the narrow stairs. There were many recorded instances where disrobing was almost necessary to rescue some poor entrapped female. To counteract this injustice, ladies adopted a slimmer garment to make the upper deck accessible to them. It is also said that when the high heel came into fashion women had their revenge for all indignities caused to them by tram design. The heels perforated the weatherproof canvas membrane between the walking slats to such a degree that severe body rot to all open top trams rapidly ensued. The upper deck of a tram was always referred to as the *outside* while the lower saloon was known as the *inside*. The rail, or part rail, over the dash was called a *harness rail*, a term going back to horse drawn days.

Most of the early electric trams, and all of the horse drawn trams, had a four wheel under carriage called a *truck*. As larger capacity vehicles were required, elongated bodies with two smaller trucks, known as *bogies* were used. Bogie trams had a shorter rigid distance between bogie wheels (known as the *wheelbase*), and could take sharper corners or curves. With extra motor accommodation, they were more powerful. Almost all modern trams are of the bogie variety. The larger bogie wheels, to which the gear wheel and motor were attached, were called the *traction set* and the smaller wheels

were known as *ponies*. Tram wheels are usually fixed to the axles and the wheel set turns by housing the axle ends in *axle boxes* which are spring loaded. On road vehicles, the wheels themselves turn on hubs fixed to the axle, which remains rigid.

Where tram tracks changed course, the choice of direction was controlled by *points*. In the early days *point boys* operated these, but later they were automatically changed by the tram itself. This arrangement was first applied in Dublin in 1903 and later adopted worldwide. Where an *outbound* tram passed an *inbound* tram on a single track section, there was a length of double line trackwork known as a *passing loop*. Usually a *halt* was associated with a loop because one tram had to stop anyway. On many systems the staff referred to the trams as *cars*.

With larger concerns, road widths permitting, double track was normal as delays were inevitable on single-line workings. On narrow streets trackwork was sometimes *interlaced*, to avoid the extra pointwork associated with loops, but on such sections trams could not meet one another.

Trams were powered by overhead electric copper cable carrying around 500 volts dc. To avoid *leakage*, a comprehensive system of porcelain *insulators* was used. The booms to carry the overhead cable were called *outreaches* and these in turn were carried on *tram poles* or *traction columns*, usually with some form of *tie rod* to provide adequate strength. The tram pole was usually topped with an ornamental cap or *finial* and, where top parts of columns telescoped into heavier lower parts, the joint was usually concealed with an ornamental *collar*. It was the practice to test all telescoped tram poles for fitness by dropping them from a prescribed height. The base of the tram pole was usually covered with an ornamental sleeve or *base*, but many of these were removed by breakage, and were not be replaced.

The track itself was special in that it carried a groove, or narrow channel, to accommodate the *wheel lipping* or *flange*. Sometimes grooved track was called *girder rail*. When the tram travelled along a *reserve*, away from the public road, it was usual to use the railway system of non-grooved railway track carried on transverse sleepers as this was more economical. Most rural tramways ran on railway type track when outside the town. This system was known as a *tramroad*, whereas the grooved tram rail, usually set in cobble stones running along a public road, was referred to as *tramway*. The tramway shared a road surface with other vehicles, the tramroad did not. Tramway personnel always called the track work the *permanent way* and those who repaired it were *gangers*. The tram driver was often called a *motor man* and the conductor was a *clippie*. Different countries had different terminology. For example, American companies called trams *streetcars* or *trolleys*; the windscreen was called a *windshield*; a bumper was called a *fender*; a lifeguard was often called a *cow catcher* and so on. Again, in America our *tram sheds* or *depots* were called *tram barns* or *stables*.

The EVOLUTION of TRAMCARS

Before turning to the detailed history of Irish trams, it might help to outline the main stages in the evolution of tramcar design. Although the cars depicted, apart from the first, will be those from Dublin, the same principles would apply wherever trams operated and evolved.

PIONEER

These were the first trams to appear and the description can apply to both horse and early electrical experiments. The designs, having no precedent of their own, tended to follow either railway or stagecoach practice. Pioneer cars were experimental and sought an identity of their own. Many were overly elaborate, with unnecessary embellishments, simply for the sake of effect. As tramcar design developed a vernacular of its own, with different needs requiring different solutions, a standard pattern of design emerged.

Seen here are:
1. John Stephenson's New York tramcar of 1832
2. A stagecoach type of vehicle which ran on the Swansea and Mumbles Tramway in Wales in the 1860s. This was probably similar to the first Fintona horse tram.
3. An early single deck Dublin horse tram.

FIRST GENERATION (Open front trams)

By the 1880s tramcar design had stabilised and was usually open fronted and open topped. The earliest horse trams were heavily ornamental but their design simplified over the years. Windows were narrower, often with arched panels over and varied in design from company to company. The platforms were short and the stairs to the upper deck were open threaded steel ladders. The early *knife board* or longitudinal upper deck bench seating had an open back rest. Lighting into the lower saloon was under these seats, forming what was known as *clerestory* lighting.

After a short while in service, the *ladder type* stairs were replaced by an enclosed *string* type with risers and treads. The position of the stairs was moved from a central location to a side one. Decency screens were added and the knife board back rests were given slats. In general, the designs were simplified and made safer. There were also single deck trams, usually on shorter routes or where low bridges prevented a double deck tram from operating, such as Bath Avenue railway bridge in Dublin.

The early electric trams introduced to Dublin in 1896 were similar to horse trams in many respects. The new electric trams usually had four or five windows in the saloon. The platforms were lengthened to accommodate the controller and the platform dashes were higher and more rounded. The knife board seating and clerestory saloon lighting became a thing of the past and the famous transverse *garden seats* with swivel back rests became the standard upper deck form of seating.

SECOND GENERATION (Open top trams)

The main departure from the first generation of tramcar design was the provision of a windscreen and the extension of the upper deck canopy to rest on the windscreen. This provided an enclosed platform or *vestibule* with the dual advantage of providing some shelter for the driver and extra seating accommodation on the upper deck.

The first enclosed platform tram in Europe appeared in Dublin in 1899. On account of the angular design of the windscreen, this tram, No 191, became know as *The Coffin* (see page 94).

THIRD GENERATION (Balcony trams)

As public comfort became the norm, it was decided to provide roof cover on that part of the upper deck directly over the saloon. This design of tram first appeared in 1904 in experimental form, but it was not until about 1916 that full production of this design began in Dublin. Originally, the upper deck platform, which was called a *balcony*, had no roof over it, but in later versions a roof was provided. The designers feared that such an exposed cantilevered roof would flex and break off in high winds. Eventually, it was extended fully over the upper deck floor area and tied down structurally with steel rods.

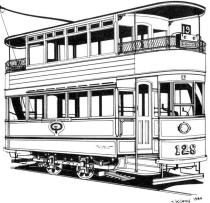

FOURTH GENERATION (Enclosed trams)

Whilst balcony cars were considered the finest in their day, with the benefits of open air travel in fine weather, the logical development was to totally enclose the upper deck. The earlier worries about doing this were structural, as the weight of the body and extra passengers, all cantilevering beyond the bulkhead structure of the lower saloon, would act as a descending lever and over-stress body components. To overcome this, the cantilevered platform was usually strengthened with steel beams tied well back into the structure as were the cant rail members above. Only five types of fourth generation tram operated in Ireland. These were the four wheel and bogie *Standards* in Dublin and the *Moffett*, *DK1* and *Chamberlain* cars in Belfast.

FIFTH GENERATION (Streamlined trams)

In the 1920s, bus competition made its presence very keenly felt and the tramway authorities had to improve the image of the trams. Many of their tramcars had been rebuilt and were ageing. The main departures in the fifth generation were the metal body structure and streamlining. The general aim was to achieve elegance and lightness. The Dublin *Luxury* trams, introduced in 1931, were an excellent design, reaching higher standards of speed, comfort and economy with plush upholstered seating throughout. They appeared in both four wheel and bogie form. The Dublin designs had very simple and elegant lines with a continuous rubbing strake wrapping around the windscreens and were very pleasing to the eye. On account of the extra width of the Dublin tramway gauge they had more copious accommodation than their British counterparts. Belfast, in 1938, also introduced streamlined trams called *McCreary* cars.

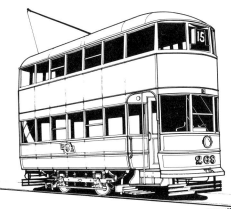

Horse Trams

DUBLIN TRAMS

The first horse tram in Ireland began operating at Fintona in Co Tyrone in 1854. This was not a street tram but ran on normal railway track and sleepers. This system was not possible on a public roadway, of course, and the grooved tram rail had not yet been invented. The first proposal for a horse tramway in Dublin was by a company called the Dublin Iron Road and Tramway Co Ltd, and the line was to run from Grafton Street to Rathfarnham, via Harcourt Street. Little is known about this pioneer company but, with a name like 'Iron Road', it had to have strong American connections as indeed had most of the early European endeavours. The most active person associated with the introduction of horse trams in Europe was George Francis Train who, as mentioned in the introduction, worked for John Stephenson. Mr Train was described as an energetic eccentric American, very determined to introduce the new mode of transport and never took 'no' for an answer, in spite of many obstacles, opposition and general mistrust of something new. He was active in introducing horse tramways not only to Dublin, Cork and Belfast, but also all over England.

In 1859 another proposal to run a tram in Dublin was put forward by the City of Dublin and Suburbs Tramway Co, but nothing came of this endeavour.

In 1867 The Tramways (Ireland) Act was passed. Under its powers a more serious attempt to introduce trams to Dublin was made by the City of Dublin Tramways Co, (possibly related to the 1859 company). This proposal was to link the railway termini of Kingsbridge (Heuston), Westland Row (Pearse) and Harcourt Street. The line was to travel along the South Quays, D'Olier Street, Pearse Street, Upper Merrion Street, St Stephen's Green and Earlsfort Terrace to Harcourt Street. Work actually started at Aston Quay to demonstrate the type of rail proposed, which was the step rail used in New York (see page 10). It is surprising that so enterprising a gentleman as Mr Train was so persistent in using the step rail which, on account of its upstand, caused havoc to other street users. It is all the more surprising since he had been run out of London some years previously for using the same rail. The rail was, of course, unacceptable and the company was instructed to abort its plans.

Although the City of Dublin Tramways Co never progressed beyond the experimental stage, and never owned any rolling stock or animals, it not only highlighted the problems associated with the step rail, but laid the foundations for future enterprise. George Train, more than likely, carried out experiments with horse traction to demonstrate the working of horse trams, possibly with one of the Stephenson or Starbuck cars used by him in Liverpool and elsewhere. The company may not have survived, but the seed of horse tram traction was planted in the minds of other businessmen and began to take root.

DUBLIN TRAMWAYS Co 1871-1881

The powers of the CDT were acquired by the Dublin Tramways Co, incorporated in 1871. This time it was proposed to use an early form of grooved rail, often called a box rail or girder rail, laid on longitudinal baulks of timber running across sleepers with tie rods to retain a constant gauge of 5'3". The rail, though still too weak in terms of design, as experience would reveal, did not cause the disruption of the step rail, and provided an acceptable solution to street rail transport at last. The DTC ran their first line from College Green via Dawson Street, St Stephen's Green, Harcourt Street and Rathmines, to Garville Avenue, Rathgar and commenced services on 1st February 1872 with six tramcars. The line was shortly afterwards extended north to Nelson's Pillar in O'Connell Street, and south to Terenure. The line proved a great success and soon other companies were making plans to lay their own horse tramways.

One problem soon to emerge was that the draught horses initially used were unsuited to the severity of work. They had not been specially bred, and the company had no option but to commence a programme of breeding their own stock to provide the necessary stamina. The original proposal of the preceding company (CDT) to link Kingsbridge Station with Harcourt Street Station (known as the Hatch St Line), was opened on 3rd June 1872. On 1st October the Dublin Tramway Co opened a third line from Nelson's Pillar to the Tower at Sandymount via D'Olier Street, Pearse Street, Westland Row, Merrion Square, Beggar's Bush, Bath Avenue, Londonbridge Road, Tritonville Road and Sandymount Road. In 1873 the company introduced a line to serve the village of Donnybrook, which ran via Merrion Square (North and East), Lower Fitzwilliam Street, Baggot Street, Waterloo Road and Morehampton Road, to the terminus at Donnybrook, near the present bus garage.

Also in 1873, this company provided another service from O'Connell Bridge along the North Quays to the gates of Phoenix Park at Infirmary Road. All the developments so far, apart from the North Quays and O'Connell Street, served the City south of the Liffey, and the chief reason for this was to attend to the needs of the better off citizens. To rectify this, the DTC laid a line down North Earl Street and Talbot Street, which turned left at Amiens Street and proceeded to Dollymount, to terminate near the present bus garage. For the time being, this constituted the empire of the DTC. In 1875 it was estimated that the company had 76 tramcars and 486 horses. Seventy of these cars were supplied by the Metropolitan Railway Carriage and Wagon Co of Birmingham, and had longitudinal seating in the saloon accommodating 20 passengers, and knifeboard or back to back seating for 26 on the upper deck. They had 10 saloon windows on either side. The earliest examples had open steel ladder stairs which proved unsafe and were later altered to the conventional string stairs.

The DTC also acquired six cars from the Cork Tramways Co Ltd when it ceased operations in 1875. Four of these were small cars with six saloon windows on each side and seated 30. The two larger cars (Nos 5 and 6 in the Cork fleet) had eight saloon windows per side and a full carrying capacity of 38 passengers. All six were built by Starbuck and Co of Birkenhead and survived on the Nelson's Pillar to Terenure route until electrification. It is possible that their handsome

blue and white livery may have been retained, and if so, may have influenced the adoption of these colours by the Dublin United Tramways at the amalgamation in 1881. It is known that the Donnybrook route used a livery of 'cream or pale yellow'. The company also operated horse omnibuses and had 55 in service in 1875. Some 6,000,000 passengers were carried in 1876.

The fares were comparatively high and outside the reach of the working classes. It would be true to say that the horse trams were really only catering for the well to do and could not yet be described as the 'poor man's carriage'. The City of Dublin Tramways Co later added linking tracks to their system, one across Kingsbridge to join the North and South Quays and another along Lower Gardiner Street and Lower Abbey Street to connect with the Dollymount line at Talbot Street.

NORTH DUBLIN STREET TRAMWAYS Co 1873-1881

A former director of the Dublin Tramways Co, William Barrington, resigned from the company and promoted a new concern, the North Dublin Street Tramways Co. He claimed that his proposals would be of great benefit to the underprivileged of the north side of the City. The areas of Glasnevin and Drumcondra were rapidly developing and it was chiefly to serve these new communities that his proposals were made. The NDST completed the construction of three lines in 1875, all terminating at Nelson's Pillar. The main line was to the Phoenix Park gate, passing through Parnell Square East, Blessington Street, and Berkeley Road to reach the North Circular Road. From here a second line turned left into Phibsborough Road and terminated near what is now known as Doyle's corner. A branch line continued from Doyle's Corner along the Phibsborough Road, over Cross Guns Bridge, via Botanic Road, to Washerwoman's Hill, Glasnevin, near the gates of the Bon Secour Hospital.

The third NDST line was laid to Drumcondra down Capel Street, Bolton Street, and Dorset Street, passing over Binn's Bridge to terminate near the junction of the Drumcondra Road and Botanic Avenue. In the reverse direction, this line was later extended to cross the Liffey at Grattan Bridge and along Parliament Street to turn left into Dame Street and terminate at College Green near Trinity College. This provided a continuous service from College Green to Drumcondra, Glasnevin and Phoenix Park.

The name 'North Dublin Street Tramways Co' was somewhat misleading, as the company immediately sought permission to extend their lines westwards to serve Inchicore by way of Dame St, Thomas St, James St, Mount Brown, and Emmet Road, Kilmainham. Some of the steepest gradients on any Dublin tramway existed along this route, especially passing Cork Hill at Dublin Castle and it was necessary to introduce an extra horse into the harness or traces. This horse was called a 'trace' or 'trip' horse and helped bring the tramcar up the hill. Trace horses were also used at Newcomen Bridge, and many of the canal bridges, at Cork Hill, Mount Brown and from Dominick Street to Granby Row.

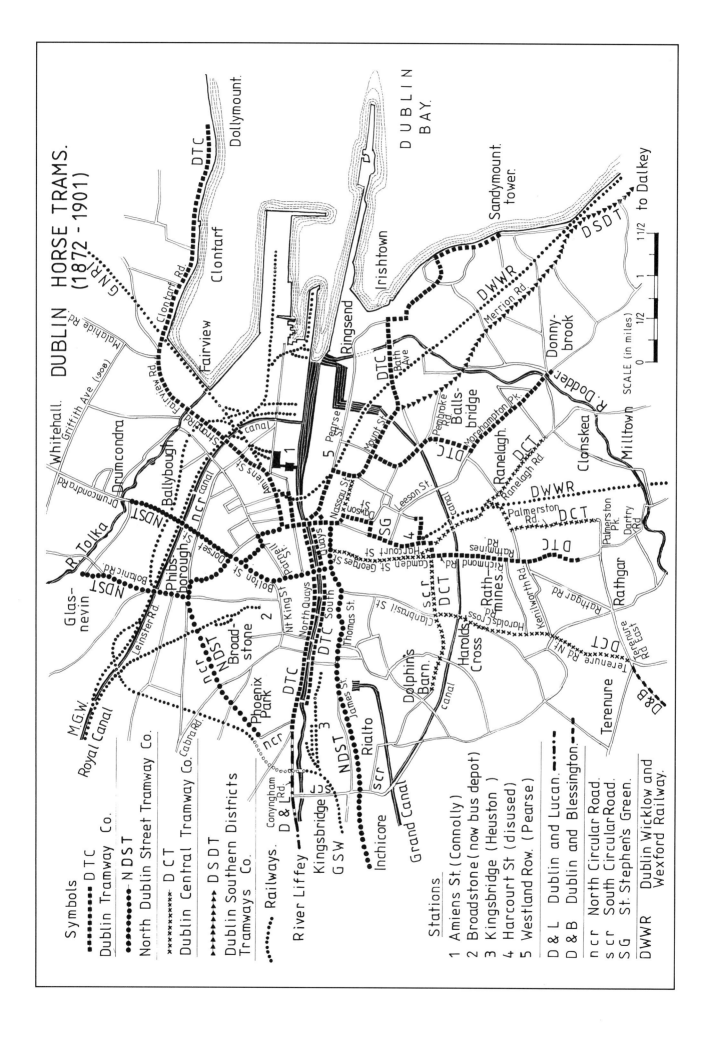

DUBLIN HORSE TRAMS. (1872 - 1901)

DUBLIN BAY.

Dollymount.
Clontarf
Fairview
Irishtown
Sandymount tower.
Ringsend
Ballsbridge
Donnybrook
Clonskea
Milltown
Ranelagh.
Rathmines.
Rathgar
Terenure
Harolds Cross
Dolphin's Barn.
Rialto
Inchicore
Kingsbridge
Phoenix Park
Broadstone
Glasnevin
Whitehall.
Drumcondra
Ballybough

to Dalkey

Symbols

DTC	Dublin Tramway Co.
NDST	North Dublin Street Tramway Co.
DCT	Dublin Central Tramway Co.
DSDT	Dublin Southern Districts Tramways Co.
	Railways.
	River Liffey
	Dublin and Lucan.
	Dublin and Blessington.

Stations

1 Amiens St. (Connolly)
2 Broadstone (now bus depot)
3 Kingsbridge (Heuston)
4 Harcourt St (disused)
5 Westland Row. (Pearse)

D & L Dublin and Lucan.
D & B Dublin and Blessington.
n c r North Circular Road.
s c r South Circular Road.
SG St. Stephen's Green.

DWWR Dublin Wicklow and Wexford Railway.

SCALE (in miles)
0   1/2   1   1 1/2

It is interesting to note that this company was the first to use 'one man operated' cars. These were single deck saloon cars seating 18 on longitudinal seats. On entering the car at the driver's end, the passengers deposited their fares in what was known as a 'Slawson's Patent Fare Receiving Box'. The driver could see the fare dropped through a glass side, and accordingly give the correct change if required. Once the fare was deposited, it was outside the reach of would-be thieves, and indeed, outside the reach of a dishonest employee. Such devices are now beginning to reappear in modern buses.

There were approximately 6 single deck horse cars with clerestory lighting, and turtleback roof and they were known as the 'American cars', possibly built by Stephenson. The NDST had a further 30 or so double deck horse cars, most likely supplied by the Metropolitan Company of Birmingham, as drawings of such a vehicle were published in a book on street tramways in 1877. They were an eight window design with a six foot wheelbase and knifeboard seating. Later versions would have been modified with the omission of the clerestory roof, and the use of typical garden seats with swivel backrests. Over 200 horses would have been required to operate the North Dublin Street Tramways system.

DUBLIN CENTRAL TRAMWAYS Co 1878-1881

In 1878 a third company was formed, called the Dublin Central Tramways Co. This company received approval to build a line from College Green to Rathfarnham. This went via South Great George's Street, westwards along the South Circular Road and, turning left into Clanbrassil Street, proceeded past Harold's Cross, serving Terenure. This line sent a branch from Camden Street to Ranelagh Village, turning right at the triangle into Charleston Road. At Belgrave Square the line turned left into Palmerston Road and terminated at Palmerston Park, near Rathgar. This line also had branches from Belgrave Square to link with Rathmines and Clonskeagh. These lines opened to traffic in 1879. William Martin Murphy, originally from Cork, was a director of the DCT. He played a major part in the evolution of the Dublin tramways and has been called the 'father' of the Dublin system. He was born in 1845 and lived to see the tramway system at its peak.

The DCT had approximately 30 double deck cars of the Metropolitan type and almost 200 horses. To assert their independence from each other, each company had distinctive liveries, with individual lettering, numbering and route identification. A model of a Dublin horse tram, constructed around this time (page 25), shows a rich livery of plum red and white for the College Green to Rathmines route, and this may be an accurate portrayal of the actual colours used. It is known that a purple livery was used on the College Green to Palmerston Park route, green livery on the College Green to Ratharnam route, and a rich livery of salmon on the 'Castle tram' which ran from Westland Row to a siding in Palace Street.

DUBLIN UNITED TRAMWAYS Co 1881

Most of the major villages and townships within a small radius of the city had by this time been reached. It must be remembered that the termini were, at that time, more or less at the city perimeter and rather than spread outwards where the light patronage would not benefit the coffers of the various companies, the trend was to improve the services within the city precincts. Of the three companies operating in the city, the earliest, the Dublin Tramways Co, was the largest, with sixteen route miles, whilst the other two companies each had about eight. As the companies evolved, they came to be recognised by their termini and so the various horse tramway companies had lines as follows:–

Dublin Tramways Co (16 miles)

1. O'Connell Street to Terenure
2. O'Connell Street to Donnybrook
3. O'Connell Street to Sandymount
4. O'Connell Street to Clontarf
5. O'Connell Street to Parkgate Street
6. Harcourt Street. Station to Kingsbridge Station

North Dublin Street Tramways Co (8½ miles)

1. O'Connell Street to Phoenix Park
2. O'Connell Street to Glasnevin
3. College Green to Drumcondra
4. O'Connell Street to Inchicore

Dublin Central Tramways Co (7½ miles)

1. College Green to Rathfarnham
2. College Green to Palmerston Park
3. College Green to Rathmines
4. College Green to Clonskeagh

The three companies saw the wisdom of pooling their resources and efforts, and on 1st January 1881 they amalgamated to form what became known as the Dublin United Tramways Co (DUTC). The new company now had an overall route mileage of 32 and carried almost 10,000,000 passengers in its first year of trade. The system was expanded and improved over the next few years and lines were laid from Clanbrassil Street (Leonard's Corner) to Dolphin's Barn, from Harrington Street to Harcourt Road, and from Camden Street to Richmond Street South.

Extra lines were laid at Lincoln Place and College Street to form valuable inter-connections. Instead of being independent small kingdoms, the three former companies unified into one large empire sharing common advantages for all concerned. Mr William Martin Murphy became the Director of the

DUTC and his careful and enterprising handling assured many years of growth.

The DUTC, when formed in 1881, had 132 horse trams on its books. Since the DTC had 76, the NDST 36, and the DCT 30, this would suggest that 10 of the earlier cars were disposed of. The earliest cars of the DTC, with ten saloon windows, dating from 1872, were rebuilt, eliminating the ornamental cusped or trefoil pattern, in favour of normal quarter light ventilating windows. It is possible, judging from some photographs, that every second window mullion was removed from some of these early cars, to provide a more modern appearance, with five side windows and larger glazed areas.

The expansion of routes and more frequent service led to a need for extra trams, and the company decided to construct these themselves at their famous Spa Road Works in Inchicore. A few cars were also constructed at the Terenure workshops. In all 181 double deck cars were built with the features typical of the later DUTC horse trams — seven saloon windows, longitudinal saloon seating, and upper deck garden seats. This was the beginning of a long history of tramcar (and later bus) construction at Spa Road, culminating with the fine luxury bogie cars of the mid 1930s.

DUBLIN SOUTHERN DISTRICTS TRAMWAYS Co

Ireland's first steam railway was constructed in 1834 from Dublin to Kingstown (now Dun Laoghaire). The purpose of this railway was to bring passengers arriving by the mail boat into the heart of the city. It is important to note that the original mail boat harbour was constructed at Howth. However, the journey from Howth to the city was along Telford's Road, (the Howth Road via Ratheny). Telford had been commissioned by the London GPO to link the City of London to the City of Dublin by good roads and harbours for the safe and speedy passage of mail. Speed was the essential factor and the rail link between Kingstown and Dublin City was one of the chief factors in the mail boat switching from Howth to Kingstown. As a result, the city stretched its boundaries towards Kingstown as large residential areas grew up. It was to serve these areas that the Dublin Southern Districts Tramways Co obtained powers to run a line from Blackrock to the city, terminating at Haddington Road, constructed to the usual 5'3" gauge. They also constructed a line from Kingstown railway station to the town of Dalkey, but for some reason adopted the gauge of 4'0". Old Ordnance Survey drawings of Dalkey show both 4'0" and 5'3" gauge trackwork side by side. This was because when the gauge was later increased, it was more expedient to simply provide an extra outer rail. In all, the DSDT operated 26 double deck horse cars, and would have needed

approximately 170 horses to operate the system effectively.

It appears that the DSDT felt it would be uneconomic to link Blackrock to Kingstown as this area was served by the Dublin, Wicklow and Wexford Railway, which in 1856 had leased the original Dublin and Kingstown Railway. The citizens between Blackrock and Kingstown were unhappy at being 'left out' so to speak and a second company, the Blackrock and Kingstown Tramways Co was formed, to link the two railway stations by a tramway. Through running, from Dublin City to Dalkey now became theoretically possible by tram, with two changes en route, and separate fares and the usual delays. However it would have taken almost two hours to complete the journey for an overall fare of 8d, whereas the railway company took little more than quarter of the time for the same fare and no changes. It is not surprising that the DSDT and BKT ran at a heavy loss and were soon seeking to be bought out by either the DUTC or the adjoining railway company, the DWWR. At the time, neither company was interested.

In an effort to overcome their problems, the DSDT introduced experiments with steam in the hope of speeding up the service. In 1882 two Kitson locomotives were purchased by the Company and two years later a further two locomotives were bought, only this time from Wilkinson. Local residents objected and trials ceased soon after. It was difficult to forsee at this stage that the misfortunes of this company would result not only in electrification of the entire tramway system in Dublin but also that these lines would carry the last electric trams to operate in Dublin.

Often a photograph of a tram is taken as part of a street scene, to which the trams are incidental. However this shot of No 59 is taken casually, but specifically of the tram, with the passengers clearly unaware of the presence of the photographer. The top hats and bowlers worn by the passengers give some indication of the usual status of horse tram passengers. The upper deck seat of No 59 is of the slatted back knifeboard type.

AV Henry, Author's collection

Top: **This scene is at College Green terminus, with Trinity College in the background. There are three cars standing at the terminus, each worthy of attention. On the left is one of the earlier DCT Metropolitan cars with clockwise direct stairs serving a central aisle with knifeboard open back seating over clerestory lighting.**

In the centre is one of the six American type turtle-back roof single deckers introduced by the NDST. On the right is a later DCT car with anti-clockwise direct stairs serving a right hand aisle with slatted backrest knife board seating.

The tram in the background crossing the picture is of the same type and is heading for Nelson's Pillar.

W Lawrence, Author's collection

Centre: **This scene shows the Nelson's Pillar terminus with three horse trams approaching from the direction of O'Connell Bridge and four horse cars ready to set off from south of the pillar. Another horse car is arriving north of the pillar. The impressive edifice to the left is the GPO. The tracks have recently been watered to reduce expansion and buckling, so this must be during a spell of hot summer weather. All the trams are of the 7 window design, although with different route liveries. The horse cars approaching the Pillar are nos 109, 56 and 34, and the latter tram is returning from Terenure via Kenilworth Square and Harold's Cross, as operated by the DCT. Of the cars waiting at the Pillar the furthest left is ready to set off for Donnybrook. The gentleman with the top hat crossing in front of No 109 is followed by a porter carrying two cases, one on his head.**

W Lawrence, Author's collection

Bottom: **This is a rare shot of the changing of the horses at the Nelson's Pillar terminus. Although every journey necessitated a change in each direction, it was seldom recorded on camera. The tram about to reverse direction is scheduled to go to Sandymount as operated by the DTC. Compare this photograph with the one above and you will notice that an entrance portico, with surrounding railings, has been added to the pillar and looks a little out of character. On the north side of the pillar you will see ladders stacked against a high pole. These were left here by the Dublin Fire Brigade in readiness for fire fighting in the city's main thoroughfare.**

John Kennedy collection

This view is taken from Bachelor's Walk, in the late 1880s, looking east over O'Connell Bridge towards the Custom House and Docks. The tram is returning from Rathmines and on the last leg of her journey to the Nelson's Pillar terminus. Butt Bridge is still a swivel bridge to allow ships closer to O'Connell Bridge. As yet the railway bridge connecting Westland Row Station to Amiens Street has not been constructed. The well known firm of Clery and Co, advertised on the tram, still exists serving generations of Dubliners. The young man and woman immediately behind the kerbside horse and cart appear very intent. The kennel-like hut on the adjoining cart is a curiosity. Cabbies await customers on the Liffey side of Bachelor's Walk.
                                                                                                W Lawrence, Author's collection

This view is worth comparison with the one above. It is taken a little further away from O'Connell Bridge, still on Bachelor's Walk, about 1898 or 1899. The Loop Line bridge is now constructed, injuring the once splendid view of the Custom House. Horse car No 111 (known as *The Sergeant*) was built for the Dublin Tramways Co and is heading towards Nelson's Pillar from Kingsbridge Station. The earlier form of knifeboard seating has been replaced with the familiar garden slatted seats with swivel backrest to enable passengers to face the direction of travel. In the background the swivel bridge is partly open permitting a tug to exit under full steam. The trams meeting on O'Connell Bridge are now electric, the one on the right being a DSDT car.
                                                                                                W Lawrence, Author's collection

Top: It is believed that this model was built as a prototype for the later horse trams with anti-clockwise direct stairs. The knife board seating however is of the original open back type which appeared with the early cars, and the upper deck surround railings with low decency screen are also of the earlier design. The model is thus transitional between the earlier and later horse tram types.

Sackville Street on the cant panel is now, of course, O'Connell Street. The Rathmines line was operated by the DTC. The top photograph on page 23 shows a Rathmines horse tram, though obviously in a lighter livery, so the livery shown here may be a proposal. The model was restored by the National Transport Museum, and two other liveries were stripped away before the livery shown was discovered.

Author

Centre: This drawing shows a typical horse tram of the later period. The stairs were usually removed from the bulkhead to permit access onto the platform from either side of the tram. The knifeboard upper deck seating is of the slatted backrest type. This tram is allocated to the Clontarf route, Clontarf being the most easterly terminus of the DTC.

The only means of lighting on the platform was by an oil lamp fixed to the outer bulkhead panel in the quarter light position. This assisted passengers to board and alight and indicated the tram's presence as it moved along the darkened streets. The underside of the canopy was usually stained with smoke and oily residue and needed frequent cleaning to avoid unpleasant smells. The livery of yellow or primrose is indicative only.

Author's drawing

Bottom: The Galway and Salthill horse tramway was the most westerly tramway in Europe. The scene here is at Eyre Square shortly after their introduction. The tram is fully crowded, both in the saloon and on the upper deck, and the conductor is about to call his horses into action.

The horses themselves are of interest, in that the further chestnut horse is taking an active interest in proceedings, while the dabbled grey has her ears back towards the driver, waiting for the word of command. In later days the rocker panel and dashes were also painted red.

From a painting by Charles Roycroft,
Reproduced by kind permission of An Post

Top left: The author (left) discussing some museum matters with Bert Brown. Bert, at 78, is the oldest working member of the museum at Howth. The tram being worked on is No 224, originally T24, an ex-London tram built by Brush Electric, and now being rebuilt as an open fronted Dublin electric car of the 1896 period.   *Bob Dawson*

Top right: Martin Wills (left) and Bill Garioch (Vice-chairman of the Transport Museum Society) carrying out the finishing touches to one of the bogies of Hill of Howth car No 9 at the PMPA depot (Private Motorist's Protection Association) at Longmile Road in Dublin, shortly before the tram was brought to Howth. The original bronze brushes and greased leather seals have just been replaced.
Author

Centre: Giant's Causeway tramcar No 9 at Broadstone bus depot in Dublin, ready for her final journey to Howth. The landward side is restructured for the greater part and is almost ready for repanelling. Around this time it was discovered that No 9 was originally an open sided car, and that the saloon roof and windows had been added at a later date.

The internal bulkhead was necessary more for structural stability than class separation for the passengers. First class had a veneered ceiling and blue moquette cushions, whereas second class had a varnished strip roof and timber slatted seats. When the line was converted to overhead power pick up, a trolley standard was located within the second class saloon, puncturing the clerestory roof. The trolley was on the seaward side.

Author

Bottom: Tram bodies still exist around the countryside, although their structural condition is usually suspect. This vehicle was No 108, a Dublin Luxury tram built in 1934, which survived on the Dalkey route until 1949.

It was purchased by the O'Brien family in Blackrock, Co Dublin, where it was comfortably rigged out and provided extended family accommodation. The land on which it sat was required for development in the late 1980s and No 108 was dragged along the ground away from the houses and set on fire.

Mrs O'Brien told me that the children on their way to school that morning, kissed the tram to bid it a fond farewell, knowing they would never see it again. Their grandfather wept to see it burn so fiercely and recalled some very happy memories about No 108, and the trams in general.

Author's collection

Top: This painting by Sean Bolan shows the Dublin and Blessington steam tram (pages 49-51) passing Russborough House as it heads to Blessington. The locomotive is *Cambria,* an 0-4-0ST built by the Hunslet Engine Co of Leeds as a contractor's locomotive in 1894, and acquired by the tramway in 1918. To protect passengers from the smoke, the locomotive is fitted with a long funnel and the tram has glazed bulkheads. The sides of the upper deck are unglazed however, leaving the third class passengers still somewhat vulnerable to smuts. Russborough House is now open to the public. It was once the seat of the Earls of Milltown, and the sixth Earl was the first chairman of the tramway.   *Reproduced by kind permission of the Lord O'Neill*

Centre: **Colour photographs of the Giant's Causeway trams are rare,** although a few have recently come to light. In this 1948 view, cars Nos 20, 16, and 10 are seen waiting at the Causeway, ready to return to Portrush. No 10, nearest the camera, was a saloon trailer, very similar to No 9. Both had seven side windows and the roof structure was identical. However No 10 lacked the ornate waist panel, hooped mouldings and crest seen on No 9 in the photograph on page 62.

These mouldings were a distinctive feature of the Causeway trams, adorning trailers and locomotives alike.

Each Causeway rake consisted of saloon car and two open cars. In this case the saloon car is a trailer, but sometimes it was a powered car.

RC Ludgate collection

Bottom: This view of a Cork electric tram is a painting by Charles Roycroft, based on a well known photograph taken around the time of the opening. The statue is of Father Mathew, a popular priest, who preached on intemperance in Cork and throughout Ireland. The statue was the equivalent of *Nelson's Pillar* in Dublin, or *Castle Junction* in Belfast, where trams are concerned, and was simply known as *The Statue.*

The yellow on the rocker panel would have been more cream-like in appearance than that depicted here. The gentleman on the upper deck was a well known reporter of the day who appeared wherever there was a good story.

Reproduced by kind permission of An Post

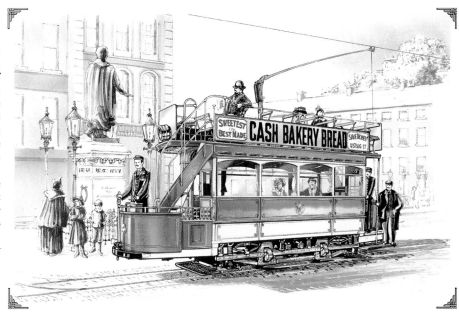

Top: **The Fintona horse tram was unique in many respects. It was the last horse tram to operate in Ireland and the second last such in the British Isles. It also had (until 1930) the highest tram number in Ireland, even though the system had only one tram! Here we see the tram inside Fintona station about to depart for the junction.**

FW Shuttleworth

Centre: **With a load of English tramway enthusiasts aboard, tram No 381 departs from the station on 8th May 1957 for a trip to Fintona Junction, some 1100 metres distant. The tram was a large vehicle, and since the line had a gradient, hauling it was no easy load for *Dick* the tram horse. Note the layer of ash between the rails.**

ColourRail IR182

Bottom: **This almost broadside view of the tram at Fintona Junction on the same date, emphasises the size of No 381, compared to most city horse trams. It was built in 1883 and had a total length of 25'0" compared to around 20'0" for most horse trams. It had a wheelbase of 10'0", as against the usual 6'0" and seated 48 passengers. The reader might like to compare these views with the top photograph on page 23 which shows a Dublin horse tram constructed by the same manufacturers —Metropolitan.** *ColourRail*

FINTONA

The Fintona horse tram, always known locally as 'The Van', was one of the most historic tramways in existence. At the time of closure in 1957 it was the longest serving horse tramway in the world. The Londonderry and Enniskillen Railway was incorporated in 1845 and the line opened as far as Fintona in 1854. It became part of the Irish North Western Railway in 1860, which in turn became part of the Great Northern Railway (Ireland) in 1876.

At the time of opening, steam locomotives arrived directly into the town of Fintona. However, the junction for Enniskillen was located three quarters of a mile from the town itself and the route taken by the railway company was chosen for reasons of economy and not common sense. Fintona Junction to the town of Fintona therefore became a branch line, and since so short a line would have been uneconomic for steam operation, horse haulage was the only viable alternative at the time. At first the people of Fintona were outraged, but gradually over the years they came to love the horse tram. The horse, always known as *Dick,* whether mare or gelding, was perhaps the most famous and best loved horse in Ireland, renowned in song and story.

The first 'van' was very similar to the vehicle used on the earlier Swansea to Oystermouth horse tramway in South Wales (see page 16) and is believed to have comprised a three compartment carriage with side stairs at both ends giving access to six transverse cross benches on the roof. The driver was perched rather precariously at high level, and accidents, fatal and otherwise, were all too common. The vehicle was in effect an enormous stage coach and not at all suitable. It was however over thirty years before something better was delivered. This followed the true lines of tramcar design, which changed little over the years, and was basically a double-deck horse tram with greater capacity on account of railway haulage. This car (No 381) was manufactured by the Metropolitan Railway Carriage and Wagon Company and was almost identical to the North Dublin Street Tramways' cars introduced in the 1870s. It had knife board seating on the upper deck located over clerestory lighting, and the lower deck was divided into two saloons. Originally first and second class passengers were carried in the saloons, whilst third class passengers were obliged to climb the stairs to the upper deck. Such was the novelty and demand to travel on the outside that the class system was meaningless and was eventually discontinued.

The fleet number itself, 381, may have conveyed the impression to the un-informed, that Fintona must have been a thriving city of some magnitude to warrant so high a fleet number. However the tram on its delivery in 1883, simply inherited the next number in the GNRI carriage list. The latter company was unusual in that at one time it operated the horse tram at Fintona, the electric trams at Howth, Co Dublin, diesel railcars, steam and diesel locomotives and rail-buses, a motley and fascinating cross section of transport motive power. On account of the gentle gradients and lighter patronage, only one horse was necessary to operate the line. In 1953, the tram was damaged in an accident, and the GNRI, planned to use this opportunity to cease operations. The local outcry and opposition to abandonment were such, that the company was obliged to repair the tram without delay and quickly usher it back into service. With the regrettable spate of railway closures in the late 1950s, the horse tram finally ceased operations on 30th September 1957, when *Dick* hauled 'the van' for the last time.

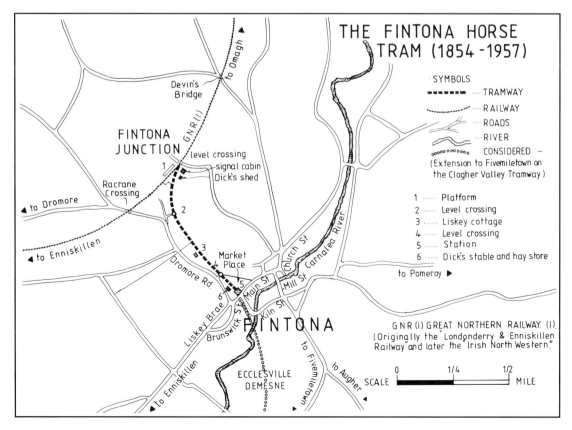

THE FINTONA HORSE TRAM (1854 -1957)

SYMBOLS
- - - - - - TRAMWAY
- - - - - - RAILWAY
- - - - - - ROADS
- - - - - - RIVER
ooooo ooo ooo CONSIDERED :- (Extension to Fivemiletown on the Clogher Valley Tramway)

1 ..... Platform
2 ..... Level crossing
3 ..... Liskey cottage
4 ..... Level crossing
5 ..... Station
6 ..... Dick's stable and hay store

to Pomeroy ▶

GNR (I) GREAT NORTHERN RAILWAY (I)
(Originally the Londonderry & Enniskillen Railway" and later the Irish North Western"

SCALE   0   1/4   1/2   MILE

to Omagh

Devin's Bridge

GNR (I)

FINTONA JUNCTION

level crossing
signal cabin
Dick's shed
1

Racrane Crossing

to Dromore

2

to Enniskillen

3

Market Place
4
Church St
Carnalea River
Mill St

Dromore Rd

Liskey Brae
Brunswick St
Main St
Kiln St
FINTONA
5
6

to Enniskillen

to Fivemiletown

to Augher

ECCLESVILLE DEMESNE

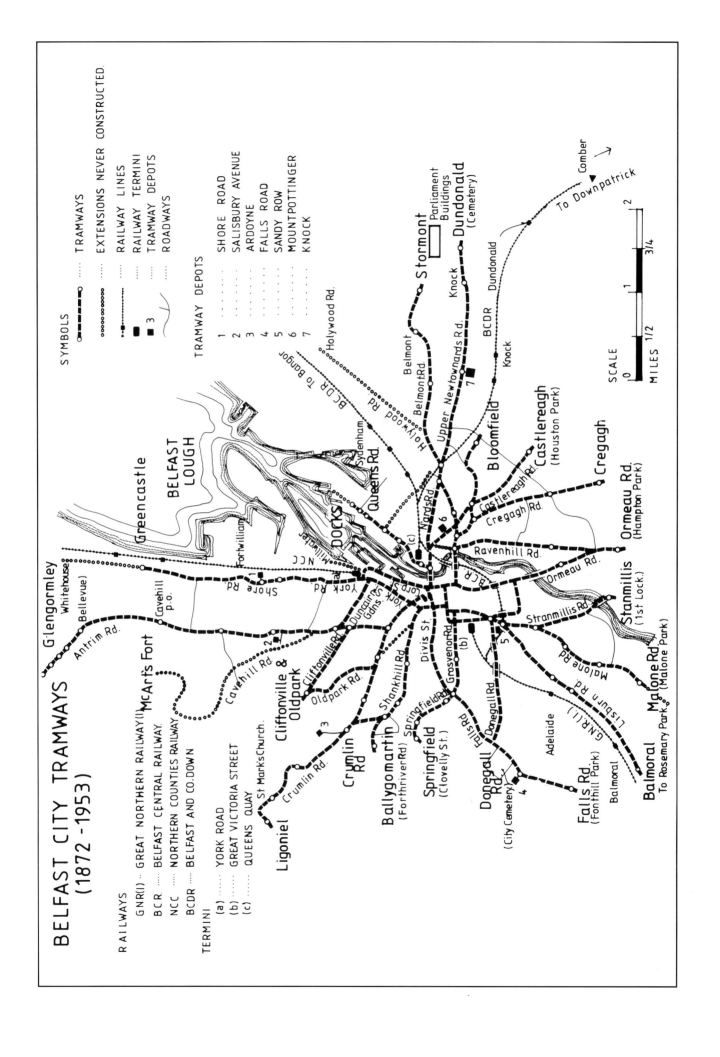

BELFAST CITY TRAMWAYS
(1872 - 1953)

RAILWAYS

GNR(I) .... GREAT NORTHERN RAILWAY(I).
BCR ...... BELFAST CENTRAL RAILWAY.
NCC ...... NORTHERN COUNTIES RAILWAY
BCDR ...... BELFAST AND CO.DOWN

TERMINI

(a) ...... YORK ROAD
(b) ...... GREAT VICTORIA STREET
(c) ...... QUEENS QUAY

SYMBOLS

TRAMWAYS

EXTENSIONS NEVER CONSTRUCTED.

RAILWAY LINES
RAILWAY TERMINI
TRAMWAY DEPOTS
ROADWAYS

TRAMWAY DEPOTS

1 ...... SHORE ROAD
2 ...... SALISBURY AVENUE
3 ...... ARDOYNE
4 ...... FALLS ROAD
5 ...... SANDY ROW
6 ...... MOUNTPOTTINGER
7 ...... KNOCK

SCALE

MILES 0 1/2 3/4 1 2

BELFAST TRAMS

Like Dublin, Belfast also introduced horse trams in 1872, as indeed did Cork. Ulster had a history of horse trams long before the South, in that the famous Fintona horse tram started in 1854. In 1855 the Londonderry and Coleraine Railway opened a branch line from Magilligan Station to Magilligan Point (to connect with a steamer service to Inishowen) with an intermediate station at Drummond. Four 'trams', believed to have been horse hauled, were operated daily in both directions. However, the branch was unsuccessful and was abandoned after a few months. It is believed that a donkey-hauled temporary tramway ran from Ballycastle Harbour to a local quarry to fetch stone around 1740. A cable and horse operated railway also transported stone from a quarry at Ballyaghan in Cavehill to the Victoria Channel in Belfast between 1832 and 1896. There were also several other small mining operations that used horse or human haulage over rails around the province and, of course, after the introduction of the Belfast horse trams others were to follow.

For the first time in Ireland the name J D Larson appears. Mr Larson was associated with a company that was involved in the successful introduction of horse trams on the continent. A local man, Mr William Morris, joined forces with Mr Larsen to obtain the necessary powers to run horse trams in the City of Belfast. By an Act of Parliament passed on 10th August 1871, permission was granted for three short lines, and a service commenced between Castle Place and Botanic Gardens on 28th August 1872. The service was operated by the Belfast Street Tramways Co, using single deck cars each pulled by one horse setting off at half hourly intervals between 8.30am and 8.30pm. The gauge selected was the standard Irish gauge of 5'3". By 1878 the system had been extended northwards to the Antrim Road and southwards to Ormeau Bridge and this brought increased traffic. The single deckers were rebuilt as double deck cars and a second horse was introduced to assist in their haulage. The fare charged was 2d in the saloon and 1d on the outside and these charges were irrespective of the distance travelled.

It was also decided at this stage that all future extensions would be in the 4'9" gauge and the existing trackwork built to the Irish 5'3" gauge was altered accordingly. In the early days of horse traction, there was no depot and the trams were stationed at Wellington Place at night time while the horses were stabled nearby in Wellington Street. The 1870s must have been untroubled by vandalism as this could hardly happen today without provoking attack.

Around this time the Company sought powers to lay lines to Mountpottinger and the Lisburn Road and with a further Act in 1875, the Company was also empowered to build a short extension along Station Street to the terminus of the Belfast and County Down Railway at Queens Quay. However none of these lines were built until after electrification.

Again in 1878, Parliamentary approval was obtained to build more extensions as follows:–
1. To Connswater Bridge on the Newtownards Road.
2. To Bedford Street and Ormeau Avenue.
3. Along the Lisburn Road as far as Surrey Street.
4. Along the Crumlin Road from Carlisle Circus to the Courthouse.
5. From the terminus at Alexandra Park Avenue along the Antrim Road to Chichester Park.

Most of the earlier lines were single track with passing loops but as the services improved, and where the road width permitted, double track became the norm. There was some interlaced track along Divis Street and Victoria Street which were too narrow for double track.

In 1884 Parliamentary approval was obtained for further extensions and new lines as follows:–
6. Extension to the Connswater Line.
7. Extension from Ormeau Bridge to Hampton Park.
8. Extension along the Crumlin Road to Leopold Street.
9. A new line along Royal Avenue.
10. A new line along the Falls Road to Falls Park.

All these tramways were operated by the Belfast Street Tramway Co. However, there were also smaller companies that obtained powers to extend the BST to serve their own areas and these small companies were as follows:–
a. Sydenham District, Belfast Tramway Co (1885) extending from the Holywood Arches to the Old Holywood Road.
b. The Belfast and Ligoniel Tramway Co (1892) extending from the Crumlin Road to Ligoniel Village.
c. The Belfast and County Down Railway Co (1892) extending from Bridge End to the BCDR terminus in Station Street.

All these systems were separately owned and funded but were worked by the Belfast Street Tramways Co who took the fares and paid a rental to each of the companies in question. The trams themselves bore a livery of blue and white with gold lining. Towards the end of horse operation there was a total of 171 cars (much the same as Dublin), operating over 33 miles of mostly double track. These provided a frequent and efficient service reputed to be on a par with, if not better than, that in Dublin. Certainly, to have an equivalent mileage and tram stock in a smaller city must have ensured an excellent service.

The early horse trams usually had 6 saloon windows and were of the first generation design with open fronts and tops. All were later rebuilt with three large saloon windows, and 'Lincrusta' ceilings (made from an embossed, painted paper), some as late as 1902. This gave the Belfast horse trams a very modern appearance. Where gradients were too steep for two horses, a third, and sometimes a fourth, trace or trip horse, was introduced to help out.

The depots of the BST were at Sandy Row, Lisburn Road, Mountpottinger, Knock, Antrim Road and Falls Park. Apart from 171 horse trams, the company also had two horse omnibuses, ten carts, thirteen four wheeled vans, five sand-distributors, four water carts, one permanent way car and a horse ambulance. The seating capacity of the trams was 18 in the saloon and 22 outside, or a total of 40 passengers.

Top: **Royal Avenue in the horse tram era, taken from Castle Junction. The approaching tram cannot be identified but the receding one is No 9. This photograph should be compared with the colour photograph on page 118. Note the Provincial Bank of Ireland on the left. The next three buildings are the Ulster Reform Club, the Grand Central Hotel and the General Post Office.**

RC Ludgate collection

Bottom: **Castle Place around 1900, with three horse trams visible. The tram in the foreground is heading for the Antrim Road, and No 94, directly behind it, is bound for the Woodvale Road. The car approaching in the distance has its sun screens down. These screens were on the exterior of the tram.**

The buildings visible in this view are not without interest and include The Empire on the left, later to be occupied by the Fifty Shilling Tailors, and currently by Clarke's. The tall building on the right is Malcolmson's, followed by Davidson and Hardy's. Further up the street is a shop known as the '6$^{1}/_{2}$d Store'. Finally, on the site now occupied by Woolworths and Burton's is the famous Foster Green's tea merchants, demolished in 1929.

RJ Welch, courtesy Ulster Museum

Top: Although horse trams tend to arouse less interest than electric trams, there are considerable differences evident in the Belfast fleet as these pictures show. This is obviously an early photograph of No 44, as it has the older six window arrangement. The upper deck has knife-board seating.

In this photograph it is on a Woodvale Road service and a pair of trace horses has been added for the climb up to Ardoyne and Ligoniel. Note how the traces of the leading horses are attached to the collars of the rear ones. The boy in the saddle has the job of leading the trace horses.

One point worth noticing about this picture is the amount of dirt on the road, particularly on the part that is not cobbled. This was very typical of roads in this period. The diamond shaped posters on the tram window are advertising the Belfast Exhibition and the Commercial Hotel.

RC Ludgate collection

Centre: The last day of horse tram operation in Belfast was 4th December 1905 and this photograph was taken on that occasion. It was taken at Fortwilliam Park on the Antrim Road service.

No 73 is one of the rebuilt trams, the most obvious difference being the provision of three large windows in the saloon in place of the previous six. The Belfast horse trams were well provided with destination indicators, including a blind above the middle saloon window.

The ribs visible on the nearest horse suggest that the animals are not all that well looked after. To the left of the driver is a notice which, above and below Castle Place, reads "The lifeboat rule is women and children first". Obviously courtesy was not taken for granted even then! The small notice on the stairs discourages spitting. After ninety years does anyone now know what Sapolio was and how it saved time?

RC Ludgate collection

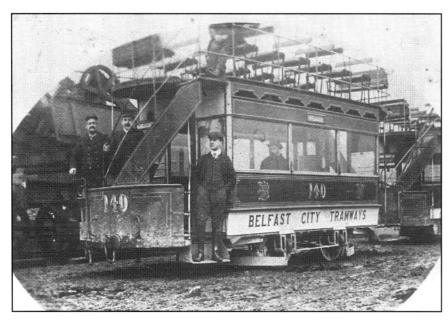

Bottom: This photograph is something of a mystery as it shows two Belfast horse trams at York Road station goods yard. Note the heavy duty railway crane in the background. The two 'crewmen' appear to be railway employees, and the three passengers may be friends of the photographer.

The picture was most likely taken after electrification of the Belfast trams, and the most intriguing explanation is that these were two of the cars acquired by the City of Derry Tramways at that time (see page 42). If so that would positively identify one of the Derry trams as Belfast No 140.

Although broadly similar to No 73 above, the reader should notice that No 140 has only seven louvre openings on the panel above the windows compared to eight on No 73.

RC Ludgate collection

CORK TRAMS

I have spoken previously of George Francis Train. As early as 1860, Mr Train carried out a detailed survey of the streets of Cork City with the City Surveyor, Henry Hugh Roche. Proposals were put forward for the introduction of a horse tramway to link the various railway termini. George Train was described as an energetic and eccentric American. He grew up at a time when horse drawn 'street cars' were beginning to take root in American cities and he worked with John Stephenson in New York. It was Train, more than anyone else, who played a major part in bringing the tram, or street car, to Europe. He had a flamboyant manner which endeared him to some but angered others. Train travelled around the world in 80 days and is believed to be the inspiration for Phileas Fogg in the Jules Verne classic. He suffered bouts of insanity and melancholia and died in relative obscurity. For many years the trams in Cork were called 'Train Cars' and this is believed to have been a result of the pioneering work done by him in the early days.

It might be opportune now to mention Mr James Clifton Robinson, who will be mentioned in connection with the introduction of electric trams to Dublin City. Mr Robinson, born in Birkenhead, was an enthusiastic follower of Mr Train, followed the latter's tram 'trials' with great interest, and joined his company. When Train set about introducing horse trams to London, the young Robinson was an office boy and soon caught the attention of Train, who quickly promoted him to a position of authority. Robinson himself was to become a leading figure in the British tramway empire and was knighted for his great services in the electric traction field. He became the first manager of the Cork Horse Tramway and while in this position he met and married Mary Edith Martin from Blackrock.

Cork in 1872 had a population of 50,000, and had no fewer than four separate railway termini. North of the River Lee were Alfred Street, terminus of the Great Southern and Western Railway and Summerhill, terminus of the Cork and Youghal (acquired by the GSWR in 1866). South of the Lee were Albert Quay, terminus of the Cork and Bandon Railway, and Victoria Quay, terminus of the Cork, Blackrock and Passage Railway.

Like the Seine in Paris, the River Lee divides into north and south channels before reaching the central part of the city and links again just beyond it, on its passage to the sea. Whilst this adds to the scenic setting of the city, bridging the river so many times also had its problems and the shortest distance between two points was often very roundabout.

The purpose of the horse tramway was to provide a service between some of the main stations to facilitate interchange, as well as catering for the normal city passenger. The proposals were put forward by Train and Roche, and were met with hostility from the jarveys and cabbies who operated small covered cabs, known as 'gingles'. Their drivers were known as 'gingle men', because of their custom of reciting gingles as they sought passengers. The gingle men naturally feared for their livelihoods and, apart from the objection to the use of the stepped rail which caused such havoc to other road users,

there was a genuine public mistrust of something so revolutionary as horse-hauled street trams. In short, nothing came of their earliest proposals.

The Chairman of the Cork and Kinsale Junction Railway, a subsidiary of the Cork and Bandon Railway, was an Englishman, MH Williams. He was very interested in having a horse tram link between their Albert Quay terminus and those north of the River Lee. He also saw a commercial role for such a tramway, bringing light wagons of fish and other freight into the heart of the city. Gradually, he won public support and the Cork Tramways Company Ltd was incorporated. The opening took place on 12th September, 1872. By all accounts, it was a joyous occasion with good crowds to cheer in the new system but was not without incident and several minor derailments took place, to the great embarrassment of the management. The Company was basically a London-based concern with directors from England and the north of Ireland. Unfortunately, some of the directors had an arrogant manner which was not very acceptable to Cork Corporation. From the beginning there existed an unease which festered into anger, and later, enmity. The system was never without difficulties and had to fight many legal battles. An incident where a local man was accidentally slain by a pick axe, while working on the track-laying, did not endear the company to local people.

The horse tramway followed the pattern of a rather distorted letter 'C', (see route map). Setting off from Victoria Road in a clockwise direction, the trams ran along Albert Quay, past the Municipal Buildings, over Anglesea Bridge, along South Mall, completing the base of the 'C' in an East-West direction. The trams now entered the busy shopping precinct rising northwards along Grand Parade until its junction with Patrick Street. The trams then turned right along the top arm of the 'C' in a rather anti-clockwise sweep, along Patrick Street, past the Father Mathew statue, crossing over the River Lee at St Patrick's Bridge. They then proceeded along Bridge Street, and King Street (later known as MacCurtain Street) to Alfred Street, finishing near what was then the railway terminus of the GSWR. At the end of Bridge Street, the tram made a right angle turn into King Street going in a west to east direction running more or less parallel to the bottom arc of the 'C', along South Mall. A short-cut linking the south and north arms of the 'C' continued from Anglesea Bridge northwards up Parnell Place (then Warren Place) along Merchants Quay to rejoin the main line at Patrick Street. The track was constructed to the 5'3" gauge with passing loops at frequent intervals.

The trams themselves were built by Starbuck and Co of Birkenhead, the birthplace of James Clifton Robinson, and there were small and large versions. They were typical early double-deck horse trams, with open-tread winding stairs, and knife board seating on the upper deck, and were not dissimilar to the early Dublin horse trams. The smaller trams, (Nos 1 – 4 inclusive), had six saloon windows with the typical ornate arched panel over and a highly decorative waist panel with

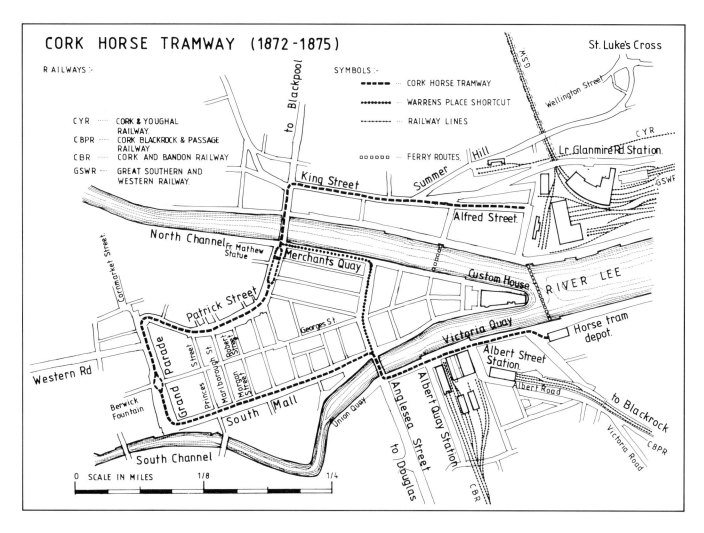

the words *Cork Tramway Company*. Nos 5 & 6 were larger cars with eight saloon windows and were to a slightly later design. Advertising panels were added in the early days of running. The livery was blue and white. Nos 1 – 4 carried 14 passengers in the saloon and 16 outside, whereas Nos 5 and 6 carried 18 in the saloon and 20 on the outside. The lower deck seats were upholstered in scarlet.

In following the pattern of a 'C' where a terminus was located at both extremities, a most circuitous route was followed and those passengers simply wishing to continue on their journey across the city were brought on a grand tour around Cork City before arriving at their destination. In essence, the tramway was an internal hub, which failed to reach outwards into the suburbs to draw passengers. The tramway failed to serve very well either the citizens of Cork or those wishing to pass through. This was quickly recognised and proposals were sought to extend the tramway to Distillery Gates, North Mall, up Mulgrave Hill to the Butter Exchange, from Albert Street to the Gas Co, from Singer's Corner to Sunday's Well, from Coburg Street to Blackpool and from Victoria Road depot southwards to the CBPR terminus, with various links in between. These extensions would have stretched the system into the suburbs and provided a meaningful service. However,

this was not to be. The clouds of gloom which always hung over this little tramway were steadily darkening. The track used was causing annoyance to other road users, and the anger of the Corporation against the offhand manner of 'foreign' directors reached its peak. The gingle men could take shorter routes between termini for a smaller fare. The system did not serve the city, which was expanding in all directions. When the horse tramway first appeared, it was met with jubilation and a popular song of the day ran:–

> *As I was going down Patrick Street*
> *I heard a lady say*
> *Oh it's jolly to be riding*
> *on the new tramway.*

But the jubilation was not to last for long. Traffic on the system declined after a short period of operation as antipathy grew. Within two years the Company was on its knees and running at a heavy loss. In early 1875 the entire system was bought out for the amazingly low sum of £510 by a Stephen O'Hea-Cussen, a local Cork man. He proposed calling it the Cork Citizens Tramway Co Ltd in an attempt to reawaken public pride in the system. He won the support of many local businessmen who saw a future in the line, but it was too late. Entrenched feelings on the part of the Corporation and public discontent could not be moved and on 22nd October 1875 the fate of the tramway was sealed. The City Surveyor was instructed to remove the tram rails without delay and reinstate the roads. One councillor said that nine out of every ten citizens felt so embittered against the horse tramway for one reason or another that they wanted it removed and the streets restored to their original condition, almost as if it had never existed. Some visionary people were amazed at the shortsightedness of the Corporation and citizens alike and a visiting former Mayor of Newark in New Jersey, who happened to be in Cork at the time of the decision, commented:– "Is it possible that your city is going to advance backwards?" Several wiser men described the tearing up of the tracks as vandalism and an act of sabotage to appease an angry mob. Protests were held in an attempt to reverse the Corporation's decision and sway public

opinion, but without success, and the little tramway, that never really had a chance, finally succumbed. The rolling stock was gladly bought by the Dublin Tramway Co and was reputed to have been used on their Terenure line surviving there for a further twenty-five years or so.

The abandonment of the horse trams in Cork City was soon regretted. In Ireland, horse tramways spread to the major cities of Dublin, Belfast, Derry and Galway but for some reason never found favour in Limerick or Waterford. The horse trams everywhere proved popular and profitable and there was hardly a major city in Europe that could not boast of this most modern and comfortable mode of railed street transport. It must have seemed a very backward step indeed for Cork to have adopted this new system and, almost before the tracks were settled, to have ripped them up. The decision to do so could not have been rationally reached, but rather must have sprung from emotional or subjective reasons.

Top: **This view was taken in Grand Parade probably around 1875 and shows horse tram No 5 (in the foreground) and No 6 (left background). The cars have just crossed each other at the passing loop round the Berwick Fountain, and both cars appear to have paused. On most British and Irish tram systems cars passed each other, on single track loops, by keeping to the left of the street in the direction of travel. The right hand running on this loop is therefore very unusual.**

Berwick Fountain itself is clearly visible and was a very ornate feature of Grand Parade. Public drinking fountains were constructed in most Victorian cities in the nineteenth century, and represented an attempt to reduce the incidence of disease by making clean drinking water freely available to all, as a municipal service.

Courtesy IRRS

Bottom: **This is an exceptionally fine study of car No 5, and is in fact an enlargement of part of the photograph above. The driver, conductor and indeed the young lad leaning against the railing beside the fountain, are all clearly very conscious of the presence of the camera and are posing for the shot.**

To convey a sense of dignity, the staff of the Cork horse trams wore smart uniforms and top hats, whereas in Dublin *only* bowler hats were used. The wheels appear to be without spokes, and the eight saloon windows are arched, with the *spandrils* or cusp-like feature over them picked out in dark blue.

The stairs are of the *ladder* type which were quite dangerous as, in wet weather, a person could slip through the rails with disastrous consequences. Side *strings* and *risers* between the individual steps prevented this.

Walter McGrath collection

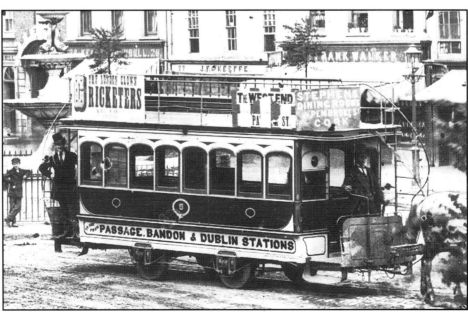

A delightful study of Cork horse tram No 1, showing how ornate some early trams were. No 1 was one of four smaller cars built by Starbuck and Co of Birkenhead. This view is at the junction of Victoria Road and Victoria Quay, Cork, with the hills of Montenotte in the background. The destination board reads 'Anglesea Bridge, Mall, Parade, and Patrick St'. As the advertisement for the London clown 'Ricketers' appears in all these views, they were probably taken at the same time. The second horse in harness has been partly touched out by the photographer, though its back and docked tail are visible. Note the prominent ribs and sunken flanks of the nearer horse, suggesting that it is not very well cared for.   *Walter McGrath collection*

This view is on the same day, and at almost exactly the same spot as the above photograph, the only difference being the arrival of a sailing ship on the left. Horse tram No 6 is seen here with most of its blinds down. The protruding ladder stairs are very visible and their danger should be apparent. The lower or rocker panel gives the destination 'To and from Passage, Bandon and Dublin Stations', whereas the smaller tram above reads 'To and from Dublin, Bandon and Passage Railway'. It was usual in many companies to print the name of the manager on the rocker panel in small script, and just below the word 'stations' on No 6 appears 'James Clifton Robinson, Manager'.   *Walter McGrath collection*

GALWAY and SALTHILL TRAMS

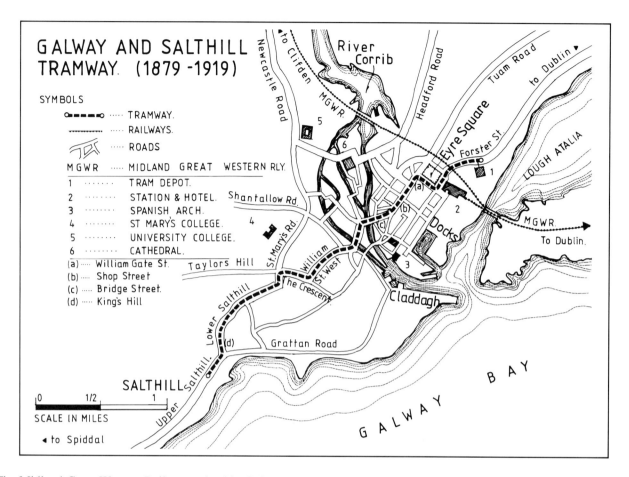

The Midland Great Western Railway arrived in Galway in 1851 when Galway was little more than a dreamy town. It was a setting-off point for tours into the unspoilt beauty of Connemara and Joyce country. In 1872 the Galway Bay Steamboat Co set up a service to the Aran Islands. The City of Galway was developing rapidly and many of the wealthy traders resided in the scenic seaside resort of Salthill. The Galway and Salthill Tramway Co was inaugurated in 1877 and opened two years later and, with it, Galway had tram transport well ahead of a great many large cities throughout Europe. There were previous attempts to set up a service which came to nothing. However, the promoters of the tramway felt confident that such a line would be profitable. The main purpose of the line was to provide a link from the city to serve the wealthy community of Salthill. Such a line would also bring the people of Galway to the seaside during the summer months, and the tram passed through the busy shopping streets, to good advantage.

The horse trams left their depot in Forster Street, passing the railway terminus and railway hotel to Eyre Square, which was the centre of the city. They then entered William Gate Street, went down Shop Street, Mainguard Street, and Dominic Street, passed the Swivel Bridge into Salthill Road, and Kings Hill and on to the village of Salthill. The line was relatively level, but, on the return journey, a third horse was provided to ascend the steep King's Hill.

The cars would pass by the grandeur of Eyre Square in its formal setting and set off down the narrow streets with a rich variety of architectural forms, the beating of the horses hooves over the cobble stones echoing against many fine stone buildings crowded with shoppers and vendors selling their wares. Gradually, the busy streets gave way to some fine residential houses as the rural character of the Galway suburbs slowly emerged. The fine views of the seaside would send a thrill of excitement through the happy summer throngs as Salthill was approached. The tram had travelled only $2\frac{1}{4}$ miles and through a rich terrain of great contrast. In the early days of the operation, the last third of the journey was virtually in the countryside with thatched cottages and green fields, but all of this was to change over the years.

The track was to the 3'0" gauge and a ten minute service was provided at peak times, reduced to twenty or even thirty minute intervals during the winter. The fare was two pence which was dear enough, especially if a whole family was travelling. The first batch of five cars were very similar to the double-deck Dublin horse trams, with seven-windowed saloons and knifeboard seating on the upper deck. These trams were drawn by two horses, and the livery was red and white. In 1888, two single-deck enclosed cars pulled by a single horse were provided for light winter use and their curved white roofs gave them the name of 'white beetles'. The name derived from a reference to them by Somerville and Ross, in a 1906 book called *Some Irish Yesterdays*. In this book, Galway was described as "an outpost of Ireland", where "little one horse trams glide along the shining road like white-backed beetles", and the name remained. In 1909 a further batch of five cars were delivered with upper deck transverse seats. Alas, the latter cars saw only short service as many of the best horses were commandeered by the British Army to serve in Flanders during the First World War. Bereft of its motive power, the line quickly succumbed and final closure was in 1919. The system was unusual in that the Gaelic language was frequently spoken, and on fair days the passengers were often accompanied by ducks and hens and the occasional piglet on the way to market. It was the most westerly tramway in Europe. The system was replaced by petrol buses.

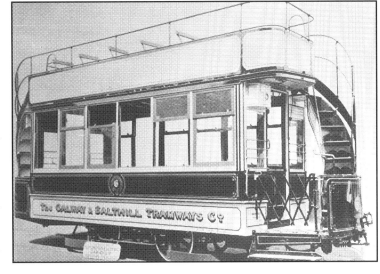

Top: **Horse tram No 3**, seen turning out of Eyre Square into William Gate Street. The large building in the background is the Railway Hotel, beside the MGWR station. No 3 was one of the five original seven window cars, built in 1879, and lacks decency screens, although the advert-isements serve much the same purpose.

Note the destination panel carried along the top of the window instead of the usual position on the rocker panel. Perhaps, since the streets the tram passed along were narrow, the company may have felt that they were more visible higher up.
Walter McGrath collection

Centre: This view truly catches the distinctly Irish character of a Galway street, as the tram slowly proceeds along Shop Street inbound, the sound of the horse hooves echoing loudly.

The gentleman to the rear left is holding on to the tram as he walks along, pulled by the tram's forward motion. The conductor stands in command of his rear platform, apparently unconcerned about the free ride. The street is busy with shoppers, and the delivery boy on the right, stepping from the pavement, certainly carries a worthy load.

Sunblinds are adorning many shops and the short shadows suggest a mid-day scene. The ladies to the front of the upper deck are carrying parasols. The shawls worn by many of the womenfolk on the pavements are very typical of the west of Ireland

The tram itself is of the same type as that in the top photograph.
W Lawrence, John Kennedy collection

Bottom: **Galway and Salthill horse tram No 6**, manufactured by the United Electric Tramway Co Ltd in 1909, probably photographed at an exhibition. There are only six saloon windows and the fenestration arrangement is unusual. The colours can be seen on page 25, though the livery shown here has more white panels. The upper deck seats are of the transverse garden slatted type with reversible backrests. The bulkhead brass window guards are clearly visible. These were to protect the corner passenger when the bulkhead window was dropped down into the bodywork.
Maker's photograph

WARRENPOINT and ROSTREVOR TRAMS

In 1849 the Newry, Warrenpoint and Rostrevor Railway commenced services between Newry (Dublin Bridge) and Warrenpoint. In 1854, the Newry and Armagh Railway connected Newry (Edward Street) to the main Belfast to Dublin line, and in 1861 the two stations in Newry were joined by Town of Newry Connecting Railway. Despite its name, the NWRR never extended the line beyond Warrenpoint. At the time, Warrenpoint was a relatively important sea port, and the railway connection added greatly to its prestige. The citizens of Rostrevor endeavoured for 30 years to have the railway extended but failed. In 1877 the Warrenpoint and Rostrevor Tramway was opened and ran for three miles along the public road as far as Rostrevor Quay, some five minutes journey beyond the village of Rostrevor itself. There were three passing loops and the track gauge was an unusual 2'10".

The tramway connected with trains at Warrenpoint, and the journey took 35 minutes. At Warrenpoint station an awning was provided to give shelter to passengers boarding the horse trams and the line was doubled along this section. The tram set off around the south side of Warrenpoint's main square, by its fine promenade and continued along the seaward side of the road, following its many curves and undulations in the lovely sea and mountain setting. The fare for the 3 mile journey was 4d in open cars, or 6d for the comforts of a closed saloon. It was often described as one of the most scenic little tramways in these islands and it was certainly one of the most photographed. As it passed under the shadow of the world famous Mountains of Mourne, the magnificent views along Carlingford Lough were breathtaking. The Company advertised in travel catalogues, offering attractive day trips, taking in the Carlingford mountains, etc. These proved most popular, particularly during the summer months and the line was quite prosperous, paying a dividend of 10% at the turn of the century.

The cars were all on four-wheel trucks and comprised ten toast-racks and three single-deck saloons. In inclement weather, canvas covers could be added to the toast racks. The saloons were very similar to the Galway saloon cars with seven side windows, curved white roofs and clerestory ventilation and lighting. The company recognised the great tourist potential of such a line and the cars were painted in a variety of bright seaside colours – yellow, red or blue. The cars were diverse, not only in colour, but also

in design and four different types of car existed. The trams were remarkably similar to those used on the Isle of Man today, and a very good idea of the joys of an open tram ride on a coastal setting can still be enjoyed along the Douglas promenade. By 1880 seven cars were in existence but, as prosperity grew, the number of cars increased and by 1900 the full complement of thirteen was in service.

An extension of the tramway to the seaside resort of Greencastle was contemplated in 1894, but was never constructed. In 1907 the Mourne Mountains Touring Co came into operation, using motor charabancs, and the tramway suffered from the competition. After a severe gale damaged the permanent way in February 1915, services were quietly withdrawn.

Open toastrack trams Nos 1 and 10 at Rostrevor. The trees are in full bloom and the short shadows suggest mid-day. Both cars are almost full and the passengers are looking towards the photographer, who has probably called for their attention. The driver of No 10 is standing, hand on the swan neck brass brake handle ready to release the horse. *Walter McGrath collection*

Saloon car No 7, also at Rostrevor, with an uncovered toastrack to the front. Note the loop in the left foreground with the turnout visible. Both cars are turned and horses are thus out of view. As with other photographs of the saloon cars, the upper deck railings of No 7 are not cluttered with advertisements, and the ornate curve of the roof is very visible. *Walter McGrath collection*

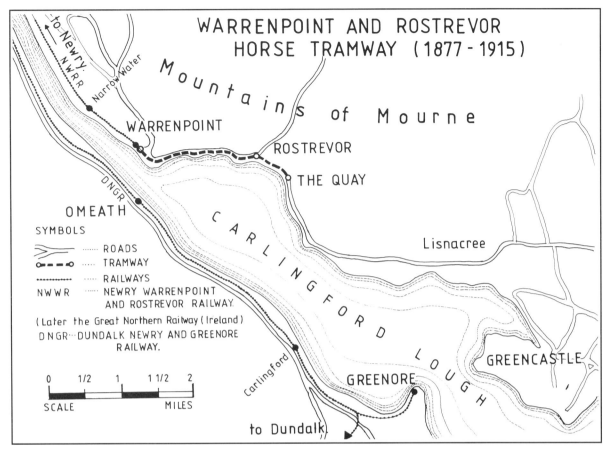

Left: **Horse tram No 3 at Rostrevor around 1905, on a Rostrevor to Warrenpoint working. In the distance is an open toastrack tram. Apart from the beautiful scenery of the area, and the fresh sea air, the Rostrevor trams were attractive for their varied colours. Car No 3 is another of the saloon cars, and has the turtle back roof, with protruding ventilators, associated with American street cars. The upper deck railings were to carry advertisements and are unusual on single deck cars. The gentlemen to the right, in their straw hats, are taking an obvious interest in proceedings.**

Walter McGrath collection

Right: **Toastrack car No 10 at Rostrevor in the early part of the century. The tram is already almost full, while a lady is contemplating boarding. The tow bar for use when the horse is attached to the near end, is clearly visible under the dash. The roof is covered by a canvas sheet with a scalloped awning. The 'opposition' on the other side of the railing looks quite unperturbed by the whole affair! The trees are not in all leaf so it is probably early spring.**

National Library of Ireland, 10155WL

DERRY TRAMS

The City of Londonderry is usually better known as *Derry*, the Irish name used for the settlement before 1609, and is also often referred to as *The Maiden City*, a reference to the siege of 1689 when the Jacobites failed to take the city. Throughout this chapter the term 'Derry' will be used where the city itself is referred to, as the tram company used this name in its own title. Conversely the railways used 'Londonderry'.

The City of Derry resembled Cork in being served by four separate railway companies. Derry is divided by the River Foyle with the Great Northern Railway (Ireland) entering at Foyle Road terminus on the west bank of the Foyle. The Londonderry and Lough Swilly Railway also arrived at the west bank descending from a north westerly direction (see map). On the eastern bank of the Foyle, the pattern was repeated in a mirrored image with the Belfast and Northern Counties Railway descending from the north east and the County Donegal Railway, which had crossed the Foyle at Strabane, entering the city from a southerly direction, alongside Victoria Road. The rather splendid edifice of the CDR contrasted greatly with the rather grim Graving Dock station of the LLSR which was located approximately 1¹/₂ miles from the GNRI station. Both the CDR and LLSR companies were 3'0" narrow gauge, whereas the GNRI and BNCR had the Irish standard gauge of 5'3". All of Derry's railways linked dual gauge tracks crossing over what was then known as Carlisle Bridge and which was renamed Craigavon Bridge when it was rebuilt in 1933. The Londonderry Port and Harbour Commissioners line, which was privately owned, opened in 1867 and operated a network of sidings on either side of the Foyle. Wagons were transferred from one side to the other across Carlisle Bridge by capstan, often with trains of mixed gauge over interlaced dual gauge track work.

Until 1887 the LLSR ran passenger trains through to Middle Quay, just behind the present Guildhall, over the goods-only lines of the Harbour Commissioners, albeit without parliamentary authority! The LLSR had rather poor relations with the Harbour Commissioners and the arrangement ended in that year. This created the need for some sort of link between the LLSR Graving Dock terminus and the City centre.

The City of Derry Tramways Co was opened in April 1897 and the tramway originally ran from the Londonderry and Lough Swilly terminus to Ship Quay near the old city walls. In the same year the line was extended to reach Carlisle Bridge, which was south of the GNRI terminus.

The LLSR had strong connections with the horse tramway in many respects. Not only did the latter obviate the need to use the Harbour Commissioner's track, but the contractor who laid the horse tramway also had strong connections with the railway company. This was the firm of Messrs McCrea and McFarland who took majority shares in the tramway and later became its owners. McCrea and McFarland were an old firm of building contractors from Belfast but were also shipping agents. They owned the Lough Swilly Steamship

Company but in 1920 sold it to the LLSR.

The tramway was single track throughout, with passing loops at intervals and, after the extension to Carlisle Bridge, had a route of almost two miles. It was a policy of the line to pick up or set down passengers anywhere en route and a half hourly service was maintained from 7.00am to 8.00pm but often services ran up to midnight, depending on the arrival of the last train at the LLSR station. The fare was one old penny (1d) irrespective of distance travelled and the tramway provided a valuable link between the LLSR and GNRI stations. The service was often increased to 20 minute intervals depending on demand.

The tram stock was identical to the earlier Belfast horse trams with seven-windowed saloons, direct stairs, garden seats on the upper deck and longitudinal on the lower. It seems likely that they were either bought directly from the Belfast Tramways or from the same suppliers. The livery also was almost identical, the main departure being that different advertisements appropriate to the City of Derry adorned the decency screen boarding. Certainly, on the electrification of the Belfast trams in 1905, further ex-Belfast horse trams, not converted to electric operation, were acquired by the Company.

The tram passed through some busy shopping streets and it was not uncommon for train loads of sightseers and shoppers to board the Lough Swilly or County Donegal Railway from as far away as Carndonagh, Burtonport, Glenties, Donegal town, Killybegs or Ballyshannon for a day's outing to Derry and avail of the horse trams to take them to the best shopping districts. After a day's shopping, the trams would transport persons and baggage, packed from stem to stern, back to the station for the homeward journey.

Another popular trip was in the opposite direction, when passengers from the GNRI and other stations took the tram to the Graving Dock terminus of the LLSR and got on to the trains for Fahan Pier to board sailing ships or steam ships to cross Lough Swilly from Fahan to Rathmullan. Originally the ships sailed from Farland Point and a regular summer service of crossings was provided. In later years a paddle steamer was used and later again smaller motor boats. Sailings were also available to Rathmelton and Portsalon.

In those days, the traveller could journey by broad gauge from Strabane to Foyle Road, pick up the horse tram to the LLSR and travel by narrow gauge to Fahan Point. From there they could board a ship to cross Lough Swilly to Rathmullen, take a horse coach to Letterkenny and pick up the County Donegal narrow gauge back to Strabane. All of this could be done in a day's outing and the traveller would have not only seen some of the finest scenery in Ireland, but a vast range of rolling stock from the powerful GNRI locomotives to the great variety of narrow gauge stock, a whole range of liveries, the fresh sea breeze of the crossing and, perhaps most enjoyable of all, (at least to the tram enthusiast) a delightful two mile journey through the narrow streets of Derry, under its historic walls, by the City of Derry Horse Tramways.

Towards the end, the horse trams, on leaving the LLSR terminus and after travelling almost 300 yards, had their first passing loop just before Boating Club Lane. The cars continued straight along Strand Road reaching a second passing loop opposite the Guildhall. On reaching the end of Shipquay Place, the line curved right and reached a third passing loop immediately after Water Street. It continued as single track along Foyle Street and terminated at the extreme south western end of John Street at the north west end of Carlisle Bridge, not far from the GNRI station.

The tramway gave good service for over twenty years. At the outbreak of the First World War, many of the fine tram horses were commandeered by the British Army to haul gun carriages and the baggage of war and the company quietly ceased operations in January 1919. The gap between the railway termini was bridged by four petrol buses and so ended a colourful little tramway, running on 4'8½" gauge in a city where 3'0" and 5'3" gauges abounded.

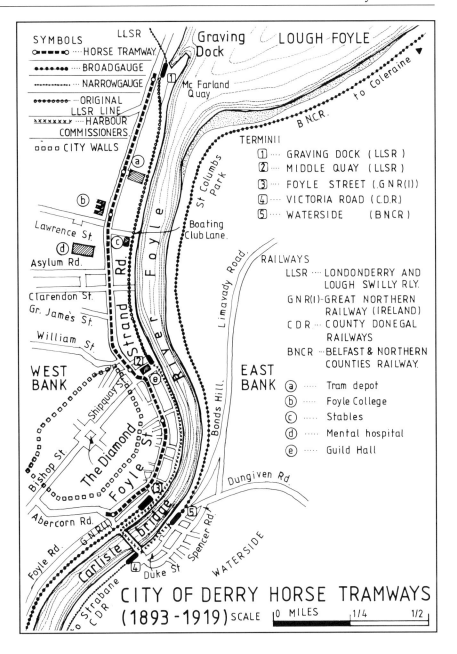

When other cities had changed over to the more practical and hygienic alternative of electric traction, the Derry Company seriously considered electrifying their system. As in most cities, opposition to electrification manifested itself, mostly from other transport concerns, particularly the cabbies. Whilst they could outpace a horse tram, they justifiably feared that faster electric trams would ruin their trade.

This humourous postcard, based on the photograph overleaf, depicts a scene of sheer chaos, with the passengers from the upper deck being thrown from the tram, which has become electrically charged. Sparks and bolts fly outward from the tracks and woe betide the passerby. The tram looks to be a standard Belfast open-topper. The statue on the City walls is of the local politician proposing electrification.

People had a genuine fear of a relatively unknown force capable of killing. When electric trams first appeared, many citizens gave them a wide berth until they were proved to be safe. In Derry the campaigners won and the trams never went electric.

T Maguire collection, courtesy Jim Tinneny

A rare view of horse tram No 6 at the bottom of John Street, near the southern terminus. In the background is Carlisle Road Presbyterian Church, which was built in 1879 in the neo-gothic perpendicular style. Note the man boarding the tram and the RIC constable outside the shop. The vast majority of people in this scene are female and no one appears to be in a hurry.   *Courtesy MacDonald and Biggar collection*

Two horse trams pass one another at Shipquay Place. Both cars are of the seven windowed saloon type, whereas the later cars had only three large windows. The cars were similar to the Dublin trams of the period and if the rocker panels and window surrounds were painted white, the difference would be hard to tell. The cannon on Derry's famous walls are a reminder of the city's turbulent past. Note the line of cabbies in the foreground, perhaps competing with the trams. The track was single throughout with three passing loops, one of which is seen here.   *National Library of Ireland, 1631WL*

GLENANNE and LOUGHGILLY TRAMWAY

People are often surprised to learn that such a tramway existed and yet its origins go back long before many other tramways. It was privately promoted by Messrs George Gray and Sons who owned linen mills in the village of Glenanne. The purpose of the tramway was to deliver the produce of the factory to the nearest railway station and on the return journey to collect raw material and coal. The station in question was Loughgilly on the GNRI, situated on its Newry to Armagh route, which was built in 1864.

There were three factories in all, known individually as the 'Main Factory', the 'Wee Mill' and the 'Upper Mill' and an earlier industrial railway hauled by hand and donkey connected the three factories with one another. Between the first two factories there was a steep section along the public road where the wagons were connected to a continuous chain or cable between the running rails and then pulled by the workers at the 'Wee Mill'. An overhead pull cord operated a bell to inform the workers, a quarter of a mile away, that the wagons were linked and ready for hauling.

The later tramway, opened in 1897, followed a more level route, and used the public roadway to achieve this, and the gauge was only 1'10". The track was bolted to iron sleepers which were slightly convex and it was necessary for the horse to walk beside the track rather like a canal barge horse with the traces linked to the roadside corner of the carriage.

The carriage was a very simple single deck affair, with knife board seating carrying seven persons back to back on each side, and a simple roof was carried on four corner pillars. The accompanying photograph shows that the horse was almost as big as the carriage it pulled and the driver-cum-conductor sat at the leading seat. This was a most unusual arrangement, as the traditional position of the driver was standing on a platform, separated from the passengers and looking straight ahead. To sit amongst the passengers craning his head to the side, leaning forward to peer around the corner post must have been most uncomfortable and prone to sore necks. Added to this dilemma was the loss of a valuable seat when the carrying capacity was already so small. The driver's function of also collecting fares as part of his duties made this one of the first 'one man operated' systems in these islands. Apart from its industrial use, the purpose of the passenger service was chiefly to bring workers to and from the railway station, but the local people also availed of the service and the fare was 2d for one direction or 3d return. The carriage also had the distinction of having been formally named *Carew* after a local family much in favour with the mill owners. The naming of tramcars was very unusual, whereas naming steam locomotives and ships was traditional. This was because such vast fleets of trams existed compared with the former. It is likely that the Glenanne-Loughgilly was one of the first such instances in Europe, and the only one in Ireland apart from the Dublin tram nicknames. From about 1917 onwards, on account of the First World War, the mill owners had difficulty in finding suitable horses to operate the line. They purchased a petrol lorry to transport the raw materials etc, and the passenger service and the horse tramway ceased operations in 1919.

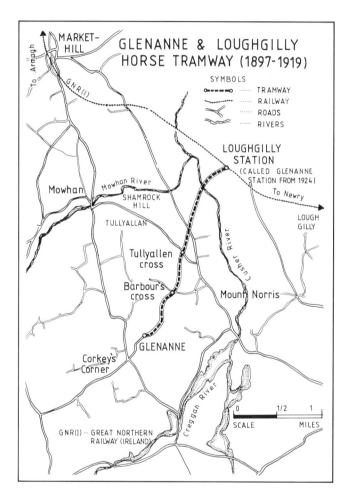

Without doubt the Loughgilly tram was probably the simplest of affairs in terms of its construction, yet it truly qualifies as a tramcar. Its most basic advantage in terms of design was its speed for loading and unloading passengers — one step and they were off! It must have been rather unpleasant in wet or windy weather, with no gutter on the curved roof and rain constantly dripping down on the passengers' laps!
Walter McGrath collection

Steam Trams

DUBLIN and LUCAN STEAM TRAMWAY

The Dublin and Lucan Tramway services had the distinction of having three different track gauges throughout their combined lifetime. The steam tramway selected the typical narrow gauge of 3'0". When the board decided to change over to electric traction in 1900, the new gauge selected was 3'6". In 1928 when the DUTC took over operation of this service, they introduced their city gauge of 5'3". This chapter will deal with the steam tramway. Electric traction will be dealt with in a later chapter on the Dublin and Lucan Electric Tramways (see page 77).

When the Dublin horse trams were introduced in 1872 the townsfolk of Lucan were anxious to be brought into the railway system. At the time, Lucan was equidistant from the lines of the Great Southern and Western Railway and the Midland Great Western Railway, both approximately $1\frac{1}{2}$ miles away. Both railways had a station at Lucan, called respectively *Lucan* and *Coldblow and Lucan* to avoid confusion. The towns between Lucan and Dublin were not well served by either railway, but none of them were important enough to warrant a railway branch line. However, a roadside tramway to Lucan would serve their needs. The line would not only provide a passenger service but also serve the farming and commercial fraternity en route. The proposals were feasible and the Dublin and Lucan Steam Tramway came into being to provide such a service in 1880. It was the first roadside steam tramway in Ireland, when the first $1\frac{3}{4}$ miles to Chapelizod were opened in June 1881. The line was opened throughout on 2nd July 1883 and had a length of just over eight miles.

Crowds from Dublin City would take the horse tram from O'Connell Bridge along the North Quays to Infirmary Road and board the steam tram standing outside the main gates of Phoenix Park at Conyingham Road. The trams were hauled by enclosed steam tram locomotives, and the number of trailers varied according to demand. The locomotives had the tall funnels typical of such locomotives and after a shrill whistle and jolt as the couplings took the strain, and a rousing cheer from the Sunday crowds, the steam tram was off on an adventure deep into the Liffey Valley. The gauge of the steam tram was 3'0", unlike the neighbouring steam tram on the Blessington route which had the Irish standard gauge of 5'3".

The Spa Hotel, with its famous health-giving waters, was a popular tourist attraction at the time, particularly for the better-off classes. The fine hotel itself was popular for weddings and functions and the proprietor valued the link with the tramway which brought good business. The steam tramway also provided early morning non-stop trams to the city and late return trams especially to serve the business clientele who stayed at the hotel. A late night 'theatre car' for the more refined townsfolk was also available. Shortly after the opening, a new company, known as the Lucan, Leixlip and Celbridge Steam Tramway, obtained powers to continue the line as far as Celbridge, but only the $1\frac{1}{2}$ miles to Leixlip were ever constructed. The two companies amalgamated to become the

Dublin, Lucan and Leixlip Steam Tramway. It was very short-sighted that the tramway did not continue from Leixlip to Maynooth which had a station on the MGWR. This would have opened the route to Midland traffic from the west and would have undoubtedly brought further revenue to the tramway. To this day the bridge over the Liffey, as one leaves Leixlip for Maynooth, has two quite different sides. I was told that the up-stream side was widened in the hope that the tram would make the crossing to Maynooth. However, this was never to be. At the early stages, the DL & LST purchased an interesting 'combined steam car' built by Manlove Alliot Fryer & Co of Nottingham, to the design of E Perett, at a cost of £950, which was a formidable amount in those days. It weighed 9 tons and could carry up to 50 passengers. However, it was not greatly successful and did not survive too long in service.

The steam trams were successful in the early years. The company watched with interest the spread of electric traction throughout the City of Dublin and its advantages as motive power were considered. It was decided to abandon the steam trams for the advantages of the cleaner and more efficient option. The steam locomotives after years of wear and tear needed retubing and serious overhauls if they were to stay in operation. The track work was also in a poor state of repair and it was the general run down condition of the line that militated against its continuance as a steam operated system. The shareholders felt that circumstances would improve if the steam trams were replaced with electric traction. A site was bought at Fonthill, near Lucan, for the construction of a power house. Then a decision was made which, in retrospect, is very hard to understand. A new gauge of 3'6" was adopted in lieu of the original 3'0". Was this to facilitate the adaptation of existing rolling stock or to prevent a takeover by the DUTC? The Board considered the idea of seeking approval to run an 'intermediate rail' between the DUTC's rails to permit their own cars to enter the city centre. Of course, this was not practicable, as all the DLER rolling stock had the deep railway type wheel flanges. In 1896 another scheme,

the Celbridge, Clane, and Donadea Light Railway sought powers to construct such a line, and extend the Clane section to Robertstown via Prosperous. They further contemplated linking Kilcock on the MGWR with Sallins on the GSWR. There was great opposition to these plans, and nothing came of them. The Dublin and Lucan Steam Tramway ceased operations in 1900 after 19 years. Many of the original trailers were converted for use on the Dublin and Lucan Electric Railway. Two of them were purchased by the Bessbrook and Newry Tramway and fortunately the body of one has survived at the Ulster Folk and Transport Museum.

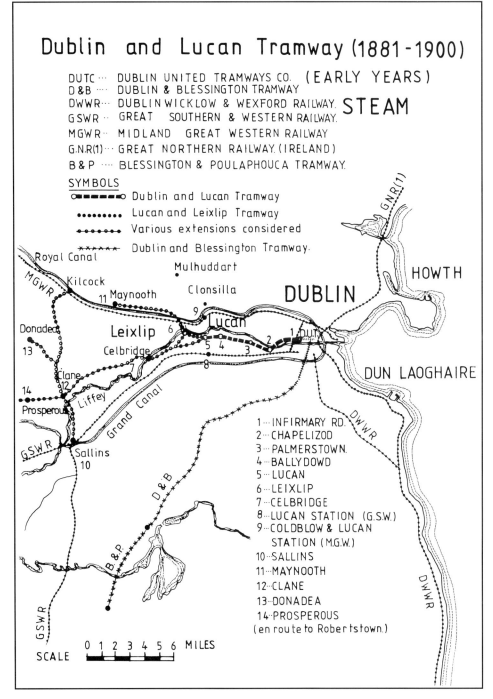

Left: A typical enclosed steam locomotive with a high funnel, linked to a full train at Conyngham Road, about 1895. The tramway staff know that Mr Mason is taking their photograph, and line up to face posterity. The burly gentleman in the middle foreground has a stance to indicate that he is someone of importance. To the left of the tram three capped youngsters sit huddled together to watch the departure.

There were six similar 0-4-0T locomotives built by Kitsons of Leeds, the last of which, No 6, was delivered in 1887, and cost £825. The leading coach carries the letters LL&C, standing for the Lucan, Leixlip and Celbridge Steam Tramway, but this was something of a misnomer.

T Mason, courtesy IRRS

Centre: Two steam trains, hauled by Kitson engines, entering the passing loop at Riverside about 1900. The nearer engine is hauling two single deck cars (Nos 5 and 11). The proliferation of advertisements on the roof, advertising Cadbury's Cocoa, Fry's Chocolate, Neave's Food, and plenty of Sunlight Soap, appeared from a distance to look like upper deck decency screening, and gave rise to the belief that the steam system also hauled double deck cars. Just out of the picture to the left, on the opposite side of the road, the new 3' 6" gauge tracks have already been laid and the system is about to undergo its first metamorphosis — electrification on the narrow gauge.

T Mason, courtesy IRRS

Bottom: Two steam trams heading off in the same direction on special school excursions around 1895. The photograph is taken at Ballydowd and the locomotives are Nos 6 and 7. Steam locomotive No 7 was constructed by Thomas Green of Leeds in 1892 and cost £825. Such was the demand for steam locomotives at that time, that the firm of Wilkinson (to whom the original order was given) were obliged to sub-contract to both Thomas Green of Leeds and Beyer Peacock and Co of Manchester.

The leading locomotive is in full steam and the staff and teachers stand around waiting for the final whistle and the continuation of their adventure into the Liffey Valley. Note the variety of tramcar types evident on these trains.

T Mason, courtesy IRRS

DUBLIN and BLESSINGTON TRAMWAY

Blessington was ignored by the various railway companies that had quickly established themselves in the middle of the 19th century across Ireland. This was a source of grievance to the populus, and various plans to put Blessington on the railway map were examined. The first proposal in 1864 was to run a line from Rathmines, Rathgar, and Rathfarnham to Rathcoole, with an extension to Ballymore Eustace and this would have brought Blessington into the railway system. However, nothing came of these plans.

In 1880 a plan for a light steam railway from Blessington to terminate at St Patrick's Cathedral in Dublin was proposed, It also fell through, as Dublin Corporation would not permit steam locomotives into the heart of the city. The possibility of running a steam tram to Terenure, then at the fringe of the city and the terminus for the horse trams was then examined. These proposals were granted approval in 1887. The gauge was 5'3" to match that of the Dublin United Tramways and it was originally hoped that steam locomotives might haul goods into the city at night time. When electrification of the DUTC (1896) took place, the more acceptable alternative of hauling wagons by DUTC electric locomotives, at night time, did occur.

The Dublin and Blessington steam tram commenced operation on 1st August 1888. A horse-drawn 'mail tram' brought the mails to Terenure from the GPO where they were transferred to the steam tram. Inspired by its early success, a second company, The Blessington and Poulaphouca Steam Tramway, proposed to extend the line a distance of 4^1/$_2$ miles to the scenic County Wicklow beauty spot and waterfalls at Poulaphouca, to encourage tourist traffic. This extension was opened on 1st May 1895. The extension was originally operated by the new company, and the spot at Blessington, where the change of company took place, is still marked by a granite stone with 'D & B' on one side and 'B & P' on the other. From 1896 onwards, through running from Poulaphouca to Terenure was in operation.

The six locomotives used in the opening years were of the all-enclosed tramway type (0-4-0T) constructed at the Falcon Works, Loughborough. Water shortages along the route resulted in saddle tanks being added to increase their water carrying capacity. On account of their appearance they were called 'kettles'. They were, however, capable of speeds of up to 40 mph on level track, but these small locomotives were severely taxed on the steeper gradients. In 1892, another type of steam locomotive was introduced with a very unusual design. They looked like two locomotives which had had a head-on collision and somehow fused into one another. There was a cab at both ends from which the locomotive could be driven. These were 2-4-2Ts.

The passengers were carried on typical double deck tram trailers with non-powered bogies situated under the bulkheads. They were open at both ends, apart from a windscreen on the upper deck. The purpose of this screen was to protect passengers from smuts and smoke emissions from the locomotives. For

this reason the locomotives had very tall chimneys or funnels to release the smoke and steam at high level.

At one stage, it was proposed to electrify the line as far as Crooksling using normal overhead trolley power pick up. After that, the journey would continue to Blessington with the tram powered by a portable petrol-electric power plant contained in a wagon. But this idea was financially outside the reach of the company. To cope with the heavy summer traffic, some of the wagons were provided with seating and surrounded with protective crimped mesh netting. These were called 'cages'.

Most of the track was single line with passing loops. In railway practice, to prevent trains entering a single track between loops, a 'staff' system applied, where only the bearer of the staff could enter the section. On the Dublin and Blessington Tramway, a piece of paper known as a 'tablet' served much the same purpose.

Other road users tended to regard the steam tram as unsafe, especially in the early years. The hissing locomotive suddenly rounding a corner sent the fear of God into many an unsuspecting horse which then bolted for its life and often risked forfeiting the life of its master. There were several cases of staff being thrown off the tram to their deaths at corners, as lurching on worn track acted as a catapult. Derailments due to speed and the poor state of the track, frequently occurred on steep sections. The tramway was often called the 'longest graveyard in the world', because of the practice of erecting crosses to mark the scenes of fatalities. Many accident were alcohol related, since public houses often served as booking offices. Whilst this may give the impression that the tramway was inherently unsafe, it should be pointed out that many of the mishaps were clearly the fault of employees who disregarded safety regulations, rather than of the system itself.

In 1915 the company introduced two experimental tramcars which were electrically powered. The electricity was generated by an Aster petrol engine, and the idea was a forerunner of modern diesel-electric traction. The cars were unsuccessful and soon withdrawn.

Bus competition in the 1920s began making its presence felt and the company examined the ways of reducing running costs. In 1925 they acquired two Ford Model T chassis, which were used to construct two petrol railcars capable of carrying 16 seated passengers. These ran between Terenure and Jobstown. They incorporated parts of the two former petrol electric tramcars, and were most economic machines to operate. Inspired by the success of these miniature railcars, a larger railcar, built by the Drewry Company, was purchased some years later. It had a passenger carrying capacity of 40 persons and could be driven from either end. It also proved successful. After the closure of the DBST, the Drewry railcar along with one of the Fords, was sold to the County Donegal Railway. It was eventually rebuilt as a trailer and happily survives in the Ulster Folk and Transport Museum at Cultra, Co Down.

In spite of the Company's best endeavours of reducing fares and introducing the rail cars, it was only matter of time before the system would succumb to the onslaught of severe bus competition. The Dublin and Blessington Tramway was closed down on the last day of December 1932.

The Blessington steam tramway provided a much valued and important service in its early years, not only conveying passengers, but bringing livestock into the city and stone from the De Selby Company quarries for construction work around Dublin. The cattle wagons were picked up at Terenure by DUTC electric locomotives and delivered to the cattle market at Phibsborough, and to Ringsend Depot near the stock storage yards of the Liverpool steamers. Electric locomotives also transported coal from Ringsend docks to provide the fuel for the locomotives.

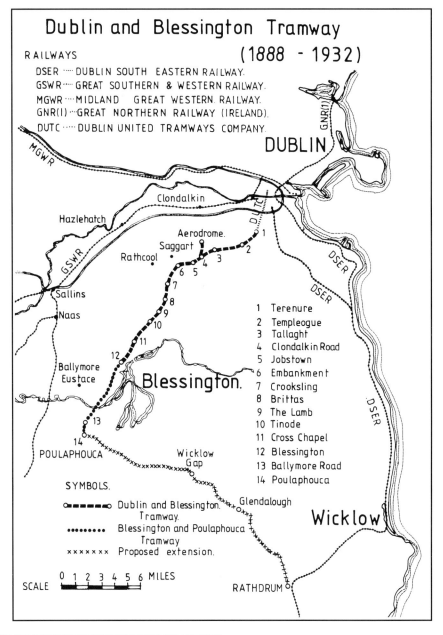

Dublin and Blessington Tramway
(1888 - 1932)

RAILWAYS

DSER ---- DUBLIN SOUTH EASTERN RAILWAY.
GSWR --- GREAT SOUTHERN & WESTERN RAILWAY.
MGWR ---MIDLAND GREAT WESTERN RAILWAY.
GNR(I) ---GREAT NORTHERN RAILWAY (IRELAND).
DUTC ---- DUBLIN UNITED TRAMWAYS COMPANY.

1   Terenure
2   Templeogue
3   Tallaght
4   Clondalkin Road
5   Jobstown
6   Embankment
7   Crooksling
8   Brittas
9   The Lamb
10 Tinode
11 Cross Chapel
12 Blessington
13 Ballymore Road
14 Poulaphouca

SYMBOLS.

○━━●━━●━━○ Dublin and Blessington.
            Tramway.
●●●●●●●●● Blessington and Poulaphouca
            Tramway
××××××× Proposed extension.

SCALE 0 1 2 3 4 5 6 MILES

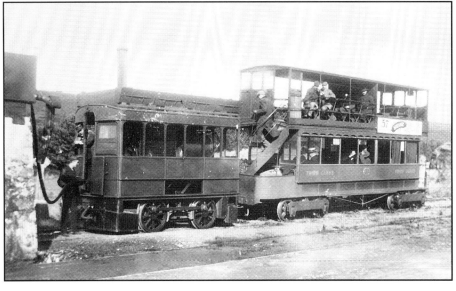

Left: **Steam locomotive No 6 (built by the Falcon Works, Loughborough in 1887, Works No 130) taking water. She is hauling one of the double deck trailers with anti-clockwise direct stairs. Apart from glazed screens at either end, the sides are virtually open to the elements.**

This locomotive was one of the first six engines (1-6) which were 0-4-0Ts, and is seen here in original condition. Only Nos 3 and 6 survived after 1912. Around 1914, No 6 received a complete rebuild at the Midland Great Western Railway works at Broadstone, when, among other changes, her windows were glazed to provide some comfort to the drivers. She lasted until the closure of the line in 1932, No 3 having been withdrawn in 1927.

GW Tripp, courtesy IRRS

Top: Between 1892 and 1906 the DBST added four rather unusual locomotives to its fleet. All were double-ended 2-4-2Ts (except for No 8, which until 1903 was an 0-4-2T), but no two were exactly alike. Nos 7, 8 and 10 were built by Thomas Green and Son, Leeds (Works Nos 179, 218, and 267), and No 9 by the Brush Engineering Works, Loughborough (Works No 284).

Here we see No 10 at Terenure in 1921. This locomotive was built in 1906 as No 2, replacing one of the original engines, but in 1915 it was renumbered 10, as the rest of the fleet were numbered in order of building.This was a strange decision as Nos 7 and 8 had been scrapped that same year, leaving only Nos 3, 6, 9 and 10 in stock.

The bogie trailer is No 9, and has had its upper deck rather crudely sheeted in, a change which must have been welcomed by the passengers.

CP Friel collection

Centre: Trailer No 6 sporting several advertisements. These were massive nine-windowed saloon cars, with the usual anti-clockwise direct stairs leading to a right-hand gangway or aisle.

The unpowered trucks were located closer to the bulkheads than with powered cars, and this was a feature with all steam trailers. The consequent large span between the trucks must have made for a rather rigid ride, and rounding a hill-top could have caused some see-sawing, similar to that experienced on Dublin trams crossing canal bridges.

This is an earlier view than that above, as the top deck has not yet been sheeted in. In high winds and rain, upper deck travelling must have been very uncomfortable.

From this photograph and contemporary descriptions, it would appear that both classes of passenger had a choice between upper and lower deck accommodation.

H Fayle, courtesy IRRS

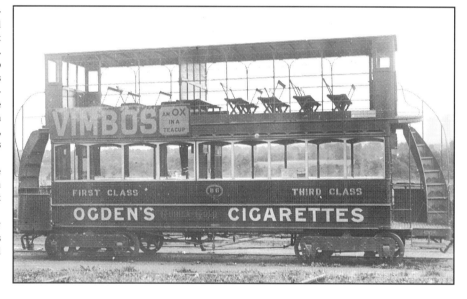

Bottom: In 1915 the company purchased two unusual tramcars from Hurst Nelson. Inspired by the spread of electric traction, the cars were an interesting, but unsuccessful experiment. They were petrol-electric cars, a forerunner of diesel electric traction.

The intention was to run the cars over the DUTC lines to Nelson's Pillar, using overhead power, and to generate electricity with the petrol engine on the non-electrified DBST route. The experiment failed for several reasons. The six cylinder Aster engine was under-powered and caused totally unacceptable vibration to the passengers. The through running never materialised, and the cars were complicated and unreliable. They were soon taken out of service and broken up. Some body parts found further use on two small railcars built in 1925, and the power bogies were used on DUTC trams.

Hurst Nelson, RC Ludgate collection

PORTSTEWART TRAMWAY

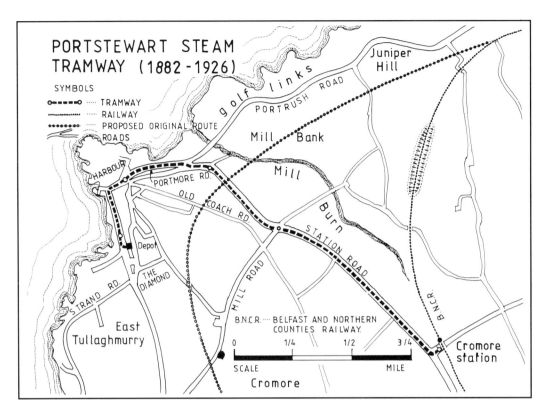

When the Ballymena, Ballymoney, Coleraine and Portrush Junction Railway put forward their proposals to construct a railway from Coleraine to Portrush it was their intention to closely follow a coastal route and serve the town of Portstewart. Portstewart at the time was an unknown dreamy seaside fishing village and the railway recognised its great tourist potential. Their plans were opposed by John Cromie, a powerful local landlord, and, as a result, the new railway by-passed the town by one and a half miles. This was a short-sighted action on the part of John Cromie, as a railway within the town would have brought prosperity, and visitors from both Londonderry and Belfast would have had easy access to a fine bathing place.

The BBCPJR arrived at Portrush in 1855. As a result of the proximity of the railway station to the town, Portrush benefited greatly and was transformed almost overnight. The citizens of Portstewart were naturally unhappy that their railway station was so distant from the town. The first attempt to link Portstewart station to the town was a horse bus, operated by a local entrepreneur some years after the opening.

A more serious attempt to introduce a tramway was made by The Portstewart Tramway Co in 1866 by Baptist Kernaghan, an agent of the famous George Francis Train, but nothing materialised, as a result of John Cromie's continued objections. The BBCPJR was absorbed into the Belfast and Northern Counties Railway in 1861.

Cromie eventually agreed to permit the construction of a tramway to serve the town and the BNCR was approached to see if they would build it, but they refused. In 1871 an application to construct the Cromore to Portstewart Tramway was lodged but lapsed. Again, in 1875, the application was revived by a group of local businessmen. All previous applications were for a 5'3" gauge line, but the latest application was for the narrow gauge of 3'0". The line was finally constructed in 1882. It was Ulster's first roadside steam tramway and the second in Ireland.

The purpose of the tramway was in some small measure an attempt to regain lost tourist traffic by linking the railway to the town along the public road. The line was single track throughout with a passing loop at Victoria Terrace and another about halfway between the Terrace and Cromore Railway station. In Portstewart, the steam trams stopped outside the Montague Arms Hotel, where many of the wealthier visitors stayed. Unfortunately most day trippers travelling on the BNCR were disinclined to leave the comfort of the train and transfer to the Portstewart tram with bags and baggage. This was because only a few miles down the track the very fine alternative seaside resort of Portrush existed, without such inconvenience.

For this reason the tramway was not very successful and went into liquidation in 1892, just ten years after its opening. It was purchased by the BNCR. They overhauled the system, acquired more tram cars and a more powerful locomotive. They advertised the virtues of Portstewart and, for a while, the tramway prospered. Shortly before its closure, the Northern Ireland government, as an unemployment measure, considered re-routing the railway to embrace the town of Portstewart as originally proposed. This was impractical at this late stage as the town had expanded considerably.

The tramway finally succumbed on 31st January 1926, after 44 years of operation.

Top: **Victoria Terrace, Portstewart, showing 0-4-0T No 3 hauling a van and an open top trailer around 1920. It appears to be a dismally wet day, but nevertheless quite a few people are about. There was a passing loop at this point, and the crew may be waiting to cross a west-bound tram. It is possible that the group of onlookers standing beside the car are seeing someone off. The luggage van was numbered 3 in the Portstewart Tramway fleet. The bogie tramcar at the rear of the ensemble was one of two built in 1897-99 by GF Milnes of Birkenhead and is either 1 or 4. The tramway ceased operations in 1926.**

Author's collection

Centre: **0-4-0T No 1 at Cromore station, 5th May 1920. The Portstewart Tramway possessed three tramway locomotives. No 1, shown here, was built by Kitsons of Leeds in 1882 (Kitsons T56) The engine had Walchaerts valve gear, driving two outside 8" x 12" cylinders. Like most tram engines, the motion was covered by long skirting to within a few inches of rail level. The boiler pressure was 150 lb per square inch and the heating surface 116 sq feet.**

Two further locomotives were added in 1883 and 1900, these being respectively Kitsons Nos T84 and T302. This latter engine had $9^{1}/_{2}$" cylinders, a boiling pressure of 160 lbs and a heating surface of 133 sq feet.

For the opening, the tramway had two cars. No 1 was a four wheel open-top double-decker, and No 2 was a single-deck open toast-rack. These, along with luggage van No 3, formed the total stock at the time of opening. No 1 was scrapped in 1899 when the new No 1 was delivered.

Locomotive Club of Great Britain,
Ken Nunn collection, 2579

Bottom: **After withdrawal, 0-4-0Ts Nos 1 and 2 were stored in the carriage wash shed at York Road, Belfast for many years. They became the only remaining examples of the once ubiquitous Kitson tram engines and both fortunately have been preserved. The famous tramway enthusiast, Dr HA Whitcombe, was instrumental in having No 1 acquired by the transport museum at Kingston upon Hull in 1939.**

No 2 survived the war, though it had a near miss when York Road was hit in the 1941 air raids. It spent some time at Cookstown, before being displayed at Ballymoney station from 1949 to 1954. It was then placed in the Belfast Transport Museum (now closed), and is now in the railway gallery of the Ulster Folk and Transport Museum, Cultra (see rear cover).

No 3 was the only engine not to be preserved. On closure of the tramway in 1926, it was sold to David Warke, a local building contractor from Castlerock who used it to power a stationary pile driver until it was scrapped in 1935.

CP Friel collection

CAVEHILL and WHITEWELL TRAMWAY

THE CAVEHILL RAILWAY

Parliamentary approval was granted in 1832 to run a mining tramway from the quarry at Ballyaghagan on the south side of Cavehill to the Victoria Channel in Belfast. Near the quarry, it was too dangerous to use animal or human haulage and on this steeply graded section the wagons were lowered by gravity and hauled back by cable. This was probably the first time that such a system was used in Ireland. Beyond the section of steep gradient, the wagons were drawn by horse to Victoria Channel. It is interesting to note that for most of the system, which was just under $1\frac{1}{2}$ miles in length, double tracks were used and the downhill track carrying the heavily laden wagons had a heavier rail than the uphill return track which only hauled empty wagons. The track was on the right hand side of the road as one travelled towards Belfast along the Cavehill Road and, where the line crossed the Antrim Road, it crossed over to the left hand side along the Limestone Road to terminate at York Street. Tramway Street is named after this little tramway and not the later Belfast trams. It was the third line in this island to be authorised by Parliament and the first to operate in what is now Northern Ireland. The gauge was 4'9", the gauge later adopted by Belfast City tramways. The Cavehill Railway closed in February 1896.

THE CAVEHILL AND WHITEWELL TRAMWAY

The Cavehill and Whitewell Tramway was the second roadside passenger carrying steam operated tramway in Ulster, the first being in Co Londonderry at Portstewart. It was incorporated in June 1881 and opened to the public on 1st July 1882.

At this time, the Belfast Street Tramways had reached as far as Chichester Park on the Antrim Road. To continue the journey further northwards on to Whitewell or Glengormley would entail either hiring a hackney carriage at great cost or taking one of the long cars which provided an infrequent and not very satisfactory service. The alternative, of course, was to walk; fine if the weather was good, but this could be all too infrequently the case. The Cavehill and Whitewell Tramway was set up to bridge this gap and was operated by three steam tram type locomotives running an overall distance of just over 3 miles and stopping just short of the Belfast Street Tramways terminus. This gap, it appears, was to demonstrate its separateness and this was also established by using a gauge of 4'8½", and using a different livery.

The locomotives were turned out in an all-over green livery with the usual gold lining. The typical double-deck open-top trailers were massive twelve-windowed saloons, with knife-board seating on the upper deck, and turned out in matching green and cream. They had a seating capacity of 80 passengers and were amongst the biggest in these islands. In 1887, three smaller trailers were purchased - Nos 3, 4 and 5. They had a two-class system: first class in the saloon and second class on the outside. The total journey to Glengormley cost 4d and 3d respectively. There was also an open toastrack tram similar to those

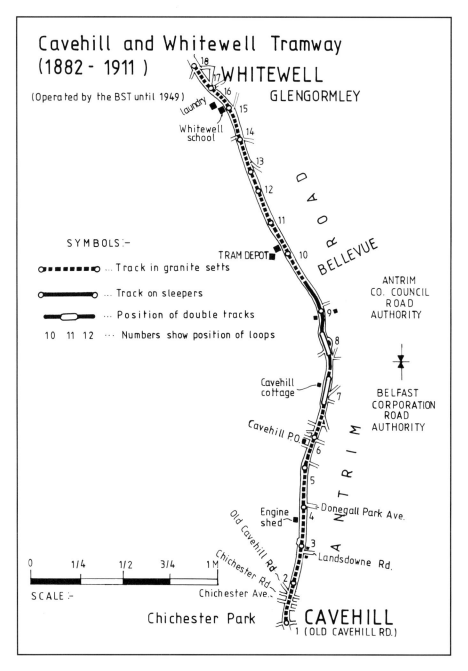

Cavehill and Whitewell Tramway (1882 - 1911)

(Operated by the BST until 1949)

WHITEWELL
GLENGORMLEY
Laundry
Whitewell school

SYMBOLS :-

⊶▪▪▪▪▪⊸ ...Track in granite setts

⊶▬▬▬▬⊸ ... Track on sleepers

⊶▭▭⊸ ... Position of double tracks

10 11 12 ... Numbers show position of loops

TRAM DEPOT

BELLEVUE
ROAD

ANTRIM CO. COUNCIL ROAD AUTHORITY

BELFAST CORPORATION ROAD AUTHORITY

Cavehill cottage

Cavehill P.O.

A N T R I M

Engine shed

Donegall Park Ave.

Old Cavehill Rd.

Chichester Rd.

Landsdowne Rd.

Chichester Ave.

Chichester Park

CAVEHILL
1 (OLD CAVEHILL RD.)

SCALE :-

0 1/4 1/2 3/4 1 M

used on the Isle of Man and the later horse drawn tram stock was similar to that of the BST, except that of course the livery was green and cream. The steam locomotives were supplied by Messrs Kitson and Co Ltd of Leeds, two arriving for the opening and a third five years later in 1887.

Originally the system was entirely steam-hauled but, gradually, horse trams were introduced and steam traction was phased out. This was a reversal of the usual situation. In 1906 the line was electrified and eventually taken over by Belfast Corporation, but more of this later (see page 110). In an effort to increase traffic, the company developed an ornamental garden which later became known as Old Bellevue Gardens and these gardens also provided band stands, promenades, figures of eight, helter skelters and other mechanical amusements. They proved very popular and brought much needed revenue to the company. The company also owned a forty acre site on the slopes of the Cavehill but it was not until the tramway's acquisition by the BCT that these lands were developed to provide the Zoological Gardens and Hazelwood.

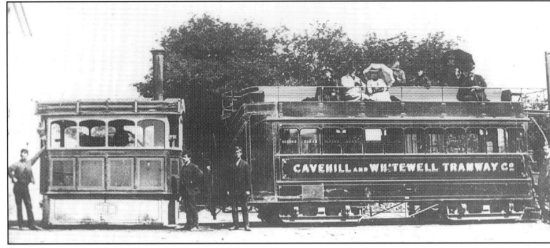

Top: **An early view of steam tram engine No 2 with one of the original double deck bogie trams built in 1882. These had knifeboard seating on the upper deck. This tramway had an unusual motive power history, in that steam power was replaced by horses in the early 1900s, before electrification in 1906.**

RC Ludgate collection

Centre: **Cavehill and Whitewell steam tram engine No 1, with one of the eight window four wheel trailers built in 1887. Note the toast rack seating, with side aisle, on the upper deck, in contrast to the knifeboard seating on the vehicle behind, which is one of the original 80 seat bogie cars.**

Courtesy IRRS

Bottom: **Cavehill and Whitewell open top electric tram No 3 at Glengormley terminus. This type of car had the full canopy extending as far as the dash, but, with no windscreen, it cannot be classed as a 'vestibuled' car. The photograph is clearly a winter scene and may have been taken when the line was electrified in 1906. Five years later the tramway was taken over by Belfast Corporation Tramways. Eight of the company's ten trams (including No 3) were bought by the Corporation and became Nos 193-200.**

RC Ludgate collection

CASTLEDERG and VICTORIA BRIDGE TRAMWAY

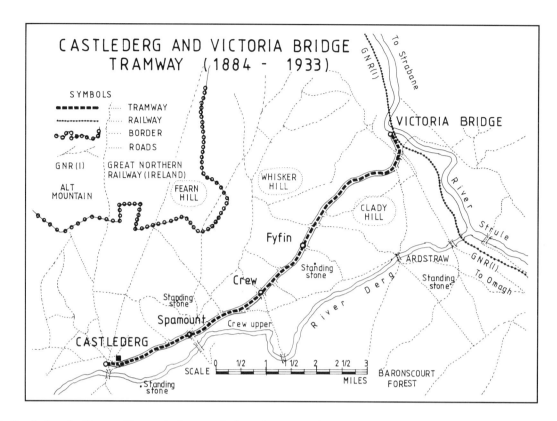

In 1884, Castlederg in County Tyrone had a population of around 900 people and the town was situated 7 miles from the nearest railway station at Victoria Bridge. This was built in 1852 by the Londonderry and Enniskillen Railway, which became part of the GNRI in 1876.

The people of the town felt cut off, and the Castlederg and Victoria Bridge Tramway was promoted to link the town with the railway network. In 1883 an Act of Parliament was passed authorising the building of such a tramway. It was constructed to the 3'0" gauge and opened in 1884. Had the tramway been introduced only a few months later, government assistance under the Tramways Act of 1883 would have made a valuable contribution to its construction costs, to the great benefit of the rate payers. This was understandably a source of some indignation, and representations were made to the government for retrospective assistance. The Vice-Regal Commission on Railways in 1910 recommended a grant of £6000 to aid the line, but for some reason or another, this grant was never received by the company. From its opening to the end of the First World War, the line was moderately prosperous and paid a small dividend of 3$\frac{1}{2}$% on ordinary stock.

The tracks were laid on reserved land on the north side of the public road, following its many curves and undulations, and gradients of up to 1 in 30 were found in places. The only passing loops on the line were at Crew and Spamount. The principle of 'one engine in steam' was usually applied to avoid two trains meeting. The Castlederg terminus was quite elaborate, providing sidings, depots and repair shops to attend to the requirements of the rolling stock. Four mixed workings in each direction were provided on weekdays only, with extra specials on certain local fair and market days. The running time for the entire journey was forty minutes, and the maximum permissible speed was 12 mph, though this was not always strictly observed.

The original locomotives were three Kitson steam tram engines and were provided with hand brakes. However, after a runaway on the steep approach to Victoria Bridge, Westinghouse automatic brakes were fitted. Replacement locomotives were all of the railway type, with skirtings to cover the moving parts. In 1925 a railcar was built by the company but proved too light and was rebuilt. The rebuild could travel at up to 30 mph and carried twenty-four passengers on longitudinal seating. It was powered by a 20hp paraffin engine, and ran until 1928. A small Kerr Stuart diesel locomotive was hired in 1929, but could not cope and was returned to the manufacturer. There were four 4 wheel passenger coaches with end platforms and a larger bogie coach. These were very tram-like in appearance. One of the 4 wheelers (No 4) has recently been recovered and restored at the Ulster Folk and Transport Museum. The company also had two luggage vans.

The intermediate stopping places, listed from Victoria Bridge, were Crew (often jokingly compared with the large railway junction of Crewe in England), then Fyfin and Spamount. With motor bus competition growing in the 1920s, the company was beginning to suffer the effects. A railway strike, involving all the Northern Ireland lines, caused a cessation of operations on the 31 January 1933. The strike was a very long drawn out affair and the line never reopened after the strike finished.

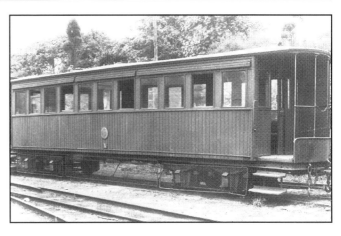

Top left: **Castlederg and Victoria Bridge 0-4-0T No 3 at Castlederg shed. The first two engines were built by Kitsons of Leeds in 1883. No 3 was a slightly larger Kitson and was supplied in 1891. In later years these small tram engines were replaced by larger railway type locomotives as seen below, although No 3 lasted until 1928.**

Michael Pollard collection

Top right: **Bogie carriage No 5 at Castlederg. This was the largest carriage on the line, the others being 4 wheelers. Note the balcony ends and the regulation wire 'skirtings' over the wheels and undercarriage. The match-board or wainscotted panelling gave them a very American appearance. London tram trailers also had this sort of panelling.**

Michael Pollard collection

Centre: **2-6-0T No 4 with the 'Fridays only' 1.15pm cattle special from Castlederg which ran on the day of the monthly fair. It is seen here at Crew, midway between Castlederg and Victoria Bridge, where there was a passing loop. The cattle special is running late and is about to cross the 2.25pm mixed working from Victoria Bridge.**

This is the only known photograph of two trains crossing on a single line that had no signals whatsoever, and only occurred because the cattle train was running late. For almost all of its route, the tramway ran along the north side of the public road. No 4 was a Hudswell Clarke locomotive, built in 1904. After the closure of the CVBT in was sold to the CVR and rebuilt as a 2-6-2T.

HC Casserley, by permission of RM Casserley
(Michael Pollard collection)

Bottom: **2-4-0T No 6 shunting wagons in the market square in Castlederg, outside the Commercial Hotel. The locomotive is a Beyer Peacock engine, built in 1878, and purchased second hand in 1928 from the LMS (NCC). The design is similar to that of the early locomotives on the Isle of Man Steam Railway.**

Note the cattle wagon, with double centre doors and four small hinged flaps for ventilation. The signpost to the right of the locomotive is rather low and might be a hazard to taller pedestrians.

Scott McFarland collection

CLOGHER VALLEY TRAMWAY

This interesting 3'0" gauge line can be classified as a tramway as it spent 60% of its route mileage on a public road. It ran for 37 miles between Tynan, on the Portadown to Clones route of the GNRI, and Maguiresbridge on the Dundalk to Enniskillen line of the same company. The largest towns served were Aughnacloy and Fivemiletown. The line was entirely within what is now Northern Ireland, but spent its first 10 miles, on leaving Tynan, closely following the course of the River Blackwater which separates Northern Ireland from the Republic. Clogher, which gave its name to the system, has been described as the smallest cathedral city in Ireland with a population of only 200 at the time. The tramway shared the GNRI stations at its termini, but also had some fine red brick stations en route.

The Clogher Valley was agricultural and the chief purpose of the tramway was to transport people and produce outwards from the centre to each terminus. The track was laid by McCrea and McFarland, who also laid the Belfast and City of Derry horse tramways. The line was relatively simple to construct with no engineering features of any significance throughout its length. The maximum gradient was 1 in 30 and this was not infrequent. The line was opened on 2nd May 1887.

The trams left the public road to seek easier gradients between Maguiresbridge and Brookeborough for about 3 miles and for 1½ miles stretches at Clogher and Aughnacloy. Where the road was narrow, the trams often travelled beside it, separated by the hedgerow, but mostly they shared the public road. After seven years of operation, the company changed its name from *Tramway* to *Railway* in 1894. Unfortunately the change of name did not bring a change of fortune. It had plans to continue eastwards to connect with the Bessbrook and Newry Tramway and southwards to connect with the Cavan and Leitrim Railway at Bawnboy Road, but the plans came to nothing. This link-up was part of an ambitious but unrealistic plan which, if it had succeeded, would have joined the town of Greenore south of Carlingford Lough, to the Western Connemara town of Clifden, from the Irish Sea to the Atlantic Ocean. This bold concept was known as the Ulster and Connaught Light Railway. One shudders to think how long the overall journey might have taken, with so many stops en route.

The system was original in many respects and was one of the first to use cattle grids, windmills to draw water, conveyors to feed bunkers and steam to heat carriages. The tram locomotives ran backwards (ie cab first) and had a massive central lamp rather like a Cyclops eye. They had the usual skirtings and condensers in the early days but gradually, over the years, these were removed. A diesel railcar and a diesel tractor, known as 'the unit' gave useful service after 1932. The carriages were like something out of the Wild West with railed platforms at each end and clerestory roof lighting.

The tramway was never very prosperous and after 1912 never yielded a profit for the Company. To increase patronage, first class was eliminated and the system operated a third class system only. In 1928 the line's operation was taken over by a joint committee of both Fermanagh and Tyrone County Councils but road competition was too severe and the last tram, or train, ran in the early hours of 1st January 1942.

Sharp Stewart 0-4-2T No 4 heading up the main street in Fivemiletown, probably in the 1920s. Note the horse and cart full of stones, and the steam roller in the foreground, which are repairing the road. The tramway was in the centre of the road and this became a problem later, when cars began to park along the pavement. The number of people visible in the photograph suggests that this may be a market day. A steam locomotive and carriages puffing up the main street must have been a stirring sight.

Norman Johnston collection

The Clogher Valley railcar slightly further down the same street on 25th June 1937. This vehicle was built by Walker Brothers of Wigan in 1932 with a Gardner diesel engine. After closure of the CVR, it was sold to the Co Donegal Railways, becoming their No 10. It is now preserved at the Ulster Folk and Transport Museum, Cultra. From 1932 until the closure the railcar operated the bulk of passenger services, though steam trams still ran, as seen on the opposite page, especially on fair days.

HC Casserley, by permission of RM Casserley

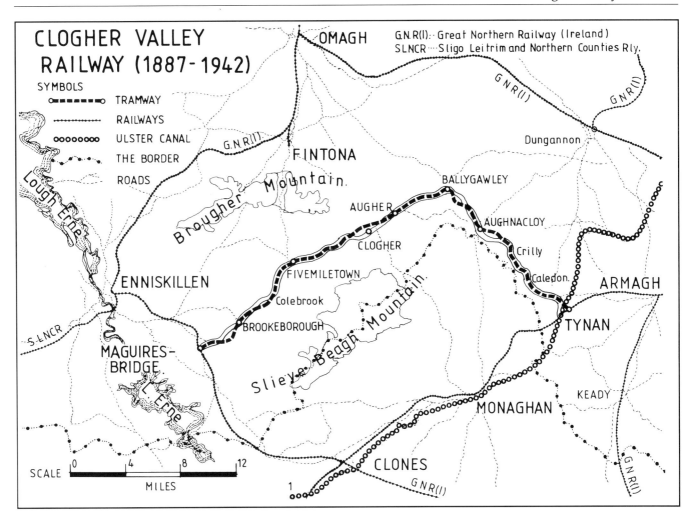

CLOGHER VALLEY RAILWAY (1887-1942)

SYMBOLS

○=====○ TRAMWAY

·········· RAILWAYS

○○○○○○○ ULSTER CANAL

·–·–·–· THE BORDER

——— ROADS

G.N.R(I).: Great Northern Railway (Ireland)
SLNCR· Sligo Leitrim and Northern Counties Rly.

OMAGH

Lough Erne

FINTONA

Brougher Mountain

G.N.R(I)

Dungannon

BALLYGAWLEY

AUGHER

AUGHNACLOY

CLOGHER

Crilly

FIVEMILETOWN

Caledon.

ARMAGH

Colebrook

ENNISKILLEN

BROOKEBOROUGH

Slieve Beagh Mountain

TYNAN

KEADY

MAGUIRES-BRIDGE.

L. Erne

MONAGHAN

S-LNCR

CLONES

G N R(I)

SCALE 0 4 8 12

MILES

Above: **For much of its route the Clogher Valley Tram ran alongside the public road, as can be seen in this view of No 6 at Stonepark Crossroads in 1937. These wayside halts had no facilities other than the timetable, seat and sign seen on the right. This view was taken on the same day as that of the railcar on the opposite page.**

HC Casserley, by permission of RM Casserley. (JD FitzGerald collection)

Left: **Some stretches of the Clogher Valley Tramway were on reserved track, where it left the public road to take a shortcut. This view, around 1930, is at an unusual location, and shows No 3 approaching Brookeborough from the north. The small 0-4-2Ts were always driven cab first. Note how the cow catcher is made of plate metal rather than a grill.**

JI Johnston. (Norman Johnston collection)

Electric Trams

GIANT'S CAUSEWAY and BUSHMILLS TRAMWAY

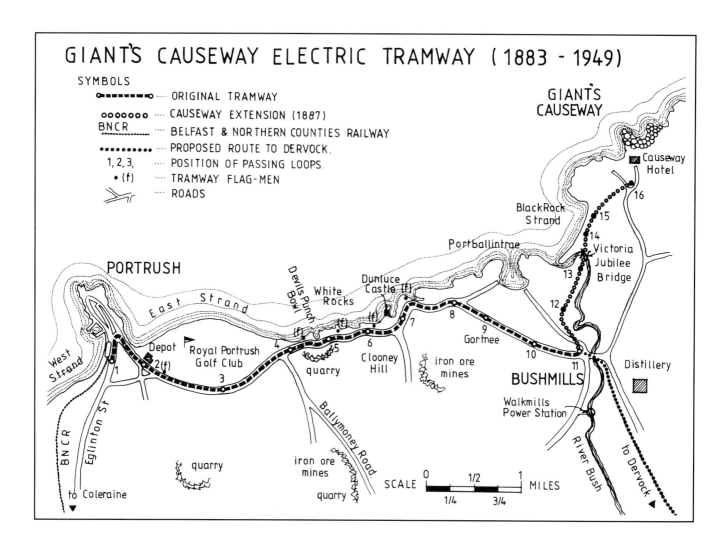

GIANT'S CAUSEWAY ELECTRIC TRAMWAY (1883 - 1949)

SYMBOLS

o••••••o ···· ORIGINAL TRAMWAY
ooooooo ···· CAUSEWAY EXTENSION (1887)
BNCR ···· BELFAST & NORTHERN COUNTIES RAILWAY
••••••••• ···· PROPOSED ROUTE TO DERVOCK.
1, 2, 3, ···· POSITION OF PASSING LOOPS.
• (f) ···· TRAMWAY FLAG-MEN
···· ROADS

GIANT'S CAUSEWAY

Causeway Hotel

BlackRock Strand

Portballintrae

Victoria Jubilee Bridge

PORTRUSH

East Strand

Devils Punch Bowl

White Rocks

Dunluce Castle (f)

Gortnee

West Strand

Depot

Royal Portrush Golf Club

Clooney Hill

iron ore mines

Distillery

BUSHMILLS

Walkmills Power Station

BNCR

Eglinton St

Ballymoney Road

quarry

iron ore mines

quarry

River Bush

to Dervock

to Coleraine

quarry

SCALE 0   1/2   1 MILES
       1/4   3/4

In my introduction, I have made mention of this little tramway, perhaps the most famous electric tramway in the world. In 1878 a company was incorporated to construct a steam tramway between Portrush and Bushmills, a distance of 6 miles, but nothing came of these proposals. Other endeavours were also made, but these also failed. Two brothers from the prominent local Traill family resolved to remedy the situation by promoting a tramway themselves. Their original proposals were to link Bushmills along the public roadway to the broad gauge station at Portrush by steam and electrically hauled carriages, and run a narrow gauge railway along the Bush valley from Bushmills to Dervock on the Ballymoney to Ballycastle railway and transport the produce of iron ore mining to Larne. However the railway from Bushmills to Dervock was never constructed. The name of the company was 'The Giant's Causeway, Portrush and Bush Valley Railway and Tramway Co'. As electric traction was in its infancy, the Traill brothers contacted Von Siemens who was operating experimental short lines in Berlin since 1881 and Von Siemens became a shareholder in the company. A steam operated generator was provided in 1882 and experimental runs with electric traction commenced that year. The tramway opened on 29th January 1883, using steam engines, and electric working began on 28th September. The gauge was 3'0".

The Traills harnessed the River Bush at a place called Walkmills to turn turbines and generate the electricity required to power the cars and the system became the first hydro-electric powered tramway in the world.

The early powered cars had one 5 hp motor located centrally under the floor, connected by chain drive to axle-mounted spur gearing. The current was picked up from a raised, live, third rail located on the seaward side of the track. As the live rail could not have been provided within the town of Portrush, two Wilkinson steam trams brought the carriages from Portrush BNCR station to the town boundary where the electric trams took over. For many years the steam trams provided a useful service over the electric line as the electric system was often a little temperamental.

The Traill brothers abandoned their mining aspirations in favour of transporting visitors, and a two mile extension to the renowned Giant's Causeway was built in 1887. During the summer months, when the tourist traffic was large, the level of the Bush river was often at a low. As a result the system became underpowered and could not cope. Overhead current collection replaced the live third rail in 1899, and at this stage trams with conventional motors and trucks were introduced.

In 1911 a second power station, to supplement the hydro-electric plant at Bushmills, was provided at the tram depot in Portrush. This was powered by a gas engine, but proved less than adequate. It was replaced in 1925 by a much more powerful generator, which had a 132hp oil engine.

At times the cars moved so slowly that they would be outpaced by cyclists. This never seemed to bother the tourists who had more time to appreciate the scenic coastline and they were probably pleased with the motor man 'taking his time'.

In spite of the system's shortcomings it provided a reliable, if occasionally a little slow, service for the local community and visitors for over 65 years. The trams themselves were very varied with both saloon and toast rack powered cars and trailers, the earlier goods wagons being converted to passenger cars as the need arose. The line is famous in song and story and whilst the community fought hard to save it, their efforts were, regrettably, unsuccessful.

At the time of its closure in September 1949 it was the longest running electric tramway in existence.

During the period when the Causeway Tramway used a third rail electric system, steam locomotives had to be used within the town boundary of Portrush. Here 0-4-0T No 3 *Dunluce Castle* looks rather the worse for wear. This photograph was probably taken shortly before steam working ceased in 1913.

HR Norman, courtesy IRRS

Dunluce Castle around 1890, showing the raised conductor rail used until 1899. Note the gap in the rail at the field entrance to the immediate left of the tram, usually crossed by the momentum of the tram. The saloon car is No 4 and the trailer is No 10.

National Library of Ireland (W Lawrence)

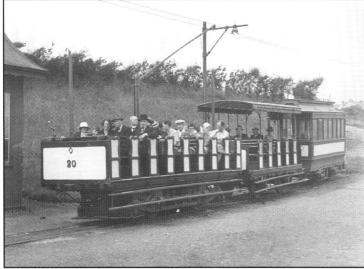

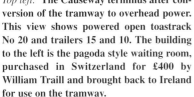

Top right: **Portrush depot in 1926. This view shows the new power house built to the right of the tram depot in 1925, and officially opened by Mrs Traill on 1st July. Power was obtained from a 132 hp crude oil engine, driving a 89kw DC dynamo, supplied by the Electric Construction Co. The tram depot still survives as a garage.** *Michael Pollard collection*

Top left: **The Causeway terminus after conversion of the tramway to overhead power. This view shows powered open toastrack No 20 and trailers 15 and 10. The building to the left is the pagoda style waiting room, purchased in Switzerland for £400 by William Traill and brought back to Ireland for use on the tramway.**

John Kennedy

Centre: **This view shows the exterior of Portrush station in 1949 during the last summer of the tramway. No 23 has just arrived from the Causeway and is about to run round its trailers, Nos 10 (saloon) and 7. The young conductor (Michael Pollard) is in the act of reversing the trolley pole. The driver is Robbie Jamieson. The partly hidden clock reads 1.10 pm. The Causeway tramway had an interesting assortment of powered cars and trailers, both open and saloon. No 23 was built in 1908.**

Michael Pollard collection

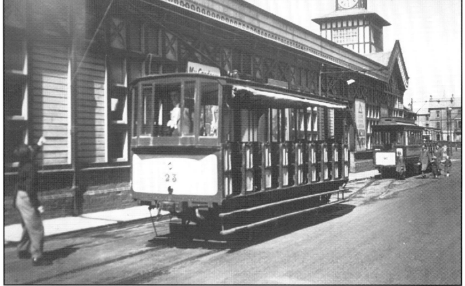

Bottom: **With driver Robert Sharp leaning out and conductor William Montgomery (driving!) car No 9 ascends out of Portrush past Craigahulliar passing loop with trailer No 5 in 1949. The town of Portrush is clearly visible in the background.**

This photograph shows No 9 as rebuilt in 1945, when it received the original ornate side panels from No 3, then withdrawn. Before 1945, this car had plain side panels as seen on No 10 (top left) and an exceedingly ugly driver's cab at each end.

After many years sitting at Youghal, Co Cork, No 9 has been rescued for preservation, and can be seen in its current, partly restored, state on page 26. Whilst some historians believe that No 9 was built new as a saloon car in 1888-90, restoration work has revealed that she was a rebuild of an earlier low-sided open powered car, probably dating from 1884.

Michael Pollard collection

BESSBROOK and NEWRY TRAMWAY

The Bessbrook and Newry Tramway was the world's second hydro-electric powered system preceded only by the Giant's Causeway. It was opened on 1st October 1885 and, like the Causeway line, had a gauge of 3'0". It was promoted by a local family, the Richardsons, who owned the Bessbrook Flax Spinning Mills and the main function of the tramway was industrial. The tramway delivered the finished mill products to Newry, where they could be transferred to the railway at the Edward Street station of the GNRI, or the wagons could be horse drawn to the docks for shipping. Raw material and coal was brought in the reverse direction. The mill gave employment to about 3,000 workers and was one of the oldest mills in Ireland. The initial proposals were for either a horse- or steam-hauled tram. However, Dr Eric Hopkinson, the engineer engaged to construct the line, had experience with the setting up of the electric system at Portrush and strongly promoted this means of traction as the best option.

In the case of the Causeway tram, when the industrial side of that undertaking failed to materialise, the tourist potential provided sufficient revenue to ensure its survival until bus competition appeared. In contrast, the Bessbrook and Newry Tramway had no such benefits and remained industrial throughout its existence.

It did, however, carry passengers from Newry to Bessbrook, but this facility was mostly for workers at the mills. The Camlough River provided the power at Millvale and the current was carried on a central live rail between the running rails. The running rails were unique in that they also had outer rails over which flangeless wheeled wagons could be hauled using the running rail as a continuous flange. This meant that, when released from the tram system, the wagons could also be street-hauled by horses.

The trams could raise and lower safety barriers automatically by tripping and emptying a water laden vessel which acted as a counterbalance, and reversing the procedure when the road junction had been passed. The trams had two pick-up shoes, fore and aft, and as long as small breaks in the live rail were less than the shoe spacing, the section of live rail could go underground at gate ways and small roads. A pick-up device on the roof of the cars made contact with overhead live cable at Millvale level crossing where the gap without current was too excessive. This is believed to be the first attempt at producing the well known 'bow current collector', popular with many later tramway undertakings.

Although opened only two years after the Giant's Causeway tram, the technological advances in electrical equipment were considerable and the system was relatively trouble free in operation throughout its existence. The Causeway trams were four wheeled and had one motor under the tram's belly. The Bessbrook trams were bogie but instead of having two bogie-mounted motors, one larger motor was housed at one end above floor level in its own compartment with chains and gearing to turn the axles. This made for ease of maintenance. To overcome the problems with turning at termini, balloon loops were provided.

The company was quick to avail itself of rolling stock made available by closures of other systems and bodies were procured from the Dublin and Lucan, bogies from the Castlederg

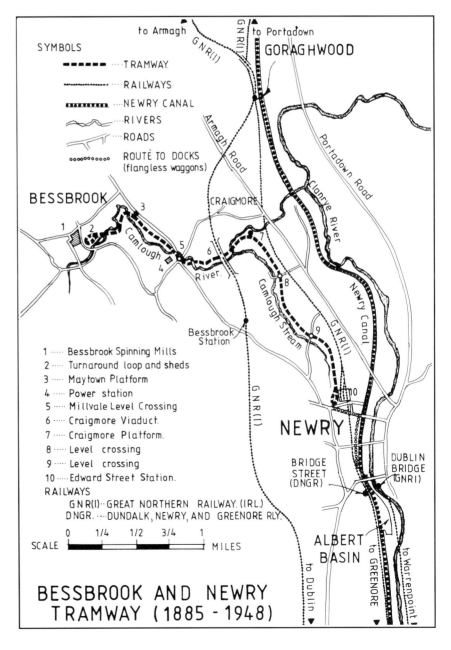

SYMBOLS

- - - - · · · TRAMWAY.
· · · · · · · · RAILWAYS
▦▦▦▦▦ · · · NEWRY CANAL
⌒⌒⌒ · · · RIVERS
⎇ · · · ROADS
ooooooooooo ROUTE TO DOCKS (flangless waggons)

1 ···· Bessbrook Spinning Mills
2 ···· Turnaround loop and sheds
3 ···· Maytown Platform
4 ···· Power station
5 ···· Millvale Level Crossing
6 ···· Craigmore Viaduct.
7 ···· Craigmore Platform.
8 ···· Level crossing
9 ···· Level crossing
10 ···· Edward Street Station.
RAILWAYS
    GNR(I)··GREAT NORTHERN RAILWAY. (IRL.)
    DNGR.···DUNDALK, NEWRY, AND GREENORE RLY.

SCALE 0 1/4 1/2 3/4 1 MILES

BESSBROOK AND NEWRY TRAMWAY (1885 - 1948)

and Victoria Bridge and wagons from the Clogher Valley. A service in each direction at hourly intervals was provided and the duration of the journey was twenty minutes.

The Company constructed a small saloon car, No 6, for the transport of the Richardson family and their friends to and from Newry. The original Car No 5 had strong similarities to the early Causeway trams. It had a platform entrance at one end only, which gave access to a low sided carriage with longitudinal seating served by a central aisle. The Causeway cars had platforms at both ends and access to the platforms was on one side only. Unlike the Causeway cars, No 5 was without any of the high ornamentation that characterised the former but had a more streamlined appearance. This open sided car was reserved for summer use only. The system closed down in January 1948.

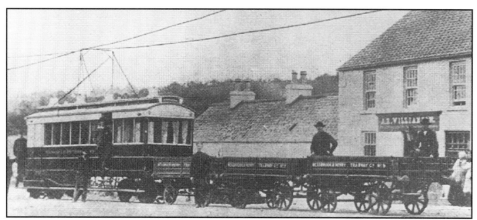

Top: **This is the original BNT No 1, constructed in 1885, by the Ashbury Carriage and Wagon Co of Manchester. It is seen at Millvale level crossing with two flangeless wagons in tow, and the bow collector is in use. Compared with the Causeway cars, introduced only two years previously, the first Bessbrook cars were a great technological advance. No 1 was divided into three compartments, occupied from left to right in the photo by the traction motor, 24 second class seats and, to the right of the entrance, 12 first class seats. Car No 2, of this type, survives in rebuilt form, at the Ulster Folk and Transport Museum.**

Author's collection

Centre left: **Motor car No 4 with trailer No 5 in tow. This vehicle originally ran on the 3'6" Dublin and Lucan Electric Tramway, but was purchased by the Bessbrook and Newry Tramway in 1928, and regauged. For a number of years it ran in the DLER livery of green and cream. Note how every other window is boarded up.**

DB McNeill, courtesy IRRS

Centre right: **Car No 6, the Richardson's private saloon, was one of the smallest tramcars ever constructed. It could carry up to 12 passengers on two facing benches. It was built around 1922, and unlike most of the other cars, had no clerestory lighting. Its simple curved roof suggested that it was constructed locally. No 6 is thought to still exist as an outbuilding at a school.**   *H Fayle, courtesy IRRS*

Bottom: **A builder's photograph of Bessbrook and Newry car No 1 at the premises of Hurst Nelson and Co of Motherwell. This car was a 1921 replacement for the original No 1, seen above. This tram was remarkable for its length (37'1¾"), and could carry up to 40 passengers.**

As the traction bogies were located under the bulkheads, the wheelbase was exceptionally long (29'8"), and this may have given rise to occasional oscillation. The windscreens were rounded and the car had quite a modern appearance, apart from the location of the bogies,

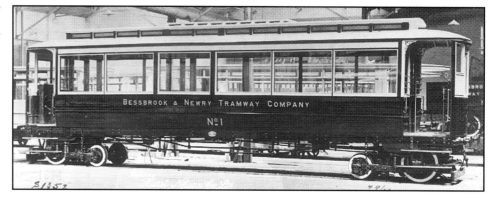

which had some affinity with steam tram trailers. The saloon was divided centrally with a bulkhead and sliding door. It had clerestory ventilation, extending between the bulkheads. Matching platforms were located at each end, unlike No 6, which had a platform at one end only.

RC Ludgate collection

Top: Motor car No 4 with van No 2 and trailer No 6 at Craigmore in 1940. This evening shot shows the tram heading towards Newry. Car No 4 was built by Messrs Hurst Nelson in 1921 and was dimensionally similar to the second No 1 (shown opposite), with the exception that a luggage compartment with roller shutter doors was provided. As a result the seating capacity was reduced to 32, and No 4 had only five saloon windows per side.

The central *live* rail, which carried the current, can be seen between the running rails of the tramway.

In the background is the impressive Craigmore Viaduct, composed of 18 masonry arches, which carried the GNRI Belfast-Dublin railway line 126 feet above the valley of the Bessbrook River.

WA Camwell, courtesy IRRS

Centre: Motor car No 4 with possibly Ex-Lucan trailer No 27 at the rear. This view clearly shows the roller shutter doors of the luggage compartment. It also shows how the system could load passengers from either platform or ground level. The motor man is looking at Mr Goldberg as he composes his shot. Two passengers about to board the tram are also aware of the camera man. This view is at the Edward Street terminus of the tram at Newry, where it connected with the GNRI railway. The condition of the station yard is unkempt and over grown, unlike the early days when everything was more shipshape.

V Goldberg, Author's collection

Bottom: Bogie motor car No 2 and four wheel trailer car No 6 at Bessbrook depot after the closure of the tramway. The car in the background is either No 1 or No 4.

In 1928 the Bessbrook and Newry Tramway purchased trailers Nos 24 and 27 of the Dublin and Lucan Electric Tramway. The body of No 24 was used to replace the original body of Bessbrook and Newry No 2. As No 24 was shorter than the original No 2, a luggage compartment, equal in length to two windows was built in front of the passenger section. This gave the tram an unusual if not a slightly ungainly appearance. No 2 is now preserved at the Ulster Folk and Transport Museum. It still has one of the original 1885 motors, probably the oldest tram motor surviving.

H Fayle, courtesy IRRS

HILL of HOWTH TRAMWAY (GNRI)

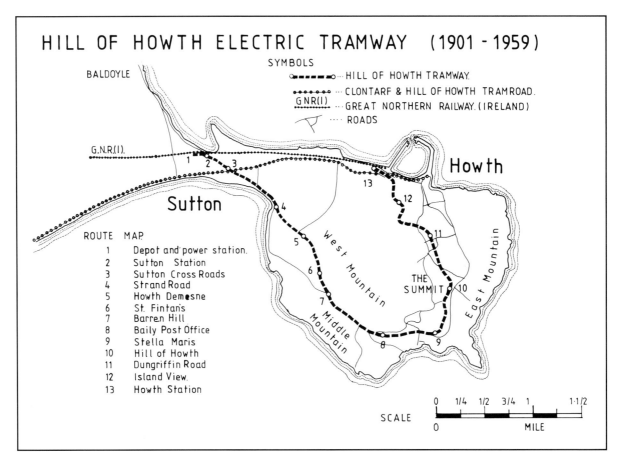

The Great Northern Railway (Ireland) first contemplated the introduction of a tramway around the Hill as far back as 1883. Electric traction was very much in its infancy and for such steep gradients, it would not have been possible at the time. Horse haulage over such hilly terrain would have entailed a team of four throughout. This would not have been a practical solution in terms of cost or indeed safety. At the time, horse drawn *long cars* seating seven passengers sitting face to face, known as 'vis-a-vis', were employed, picking up passengers from the steam trains at Howth terminus and, bringing them to the village or around the hill. This service started in 1867.

During the summer months the long cars continued up what is now Thormanby Road and turned into Dungriffin Road and entered the region of the West Mountain to emerge beside an old cottage (which still exists) near St Fintan's Cemetery and down to Sutton. In many ways this was the precursor of the electric trams, excluding the area of the summit. The 'vis-a-vis', known locally as 'visabees', were housed where a modern housing estate called Mariner's Cove is situated. This was the site of the old Howth Riding Stables operated by Jerry O'Brien.

The route followed by the tramway was prepared by the company's engineer, W H Mills, and it used the Irish standard gauge of 5'3". The track gradient was reduced by 'serpenting' the permanent way from the summit down to Howth Station. The purpose of the tramway was to pick up passengers and deliver them to the line's railway stations at either Sutton or Howth. Regrettably the village of Howth was poorly served by the route adopted. The company presumably hoped that the village would expand along the route of the tramway, which was quite usual in more built-up areas. Sadly it was not until after the had line closed, that sufficient development of the residential area took place to warrant the survival of such a tram route.

The long survival of the tram owed much to the fact that the hilly nature of the route was unsuited to the under-powered motor buses of the day, so there were no mechanical predators to offer much competition until the mid 1950s.

On 17th June 1901, the line opened from Sutton to the Summit (just over half of the route) and the balance of the line to Howth Station was opened to the public on the 1st August. The original rolling stock consisted of eight six-windowed open-top bogie saloons, with longitudinal seating in the saloon and reversible garden seats on the outside with a total of 67 passengers. They were built by Brush Electric of Loughborough and the bogies were Brill 22E. The livery of these trams was crimson lake and ivory.

The Board of Trade insisted that the upper deck surround caging be increased in height to protect a standing person on account of the closeness of poles and trees en route. These trams could boast of being the highest open-toppers ever constructed.

The patronage was very good in the first months of the service and the company decided to purchase two 'Summer cars' without fenestration in the saloon. These cars were designed at the GNRI railway works in Dundalk and were influenced by carriage design principles with nine vertical windows which were more than a little reminiscent of a railway carriage. The internal seating arrangement was to afford the best possible views to the tourist and had a centrally located knife board seat with passengers sitting back-to-back facing outwards. These cars, Nos 9 and 10, were glazed soon after. They were built by G F Milnes on Peckham 14 D-5 bogies and seated 73 passengers.

During the First World War years the trams were in need of painting. On account of the shortage of pigments the company decided on an austerity livery of grained mahogany and all trams and coaching stock were painted accordingly. Later in the 1930s when the GNRI introduced their diesel rail cars, a third livery of Oxford blue and cream was adopted, and all the trams, with the exception of numbers 9 and 10, were turned out in the new colours. One of the conductors, Willie O'Brien, was so incensed with the 'gaudy garb' of the new trams that he surprised his morning passengers on the first day of their appearance. He constantly clanged the gong and shouted at the top of his voice, "Stop me and buy one," the

usual call of the ice cream vendors! As it turned out the new livery grew in popularity and eventually even Willie himself grew to like it. As Nos 9 and 10 were only in use in peak summer traffic they were not in need of repainting and the GNRI, as a measure of economy, retained their grained mahogany livery until the closure.

Apart from the summer tourist traffic and morning peak hours, the trams provided a regular service at twenty minute intervals all day long. The aspiration of the company to serve a built-up community never came to fruition. In spite of this, the heavy summer traffic often yielded an overall profit for the year. The trams provided something of a social service in the area, never charging poor folk the fare, transporting packages free of charge and sounding the gong by request when passing certain houses to act as a morning alarm clock. The same crew manned the same trams over the years and conversations and gossip continued from morning to morning almost uninterrupted for generations.

When the line closed down on 31st May 1959, Howth lost part of her charm. On that fateful last day of operation, when conductor Billy Rankin called: "Last fares please!", grown men were seen to weep.

The closure of the Hill of Howth tram also marked the end of the electric tram era in Ireland.

Left: **Brush Electric car No 8 inside Sutton tram shed. Although of timber structure, the sheds were impressive and gothic-like with massive pitch pine stantions secured to 1" thick gusset plates anchored into poured ground beams. The stantions or columns carried a railway type wrought iron roof with patent glazing and ventilation. Large round headed windows in each bay conveyed a sense of lightness and provided pleasant working conditions. The structure was clad with timber ship lap sheeting. After closure the building survived as a store and then lay derelict for many years. At one stage the Transport Museum Society had hoped to set up a museum depot here, but no firm would insure the timber structure.** *John Kennedy*

Right: **This is an early photograph of one of the eight Brush Electric cars in its original crimson lake and ivory livery, circa 1904. The platform opening has not yet been infilled with a window, as can be seen by comparison with the tram above. The motorman, conductor and three other staff, some standing on the upper deck seats, face Mr Welch, the photographer. He is standing in Bellingham's Field at Red Rock. In the background is Shielmartin Mountain, and behind the photographer is a hill known as the Middle Mountain, though it is not much higher than the tram itself. Notice the four tents halfway up the mountain, from which magnificent views of Dublin bay would be enjoyed.** *R Welch, courtesy Ulster Museum*

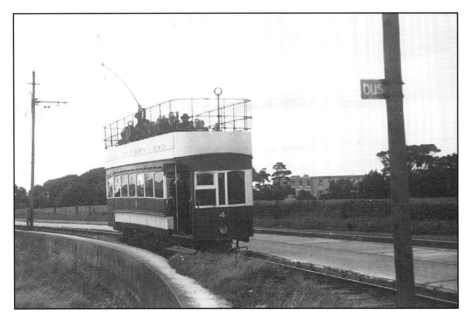

Centre: No 9 and No 6 standing at the Summit in the late 1950s with conductor Billy Rankin facing the camera. The building to the right of No 6 is now the *Summit Stores*, but at the time was a domestic dwelling. The corner of *Gaffney's Summit Inn* can just be seen to the far right above the hedge. This was a favourite watering place for both staff and passengers. Judging by the position of the trolley poles, No 6 is returning from Howth station and No 9 is ready to proceed to Howth. Both trams will start to descend as this is the Summit. Very often the trolleys of Nos 9 and 10 were reversed at the summit to return to Sutton, as these massive cars were difficult to handle on the steep gradients and switch-backs between the Summit and Howth. Only the most experienced motormen had the privilege of driving on this section with the big cars.
RC Ludgate

Bottom: No 2, one of the Brush Electric cars, ascending the steep climb from Howth station and about to continue its journey to the Summit. The loop is at Dungriffin Road, and a shelter can be seen just to the left of the team. The appearance of a second trolley pole betrays the presence of a hidden tram behind No 2, about to descend to Howth. The tram track from Dungriffin Halt to Howth station was a popular walk for the more energetic locals, as the well worn track indicates. This was against Company rules, though no one appears to have objected. At times, especially during off peak hours, the trolley pole was disconnected just beyond the Summit and the trams coasted by gravity down to Howth. This was a measure to save money but could not be done at night when lighting was essential.   *RC Ludgate*

Car No 8 descending towards Howth from the Summit. This part of the line was very picturesque, and was popular for walks as described earlier. Howth village is out of sight behind the trees and the sea is just visible to the right of the bushes. The wooded area in the background is Offington Wood, after Lady Offington, who was related to the owners of Howth Castle. Howth Castle Estate itself is to the left. Note the inside-keyed track.

Leeds Transport Historical Society

This view, taken outside Sutton tram depot, shows No 6 ready to enter service with the trolley in position. The depot was adjacent to the Howth branch of the GNRI and an old grained mahogany railway carriage can be seen in the left background. Just beyond the signal cabin, the public road crosses over both the railway line and tram tracks. The railway line and tramway run parallel up to this point and then separate as they reach Sutton and Baldoyle railway station. The bridge on the right links the up and down platforms and originally had a roof over it, which was unusual. Holiday makers, arriving from Amiens Street, wishing to travel around the Hill by the electric cars, would leave the train at this station, cross over the foot bridge, and board the tram in the station yard. This view shows clearly the blue and white livery used on cars Nos 1-8.   *C Banks collection, ColourRail*

Top right: **Preserved Hill of Howth tram No 9 outside the Transport Museum at Howth Demesne. Tom Redmond, seen here, was the chief motorman with the company in the 1950s, and was known to his fellow staff as 'The Manager'. In 1959, Tom, in car No 1, was the last man to take a tram out of Howth railway station. Both cars 9 and 10 are preserved, and on the occasion shown here, the partially restored No 9 was rolled out of the depot for the launch of the 1985 set of postage stamps depicting trams, and issued by An Post. No 10 of this class is preserved in running order at Crich, in Derbyshire.**   *Michael Corcoran*

Top left: **This photograph could understandably cause some confusion unless one knew the background. After the closure, car No 2 was bought by the Orange Trolley Museum of Perris in California, where it was regauged and left in the open, slowly deteriorating, for many years. In 1986, the author brought out a book called *Howth and Her Trams* in which he described No 2 as 'decaying in the California sunshine'. To his surprise a certain Jim Fulton rang from Perris to say that he personally would like to make up for his society's negligence, and undertook the full restoration of No 2. It was restored to excellent condition and is proving a most popular tourist attraction, with an Irish pipe band occasionally serenading the passengers. In contrast to the trams on the previous page, the livery is not quite Oxford blue, as the repainting was based on the faded paint stripped off the tram during its restoration. This photograph was taken on 20th October 1990.**   *Jim Fulton*

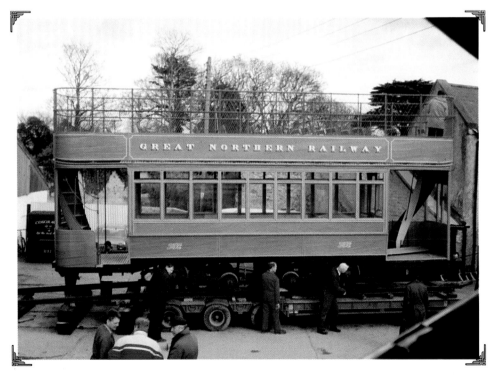

Bottom: **No 9 at the Transport Museum, Howth, being raised onto a low-loader for transport to Dublin for the St Patrick's Day parade in 1992. In contrast to the earlier view above, No 9 is now fully restored. On occasions such as these, Danny Maher of CIE, seen beside the driving wheel of the right hand bogie, usually takes charge.**

The tram was raised on rails running up a steep incline from the tracks inside the museum to the low-loader. Great care had to be taken at all times, as a derailment could have had serious consequences. Once secure and the tying wires are carefully checked, everyone breathed a sigh of relief!

Nos 9 and 10 were both built in 1902 by GF Milnes on Peckham bogies. As they were intended for summer use the saloons were initially unglazed. When the other cars were given the Oxford blue and cream livery, Nos 9 and 10 were not in need of a repaint and remained in varnished grained mahogany until the closure.   *Michael Corcoran*

CORK ELECTRIC TRAMS

An earlier chapter of this book told the story of the short-lived horse tram system in Cork. When electric traction appeared and began replacing the horse as a motive force, the idea of tramways once more came to the fore. In Cork, the bearers of such an idea had to tread very carefully, knowing the history that preceded. The use of electricity in the early years was geared towards public lighting supply and other uses. Traction was, to some extent, left in abeyance. The proprietors of a tramway company would be required to produce surplus electricity, not just to power the tram line, but also to serve the electrical needs of the city.

With the introduction of the Cork horse tramways, names such as Train and Robinson, which became famous world-wide, were deeply involved in the early years, and the introduction of the electric trams to Cork was no different. Dr Theodore Merz, a director of the world-famous British Thompson Houston Co (BTH), which played a major part, not only in developing motors for electric tramcars but with pioneering electricity in general, had a son, Charles H Merz, who followed him into the firm. Charles Merz was commissioned to set up the whole system in Cork, although only a young man at the time. He became chief engineer and secretary of the company.

To emphasise the aspect of public lighting, the new company was called 'The Cork Electric Tramway and Lighting Co'. This may also have been to sweeten the tramway pill, so to speak, and make it more palatable to a hesitant community. Charles H Merz was also destined to achieve worldwide fame and was called one of Britain's most illustrious engineers. It was while working in Cork that he was introduced to Mr William McLellan. Mr McLellan worked for another world-famous company, Siemens, and joined Merz in Cork to set up the system. Together they formed not only a lifelong friendship but set up the firm of Merz and McLellan Ltd which achieved international recognition. Merz, it could be said, was to Cork's electric trams what Robinson was to her horse trams many years previously, both going forward after their experience in Cork to greater things. Merz was killed tragically in 1940 when his home in London received a direct hit from a German bomb.

The chairman of the Company was none other than William Martin Murphy, who was born in Berehaven in West Cork and he was also responsible for laying the tracks. The gauge selected — 2'11$\frac{1}{2}$" — was unusual and was chosen to permit shared running with the 3'0" narrow gauge railways through the city. The difference of $\frac{1}{2}$" resulted from the transition from normal railway practice, with sleepers, to over street grooved track running. For this reason, Dublin City trams could never operate over the Hill of Howth tramway as the GNRI was based on railway practice, and the DUTC on grooved track running, even though both were nominally 5'3" gauge. Although the gauge between train and tram was suited to interchange in Cork city, this never actually took place in practice.

One of the more difficult tasks was the construction of the power station with its high chimney, as the ground was marshy. A base of closely-laid pitch pine columns or piles set in a staggered formation to a depth of almost forty feet was necessary to provide a non-shifting foundation. The tall chimney was one of the first of its kind in these islands in that it was steel framed to reduce its overall weight.

In all, 35 tramcars were ordered from the firm of Brush Electric of Loughborough and they were delivered in three batches. The first batch of 18 cars, delivered for the opening on 22nd December 1898, were numbered 1-18 inclusive and had the shorter canopy, common in early tramcar design. The second batch of 10 cars were very similar and recognisable by the fact that they had only two louvred vents over each window compared to three on the first batch. They were delivered in 1900 and numbered 19-28 inclusive. These cars also had the shorter roof canopy. The third batch, 29-35, delivered in 1901, were an advance on the previous two batches in that the canopy was extended to cover the entire platform area and they had a more rounded and streamlined frontal appearance. These were popular with both conductor and motor man and the extra shelter was appreciated over the years. The design not only provided extra shelter, but also extra passenger accommodation on the upper deck. The last batch also had *reversed* stairs, more usual with the full canopy design, but these restricted the number of passengers on the outside and shortly afterwards the stairs were altered to the *direct* or anti-clockwise arrangement of the first two batches.

One of the trams eventually had the distinction of being entirely built in Cork, and this was No 3 of the first batch. This resulted from the tram's destruction during the famous burning of Cork on Saturday 11th December 1920, when the crew and passengers were ordered off by the Black and Tans at gunpoint and the tram was set on fire. The new tram had the full canopy and, as with modified cars, had opening ventilating windows instead of the earlier louvres. It was recorded that the tram staff in Cork were very proud of this fully Cork-built tram, the only one ever to be so built.

Another feature of the Cork electric cars was that they continued the practice of locating the head lamp at high level, built into the upper deck dash. It will be appreciated that horse trams had no need for platform dash headlamps as all that would be illuminated would be the horses posterior, hardly to the gratification of the passengers or the safety of the cars. Oil lamps, however, were carried on the bulkhead under the canopy to shelter the flame. With electric cars no such shelter was required and originally the lamps were located on the short canopy itself. When the short canopy was extended the lamp was usually set into the lower platform dash by most companies, but the Cork trams retained them in the upper deck position throughout their life. The trucks were manufactured by Peckham, (8A type with 5'6" wheel base), but in the latter years some of the trucks were replaced with Brush radial 7'6" wheel base, which must have given a smoother ride.

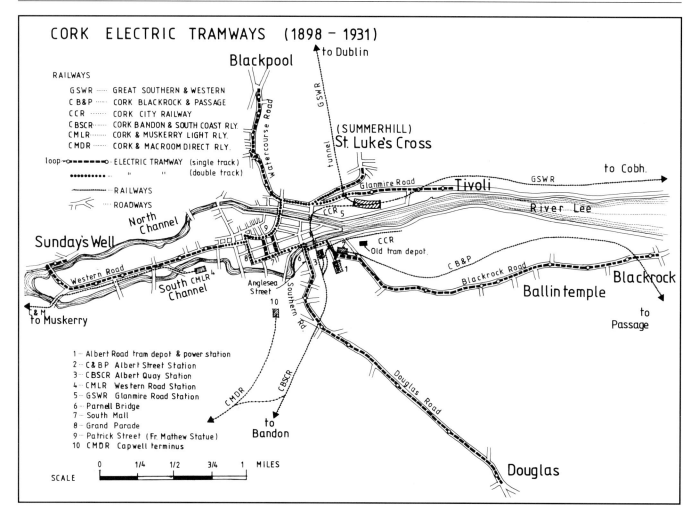

CORK ELECTRIC TRAMWAYS (1898 – 1931)

RAILWAYS

GSWR ---- GREAT SOUTHERN & WESTERN
C B & P ---- CORK BLACKROCK & PASSAGE
CCR ---- CORK CITY RAILWAY
CBSCR---- CORK BANDON & SOUTH COAST RLY.
CMLR---- CORK & MUSKERRY LIGHT RLY.
CMDR ---- CORK & MACROOM DIRECT RLY.

loop ---o—▪—▪—▪—▪— ELECTRIC TRAMWAY (single track)
         ▪▪▪▪▪▪▪▪▪▪   "   "   (double track)
         ------ RAILWAYS
         ʃʃʃʃʃ --- ROADWAYS

1 - Albert Road tram depot & power station
2 - C & B P Albert Street Station
3 - CBSCR Albert Quay Station
4 - CMLR Western Road Station
5 - GSWR Glanmire Road Station
6 - Parnell Bridge
7 - South Mall
8 - Grand Parade
9 - Patrick Street (Fr. Mathew Statue)
10 - CMDR Capwell terminus

SCALE   0   1/4   1/2   3/4   1   MILES

As with most systems which penetrated into what was then countryside, there were long stretches of single line track with passing loops at intervals. Within the city itself, the track was doubled. On single line workings, where one loop could not be easily seen from another, it was necessary to introduce a signalling system to avoid two trams meeting head on. The conductor of the first tram to reach a loop would dismount and turn a key in a signal box which showed a red light on the approaching loop out of view. This prevented another tram from entering the single section of track until the first tram reached the second loop.

This usually worked, but it could happen that opposing signals were turned simultaneously, as both trams entered the single track section towards each other. Inthat case, the usual practice was that whoever had travelled furthest had the right of way. This did not necessarily hold true, if the opposing conductor was a burly man of mean disposition, in which case common sense normally prevailed. Whoever had to retreat had to turn the trolley pole and suffer the rebuffs of the passengers who would have to endure the delay. There was at least one occasion where 'midway' meetings were resolved unanimously by the transfer of passengers and a reversal of the trolleys!

Within the city core the tram route followed that of the earlier horse tramway quite faithfully, and the extensions sought by the horse tram authorities, almost a quarter of a

century previously in an effort to save the system, were put into effect for the greater part and extended. I described the horse tramway as a somewhat distorted letter 'C'. The various new extensions introduced by the electric tramway now looked like a spider, with six legs setting off in different directions.

Keeping to a clockwise direction, the first leg moved due east along Blackrock Road, via Ballintemple, to Blackrock. Originally the trams terminated at Ballintemple, but by the arrival of the last batch of cars in 1901 the new terminus was reached. This line reached the city centre via Albert Road and passed the power station where the tram depot was also located.

The second leg left the city along Anglesea Street, through Southern Road in a south east direction along Douglas Road to Douglas, then just a village.

The third leg left Grand Parade near its junction with Patrick Street. It went along Washington Street and Western Road, between the North and South Channels of the Lee. Then it turned north to cross the North Channel just before the point where the channels divide in two. Finally a short distance after crossing the channel, the line turned sharply eastwards to terminate at Sunday's Well. As the name suggests, the area is associated with a holy well, now covered over.

The fourth leg was to Blackpool due north of the city, turning left at the junction of Bridge Street and MacCurtain Street (then King Street), to run along Leitrim Street and Watercourse Road to the terminus at Blackpool.

The fifth leg turned right into MacCurtain Street and then separated from the Tivoli route at Lower Glanmire Road where it followed Summerhill to St Luke's Cross. The terminus was usually referred to as Summerhill. This was the shortest leg. The final or sixth leg, after sharing MacCurtain Street with the Summerhill route, went along Lower Glanmire Rd to its terminus at Tivoli. The total route mileage was ten.

In the early years short cuts were introduced from South Mall to Patrick Street, via Marlborough Street and through Morgan and Robert Streets. These streets were very narrow and one can imagine the problems of attempting to reverse horse drawn vehicles when confronted by a tram. The short link lines were equally short-lived and were removed at the turn of the century.

In the earlier years, the trams carried large easily-read letters on their platform dashes indicating the route traversed.

DS	Douglas to the Statue
WS	Western Road to Summerhill
BS	Blackrock to the Statue
BP	Blackpool to Grand Parade

These large letters were a feature of the trams until sometime after the First World War and appear on many of the photographs taken during these years.The Father Mathew Statue, known as 'The Statue', was the main hub from which one could board any tram for any terminus.

Eventually the tram company, rather than terminating at the Statue, reversing the trolley and necessitating a change of passengers each time, introduced through-running as was happening in Dublin and other cities. For through-running the trams made for those diagonally opposed termini, apart from the easterly routes. The north terminus of Blackpool made for the most southerly terminus at Douglas and this was the longest route, crossing the city from north to south. The north east terminus of Summerhill made for the most westerly terminus at Sunday's Well and this was the shortest route. Finally, the easterly terminus north of the River Lee at Tivoli simply set off west towards the city, along the 'C' and continued out again in an easterly direction to Blackrock.

After the large letters a new system was adopted. Small rectangular destination plates were dropped into slots immediately above the fleet number. These plates were also painted different colours and these were as follows:

Blackpool	Dark Blue
Summerhill/Sunday's Well	Red
Tivoli	Yellow
Blackrock	Brown
Douglas	White

At night time the front platform carried a small light, bearing the colour of the destination. However, it was found that the brown lamp was not easily seen and Blackrock could boast the distinction of having a lamp a different colour than its destination board, in this case, green. This idea may have derived from DUTC practice.

The Cork electric trams certainly redeemed any loss of favour incurred by their equine-hauled counterparts one generation previously. Their record was excellent, safe, efficient and profitable until the 1920s. In the case of most cities, the population grew outwards in the direction of suburbia and usually along the route of the tram or train lines or good roads on account of the convenience of travel. Cork did not appear to develop as rapidly as other cities, at least not in such a manner as to benefit tram patronage and, sadly, not before their demise.

When bus competition appeared, from the 1920s onwards, the tramway was in serious trouble. There was not enough patronage to sustain both tram and bus systems in a small city of 50,000 people or so, and it was decided that the trams should be sacrificed. In most cities, tramcar design had progressed to a more advanced generation of design with fully enclosed vestibules and often part enclosed upper decks. In Cork, apart from extending the upper decks, and fitting more comfortable interiors, little else had changed. The bus was seen as modern and state-of-the-art transport. The image of the trams, unfortunately, was that of obsolescence. An ageing fleet of open front cars could not retain its regulars, who were gradually drawn away by the fierce bus competition. Incentives such as reductions in fares, concessionary tickets, and reduced return fares were all attempted but to little avail. The cost of modernising the fleet and repairing worn trackwork was too major an obstacle to overcome. The bus and tram authorities met to discuss the transition. The tram company, which had the full loyalties of one generation and part of another, sought the best they could for their staff.

In the early days the tramway had brought the facility of public lighting, and the surplus electricity sold by the company had been a real advantage, justifying the tramways' very existence. With the nationalisation of electricity and the construction of the Ardnacrusha power station, small suppliers of electricity gradually lost ground. With the Electricity Supply Board providing a full electrical alternative, the last vestige of power, in every sense, was lost to the Cork tramways and the close down was inevitable.

The closure was scheduled for 31st March 1931 and crowds of well-wishers thronged the streets to bid them farewell. It transpired, however, that the replacement bus service was unable to cope and, after six days, the trams were hurriedly ushered back into service. As the bus numbers grew and the bus service improved, the trams were gradually withdrawn on a one-by-one basis. The final closure did, however, take place on 30th September 1931 after a six month reprieve and the same throngs reappeared to bid them an even fonder farewell. And so ended the era of the tram in the southern capital.

FATHER MATHEW STATUE CORK. 2828.W.L.

Top: **This is a delightful study of both the Father Mathew Statue and a tram side by side. Father Mathew was a mid nineteenth century campaigner against excessive drinking and a voice for the poor of Cork. This monument was a testimony to his popularity. The ornate railings and corner lamps were short lived, as they became an obstacle to traffic. Tram No 12 was one of the original batch of 18 Brush Electric cars, delivered in 1898. Note how the top hat worn by tram staff in horse tram days has given way to more casual attire. The motorman is evidently posing for the photographer, while a young boy looks on with interest. The double span of the ornamental tram pole, which doubles as a lamp standard, is most impressive.**

National Library of Ireland (W Lawrence)

Bottom left: **This view was taken from the opposite side of the Statue to the one above, and is later, since the original ornate railings and lamp standards have been removed. Car No 1 stands, while a woman in her Youghal cloak prepares to board. The motorman is in deep contemplation while he awaits the conductor's bell to proceed. A car from the same batch is passing on the opposite side of the loop, its upper deck passengers evidently watching the photographer. The destination board of car No 1 reads 'DS' telling us that it is working the route from the Statue to Douglas and back. The photographer appears to have masked out the trolley pole in his print.**

Alec R Day, Michael Pollard collection

Bottom right: **This picture has been taken from an elevated position and gives an excellent view of the loop arrangement in central Cork. Car No 3 has just left the loop at the Father Mathew Statue and is approaching the camera. Cars 30 and 16, in the background, are from the 1901 and 1898 batches respectively. The picture also includes a rare sight of the tramway's watering car in the centre road. It was necessary to wet the trackwork to reduce track expansion and keep down the dust in dry weather. A side car with seating for six, passes in the foreground. The purposeful walk and the attire of the man following No 3, suggests that he is one of the tramway staff, possibly attending the watering car or in control of the points.** *W Lawrence, Michael Pollard collection*

Top: **Almost the entire Cork City tram fleet is in this view, taken at Patrick Street in October 1920, when the entire workforce marched to St Mary's Cathedral to recite prayers for the Sinn Fein Lord Mayor, Terence MacSwiney, then dying on hunger strike in Brixton Prison, London. Amongst the trams visible are (left to right) Nos 22, 16, and 20. At least eighteen trams are visible in this view. The photograph was taken by Thomas Barker, a photographer with the Cork Examiner newspaper. A documentary film, depicting the scene, was made at the time and constitutes a piece of rare movie footage of the Cork trams.**
Walter McGrath collection

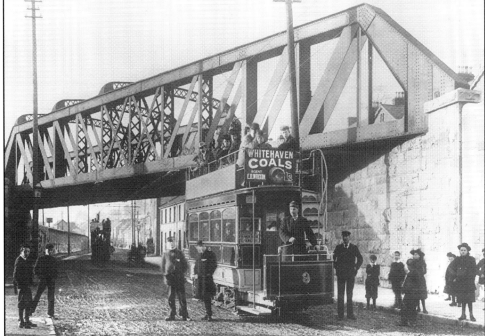

Centre: **Car No 9 passing under the bridge which carries the GSWR line from Cork to Cobh. The tram has just passed under the bridge from the city centre, and is passing along Glanmire Road towards its Tivoli terminus. On account of the height of the bridge, the trolley pole would have dipped to an almost horizontal position. The car is fully packed, and crowds on both sides of the road stop to face the camera and join in the general excitement of the occasion. No 9 is one of the first batch of 18 cars delivered from the Brush Electrical Co in Loughborough, and can be identified by the three louvre openings per window. The second batch, Nos 19 to 28 inclusive, had only two louvres per window, whereas the last batch, Nos 29 to 35, had a total of six louvres.**
Maker's photograph
John Kennedy collection

Bottom: **This picture became a well known painted postcard of the day. Several postcard companies featured trams in their views to emphasise that the city was large and enterprising enough to support a tramway, and to express the commercial prowess of the city. This was fine when the trams were modern and freshly painted, but old worn-out stock appearing on a postcard would have injured the commercial image of the town. The scene is in South Mall and shows the swivel bridge over the River Lee, over which the tram is about to pass on its way to the Douglas terminus. The bridge was named after the famous Irish politician Charles Stewart Parnell. It was the policy of the newly-formed state, after 1922, to rename many streets and city features to establish its new national identity. The fine structure on the opposite side of the Lee is Cork City Hall.**
National Library of Ireland, 2588WL

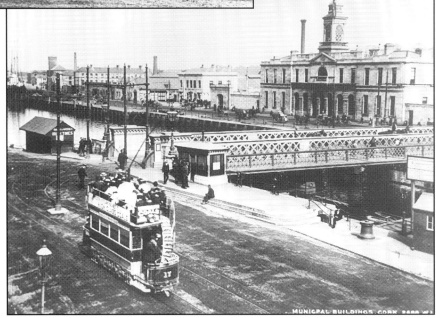

Top: **No 29 at Tivoli terminus in 1902 with its trolley pole reversed and setting off on its return journey to the city centre. In the background, car No 10 has just entered the loop.** The colourful occasion is the annual Cork regatta, as crowds of spectators line the banks of the River Lee to cheer on their team. This view was taken shortly after the final batch of tramcars, Nos 29 to 39, arrived to take up service in the fleet. The more 'modern' appearance is due to the extended canopy and dash over the driver's platform, and the next evolutionary stage would have been the introduction of a windscreen to protect the driver. However, this never occurred in Cork. The drivers remained exposed to the elements long after their counterparts in most other cities were afforded the protection of a screen.

RC Ludgate collection

Centre: **This peaceful setting is the Blackrock terminus. No 33, one of the final batch of trams, has reversed its trolley pole and is waiting to return to the city. The year is 1901 and Blackrock village is still very rural in character.** The proprietor of the establishment to the left of the tram has changed the name of his premises to the Tramway Restaurant. It is likely that the tram crew are sitting in the tram saloon, waiting for the appointed time of departure. One assumes that they are not in the other saloon in the background! Note the horse-drawn delivery van outside the restaurant. The tram looks strangely out of context with its setting. The letters BS on the dash advise intending passengers that the tram runs from Blackrock Village (B) to the Father Mathew Statue (S) in the city.

Walter McGrath collection

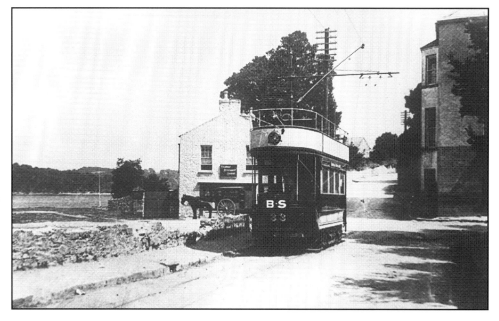

Ballintemple, CORK

Bottom: **No 7, of the first batch of trams, passes through the village of Ballintemple on its way to Blackrock, in 1905.**
The state of the roads and general dilapidated condition of the footpaths and cottages to the right contrast strikingly with the gleaming modernity of the electric tram. One can imagine the excitement of the villagers when they first heard that their village was to be connected with Cork by the most advanced means of public transport of the day. The two young lads watch the tram as she passes. The horse and cart opposite the tram on the other side of the road look more in keeping with the dreamy character of Ballintemple.

Walter McGrath collection

DUBLIN and LUCAN ELECTRIC TRAMWAY

The origin of the Dublin to Lucan service goes back to 1881 with steam traction on the 3'0" gauge. The chapter on the Dublin and Lucan Steam Tramway (page 46) also gives an introduction to the early electric tramway service, which was to all intents and purposes, operated by the former steam tramway company. However, the name was changed to the Dublin and Lucan Electric Railway which, as mentioned, ran on a 3'6" gauge. The reader may wish to refer to the earlier chapter before continuing. This chapter picks up more or less where the former ends.

The new powered rolling stock purchased by the Dublin and Lucan Electric Railway comprised five double-deck open-top bogie cars, the first such cars to operate in Ireland on the narrow gauge. An early attempt was made to provide a cover for the upper deck, to improve standards of comfort. However, the Board of Trade was unhappy with the idea of such large cars on so narrow a gauge, buffeted by high winds on very exposed sections of track, and approval was refused. The line was destined to operate with a fleet of open toppers until its closure in January 1925.

The DLER commenced operations on 8th March 1900. The trams were built by GF Milnes, on Brill 22E bogies. In 1905 one of the original bogie steam trailers was motorised on an extended 4 wheel truck, converted to a single decker and used for the transportation of the Royal Mail. A further two of the original steam trailers were also converted to electric traction, one being used for shunting. Most of the former steam rolling stock was regauged and found a second lease of life after electrification. The original extension to Leixlip was closed and the new trams terminated at the town of Lucan. The Spa Hotel operated jaunting cars to bring passengers up the hill from the terminus to the hotel. In a bid to reopen the Leixlip extension, the Lucan and Leixlip Electric Railway was formed and obtained approval in 1910. However, the line was only built as far as Dodsboro and achieved the distinction of being one of the smallest railways in the world, less than half a mile in length. Later attempts were made to extend the line at least as far as the Spa Hotel, but without success.

On the outbreak of the First World War, the Government took control of the Irish railways. The DLER was ignored, much to the consternation of the company. A takeover by the Government would have meant that the wages of the staff, (approximately 30 shillings a week) would have been brought into line with higher railway emoluments. Eventually the demands of the DELR were acceded to. During the war years, with its resulting shortage of petrol, the tramway did quite well. After the war however, the situation was less favourable. The company now had to continue paying the higher wages set by the Government. Moreover many surplus army lorries were sold to private operators and hastily converted into petrol buses and fierce road competition

ensued. The tramway could not compete and ceased operation at the end of January 1925.

One character associated with the tramway, a man of many parts and qualities, was a Mr D McDowell Grosart. Mr Grosart originally worked for the DUTC as an engineer and had joined the DLER with three posts, Engineer, Manager and Secretary. It is not clear whether or not he had three salaries. On the bankruptcy of the company he acted as Receiver. On the sale of the company's assets he was appointed Liquidator. He certainly served his company to the fullest of his potential.

The DLER had made vain attempts to have their ailing company taken over by the DUTC, but failed. Bereft of their line, the inhabitants of Lucan and influential citizens of Dublin put pressure on the DUTC to rerun a tram to Lucan. The DUTC finally agreed and relaid the track to their 5'3" gauge, with through-running to the city centre. The new line was opened as far as Chapelizod on 14th May 1928 and to Lucan on 27th May 1928 with a 25 minute service frequency. The total distance, measured from the City centre, was approximately $9^1/_2$ miles. This time the terminus was just outside the town on the south side, where a modern petrol filling station is now located.

New tramcars were built in the DUTC workshops at Spa Road. They were similar to the four-wheel all-enclosed DUTC standards introduced in 1924, but were stretched-out versions, on bogies. They were called the 'Lucan cars', and were numbered rather haphazardly as numbers became available on the withdrawal of earlier cars. They were Nos 181, 184, 252-255, 278, 284 and 314. In addition, a 1906 balcony car, No 313, was similarly rebuilt for use on the route, and at peak times other DUTC cars were pressed into service.

Bus competition accelerated rapidly in the inter-war years and soon the line was in trouble again. Within ten years of reopening, the DUTC decided to replace the entire tram network with buses. The first system to go was the line along the North Quays at Easter 1938, effectively severing the Lucan system from the city centre and the final tram to Lucan ran on 31st March 1940. The Lucan cars ended their days giving good service on the Dalkey route but instead of bearing route Nos 24 and 25 they now bore route No 8. Two of the Lucan cars have survived — Nos 253 and 284 — having been rescued by the National Transport Museum. No 253 features at the top of page 90 and it is hoped that, in years to come, No 284 will be converted to a balcony car, similar to the original car No 313.

Over the years, the Lucan tramway system changed three times to meet the challenge of difficult circumstances. If the city had spread its development more rapidly along the line, the trams might have survived a little longer but the line was always sparsely inhabited and once the DUTC capitulated to pressure from the bus lobby, the end was inevitable.

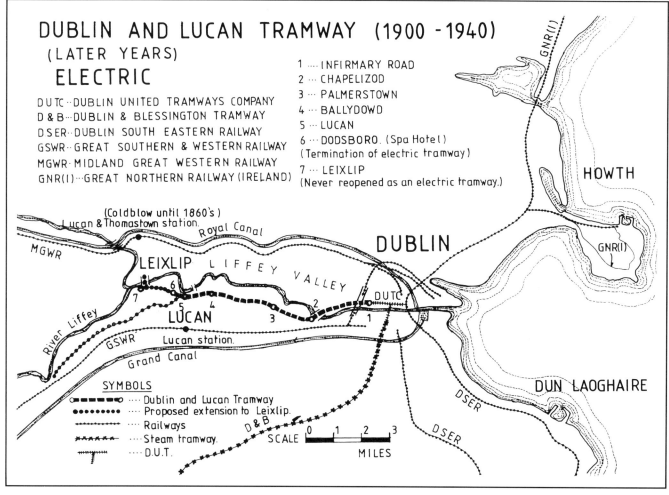

DUBLIN AND LUCAN TRAMWAY (1900-1940)
(LATER YEARS)
ELECTRIC

DUTC··DUBLIN UNITED TRAMWAYS COMPANY
D&B···DUBLIN & BLESSINGTON TRAMWAY
DSER·DUBLIN SOUTH EASTERN RAILWAY
GSWR·GREAT SOUTHERN & WESTERN RAILWAY
MGWR·MIDLAND GREAT WESTERN RAILWAY
GNR(I)···GREAT NORTHERN RAILWAY (IRELAND)

1 ····INFIRMARY ROAD
2 ·· CHAPELIZOD
3 ·· PALMERSTOWN
4 ··· BALLYDOWD
5 ··· LUCAN
6 ··· DODSBORO. (Spa Hotel)
(Termination of electric tramway)
7 ··· LEIXLIP
(Never reopened as an electric tramway.)

SYMBOLS
— Dublin and Lucan Tramway
···· Proposed extension to Leixlip.
···· Railways
xxxxx Steam tramway.
···· D.U.T.

On February 27th 1900 the newly laid 3'6" gauge was inspected and passed by the Board of Trade. The public opening of the electrified line was scheduled for March 8th. For the occasion, five new cars, Nos 12 - 16 inclusive, were ordered, constructed by GF Milnes & Co of Birkenhead, with Dick Kerr motors and Brill 22E bogies. These cars carried 30 passengers inside and 32 outside. However, No 14, shown here, carried an extra four passengers in the saloon. The livery was green and white with the main stops painted on the cant panel just above the louvres. The saloon was separated into 1st and 3rd class by an internal bulkhead. The steam trams also had a 2nd class. However this class was not continued into the electric era. The trolley pole was deliberately bent to meet the powered cable at an acute angle. Many trolley booms on old cars took on a natural bend over years of use, not dissimilar to the pre-distorted boom shown here.

H Fayle, courtesy IRRS

Top: No 13 was one of the batch of five cars (12-16) delivered in 1900. In 1903, No 13, seen here with toast rack trailer, was provided with a covered top but virtually no canopy. The cover had glazed screens at both ends with access doors from the stairs, but the sides were open to the elements. The cover was one of the first to be tested in Dublin. However, after an accident where a similar narrow gauge car in Halifax overturned in high winds, the Board of Trade withdrew permission, and No 13 was returned to its former condition. The line was destined to operate with single deckers or open-toppers until the arrival of the DUTC 'Lucan bogies' in 1928.

Between 1917 and 1918 a number of the original double-deck cars were rebuilt with extended upper deck canopies to equal the platform length. This provided accommodation for extra passengers. However, no windscreen was added for the motorman's protection. No 13 was renumbered 17 when the original car of that number was scrapped.

H Fayle, courtesy IRRS

Centre: No 17 was a rebuild of one of the earlier single deck cars, and was very unusual in appearance. As it did not transport passengers it was called an electric locomotive, and was used to haul goods along the line. It was capable of carrying 18 tons up a 1 in 20 gradient, and was known to have hauled a disabled double-deck car on at least one occasion. The truck was a Brill 21E and the motors were $37^{1}/_{2}$ horse power, supplied by British Thompson Houston Co the original car having had a United Electric Car Co's body. The driving cab was in the centre and, unlike most electric track-bound vehicles with controls at each end, only one was required. The deck was surrounded with iron railings, and it was said that on the other side of a hedgerow, it looked like a floating glass house.

CP Friel collection

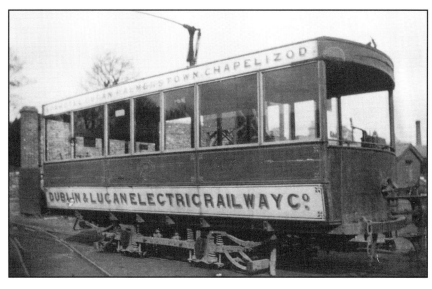

Bottom: No 19 was unusual in many respects and looked completely different from either side and end. It was constructed by Milnes Voss and was purchased secondhand by the company. From the view shown, No 19 looks very much like a normal enclosed saloon car, but with a platform only at the end farthest from the camera. However the opposite side was completely open with a continuous step giving access to cross bench seating. The conductor usually collected the fare by walking along the continuous step, even though the tram was in motion.

Open-sided cars were designed for swift loading and such cars were popular at sea-side resorts, like Douglas, Isle of Man, with frequent stops along a promenade. In the case of No 19, it is likely that the side nearest the hedge was filled in to reduce draughts.

W Gratwicke, courtesy IRRS

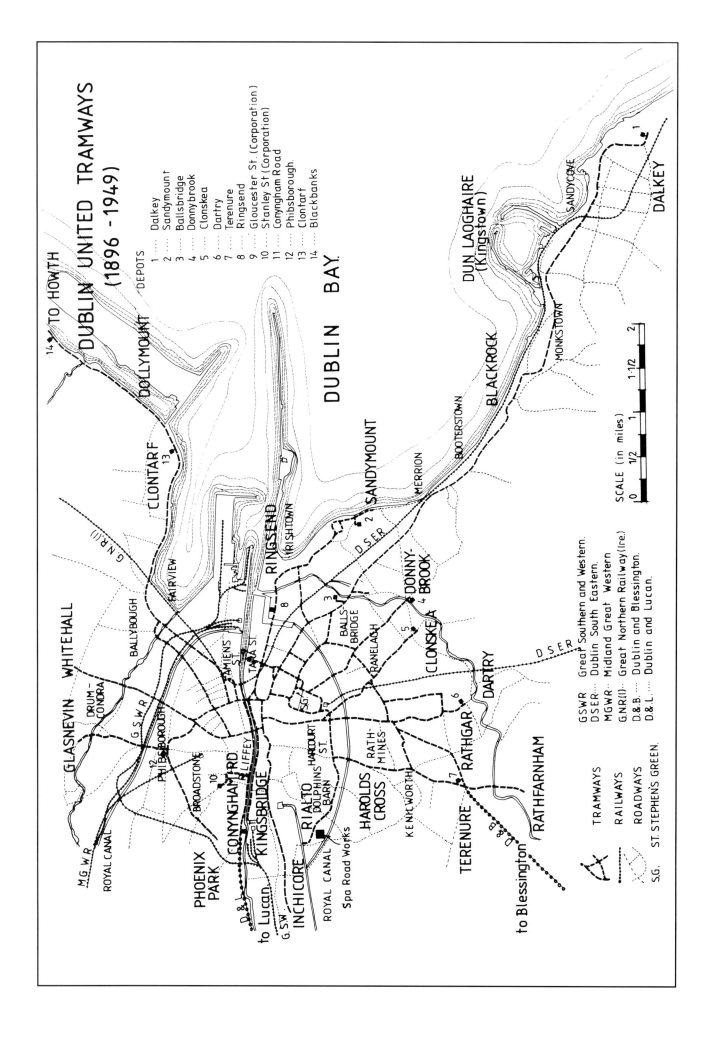

DUBLIN UNITED TRAMWAYS
(1896 - 1949)

DEPOTS

1 ..... Dalkey
2 ..... Sandymount
3 ..... Ballsbridge
4 ..... Donnybrook
5 ..... Clonskea
6 ..... Dartry
7 ..... Terenure
8 ..... Ringsend
9 ..... Gloucester St. (Corporation)
10 ..... Stanley St (Corporation)
11 ..... Conyngham Road
12 ..... Phibsborough.
13 ..... Clontarf
14 ..... Blackbanks

DUBLIN BAY.

TO HOWTH

DOLLYMOUNT

CLONTARF

FAIRVIEW

RINGSEND

IRISHTOWN

SANDYMOUNT

MERRION

D S E R

DUN LAOGHAIRE
(Kingstown)

SANDYCOVE

DALKEY

MONKSTOWN

BLACKROCK

BOOTERSTOWN

BALLS
BRIDGE

RANELAGH

DONNY-
BROOK

CLONSKEA

DARTRY

D S E R

RATHGAR

TERENURE

RATHFARNHAM

to Blessington

GLASNEVIN WHITEHALL

BALLYBOUGH

DRUM-
CONDRA

G.S.W.R

PHIBSBOROUGH

BROADSTONE

LIFFEY

KINGSBRIDGE

CONYNGHAM RD

PHOENIX PARK

INCHICORE

to Lucan

G. SW

ROYAL CANAL

Spa Road Works

RIALTO

DOLPHINS
BARN

HAROLDS
CROSS

RATH-
MINES

KENILWORTH

G.N.R(I)

M.G.W.R

ROYAL CANAL

AMIENS
ST.

TARA ST.

S.G.

HARCOURT
ST.

GSWR ..... Great Southern and Western.
DSER ..... Dublin South Eastern.
MGWR ..... Midland Great Western
G.N.R(I) ..... Great Northern Railway(Ire.)
D.&.B. ..... Dublin and Blessington.
D.&.L. ..... Dublin and Lucan.

TRAMWAYS

RAILWAYS

ROADWAYS

S.G. ST. STEPHENS GREEN.

SCALE (in miles)

0   1/2   1   1-1/2   2

DUBLIN UNITED TRAMWAYS

The first electric trams to operate in Dublin were those of the Dublin Southern Districts Tramways Company which electrified in 1896. The origins of this company are explained on page 22, and I will now tell the story of its decision to electrify.

Electric traction was gradually spreading as confidence in the new system of transport grew. The main problem associated with electric traction was the method of current pick up. All the early experiments used the *third* or *live* rail system for current collection, but other forms of collection were also being examined. A third rail could only operate on reserved track, such as the metro or underground systems, on account of the dangers of electrocution. When the overhead power cable was first introduced, the method of collection was by a wheeled device sitting on top of the cable, known as a *troller,* and this was connected to the tram by a flexible cable. Mr Daft, previously mentioned, was in the forefront of these experiments but the wretched things had a habit of falling off the overhead cable. This was not found to be too enjoyable by the upper deck passengers and many of his ideas were considered 'daft', giving us a new word in Anglo-American. Eventually, the wheeled device was attached to a rigid arm called a *trolley mast* or *pole*, which was spring loaded to compress the wheel or trolley head up against the cable. This proved much safer, as a dewirement did not mean near-decapitation! In 1885, a Belgian, named Charles Van Depoele, used a wooden trolley pole at the Toronto Industrial Exhibition. The spring loaded trolley boom system was further developed by an American, Frank Sprague, in 1887 and was not long in reaching Europe. This system was first successfully tried in England on the Roundhay Tramway (in Leeds) in 1891 and this is often seen as the date when serious and safe development of electric traction commenced in Europe. In the new system, trolley heads could be either fixed or swivelled; the latter was

used in Dublin. Incidently, in the United States, Frank Sprague is regarded as the 'father of electric traction', a title which, in Europe, is more usually given to Von Siemens.

The Dublin Southern Districts Tramways were linked with the 'Provincial Tramways of London' and this did not add to the popularity of what was often referred to as 'The English Company'. This link, however, soon proved an advantage, as another English company, 'Imperial Tramways' of Bristol, bought out both the DSDT and the Blackrock and Kingstown Tramways in 1893 and appointed Mr James Clifton Robinson as the Managing Director.

Mr Robinson, born in Birkenhead, had been involved with the evolution of horse trams and had worked as an office boy for Mr Train, when the latter set up his horse trams in London. He was an engineer by background and was married to a Cork woman. His first and most obvious moves were to replace the 4'0" gauge section from Kingstown (Dun Laoghaire) to Dalkey with the conventional Irish gauge of

Our first view of Dublin electric trams shows Grafton Street with College Green in the background. As illustrated on page 87, Dublin trams at this time carried symbols rather than numbers to identify the routes. The nearest tram, No 279 (DUTC 1901), carries two diamonds with a horizontal flash, and is on its way from Donnybrook to Phoenix Park via St Stephen's Green and Dawson Street. Eventually when the numbering system appeared, this route became No 10. If the flash was absent, the tram would have passed via Merrion Square instead of Stephen's Green. The approaching single decker, No 252 (a 1900 conversion of double deck horse car No 4) is destined for Sandymount Green via Bath Avenue (later the No 4 route). The furthest receding car, No 231 (ex horse car No 101), carries a shamrock and therefore is bound for Nelson's Pillar from either Blackrock, Dun Laoghaire or Dalkey (later routes 6, 7, and 8 respectively). The enclosed railed area in front of Trinity College (in the distance) projected well into College Green causing disruption and was later reduced in size.

W Lawrence, Author's collection

5'3", and to use heavier track throughout the entire line. He knew the advantages of electrification and lost no time in converting the system to electric traction. The new company retained the name of the Dublin Southern Districts Tramways.

On May 16th, 1896, the first electric tramcar (No 2), in a convoy of five trams hauling trailers, set off from Ballsbridge to Dalkey with Mr. Robinson at the helm. The press accounts were favourable and the economic advantages, safety and greater speed of the cars proved popular. Most popular of all was the reduction in fares, which resulted in greater patronage and lower running costs. It would be true to say, that not until the arrival of the electric trams, did the so-called 'poor man's carriage' also arrive. The new fares were within the reach of the working classes and, for the first time, a system of transport which served all the citizens of Dublin had been created. Whilst the horse trams had their advantages, served the commercial concerns of Dublin, and helped push out the frontiers of the city, high fares placed them firmly outside the reach of Dublin's poor. The electric tramways redeemed this injustice.

DUBLIN UNITED TRAMWAYS Co (1896)

One may be surprised to learn that one of the honoured guests on the occasion of the first electric tram run was none other than William Martin Murphy, the Managing Director of the DUTC. In 1894 he had seriously considered electrification of the horse tramways, but was complacent as they were extremely profitable and there were no competitors in that field, at least not until the DSDT's electrification. I often wonder what was passing through his mind as the new electric cars passed the traction poles safely and swiftly. He surely regretted not buying out the DSDT when they were at his mercy. The DWWR would also have harboured such regrets as the electric tramway from Dalkey to Dublin took much needed revenue from their railway. Was William Martin Murphy plotting his takeover on that fateful day?

When the DSDT sought powers to run their electric trams over the canal bridge and into the city, the DUTC was naturally apprehensive, to say the least. The small 'English Company' invading their preserve, was a threat that could not be ignored. It was not just the DUTC that was concerned. The Dublin Car Men's Union (the jarveys or cabbies) and other horse-drawn passenger services,

viewed the new system with grave doubts. They could cope with the horse trams, in terms of speed, and could serve those streets without tracks. The new system was much swifter and they feared that it would spread like wildfire throughout the city and put them out of business. They threw in the usual red herrings about terrorising horses, unsightliness of overhead cables, dangers of electrocution and the threat of great speed. In the meantime, not far from the court room set up to investigate the DSDT proposals, the new system itself was operating successfully and proving popular and safe. It was only a matter of time before the fears of the competitors would fail to have a hearing, no matter how eloquently their cases were presented.

Gradually, Robinson, who proposed running a parallel course to the existing horse trams into the city, was winning favour, and was supported by the Trades Council, who saw personal benefits for themselves. To promote his proposals, Robinson, a keen businessman, began offering cheap rates, return ticket reductions and other inducements and soon he received great public support. The DWWR opened two new stations at Sandymount and Merrion Halt in an effort to redeem some lost revenue. The DUTC also fought all the way to prevent the advancement of their competitor. and began reducing fares. It was obvious what the DUTC had to do, and that was to buy out their competitor and end the threat.

A new company, called the Dublin United Tramways Company (1896) Ltd was set up with this intention. The

This photo shows two open-front cars on the north side of St Stephen's Green around 1900. The nearest car, No 101 (DUTC 1900), which is bound for Nelson's Pillar, is unusual in that it has five saloon windows. In 1897 Milnes constructed 12 electric cars, each with five saloon windows, numbered 21-32, which were originally allocated to the Clontarf line. Other five window cars were Nos 41-45 and 99- 08. The side panel reads "Terenure-Rathmines-Nelson's Pillar". The further car, No 156, is a typical 4 window car and was built by the American Car Co in 1900. Directly above No 156, on the upper floor of an adjoining building, at least six Union Jacks are flying to celebrate some occasion, and a further unidentified flag is on the roof. Unlike today, the trees along the Green are still quite immature. Notice the ornamental tram poles located in the centre of the road. Poles where trams stopped were partly painted white as shown here.

W Lawrence, Author's collection

operation of the DSDT were taken over by the DUTC later in the year, though the former remained in existence until 1905, when it was eventually absorbed and quietly vanished from the scene. Due to legal complications, it remained in nominal existence until 1931.

The DUTC lost no time in seeking to convert the horse tramways to electricity, but they met with considerable opposition from Dublin Corporation, who at first would not permit electrification within their area. Consequently the first section of the DUTC (1896) empire to be electrified was from the Clontarf Depot to Annesley Bridge on 11th November 1897.

It was not until 19th March 1898 that the first electric tram arrived at Nelson's Pillar in the city centre. The company decided not to highlight the occasion and early morning citizens watched with surprise as the first of the trams appeared. The remainder of the system was quick to follow and the first tram to reach the Pillar from the south side was on 12th July 1898. The North Quays went electric on 1st October, the Phoenix Park line on 22nd November and Donnybrook was reached on 23rd January 1899. The Inchicore route was electrified on 4th September, Palmerston Park on 12th September, and Terenure, via Rathmines, on 20th October 1899. Rathfarnham was reached by the new system on 4th November and Clonskeagh on 4th December 1899. By the end of the decade the changeover was almost complete. The Drumcondra route was electrified on 5th January 1900 and Rathfarnham, via Harold's Cross, was reached on 16th January.

The last horse tram to run was on the Sandymount line, on 13th January 1901 and, in true reflection of the unlucky date, the occasion did not pass without incident. The event, which was well-reported at the time, was something of a sad note on which to end horse traction in Dublin. A gentleman's gentleman named Ralph Patterson was knocked down and received two broken legs. The driver, Thomas Tracey, was charged by the constabulary but later released and subsequently exonerated from all blame. No one knows if Mr Patterson survived the accident, but his tragedy will always be associated with the horse trams' last day in operation. They had served the city and the suburbs well for almost twenty years. Many people

were sad to see them go but progress waits for no man or indeed, for no horse.

There is one sad story told about an event which took place immediately after the closure, when vast stocks of tram horses were being transported to England, many for slaughter. Serving all their lives between tracks and obediently serving their masters without hesitation, many of the poor horses were confused about boarding the various vessels which were to transport them to pending doom. It is reported that the problem was overcome by laying rails over the gangway to the ship. Then some of the old drivers, who were helping with the loading, called "Rathfarnham" or "Sandymount", as this was the usual cry when the tram was setting off on its journey. The animals blindly obeyed and boarded the ships, never to be seen in Ireland again. The drivers suffered greatly and many wept openly, as they felt that they were betraying their loyal and hardworking friends. Thus ended the horse tram era in Dublin.

Rather than end on a sad note, permit me to recount one of the many humourous anecdotes associated with horse trams. One of the tramcars mysteriously disappeared without trace and the poor depot foreman could not account for its absence. Search as he might, no inkling of its whereabouts was found. How could such a bulky item as a horse tram evaporate into thin air? At that time Kingsbridge tram depot (now part of Guinness' Brewery) was the point of delivery and storage for much of the fodder and animal feed. Somehow, the tram in

This view in College Green is taken from Trinity College, looking west down Dame Street. The impressive building to the right was Ireland's Parliament until 1801, but is now the Bank of Ireland. It is unusual in that there are no windows in the entire facade, and the rooms are lit from an internal courtyard and lighting wells. The car to the right is returning to Nelson's Pillar and was originally a horse tram converted to electric traction. The car on the left is No 192, a 1900 conversion of a Milnes trailer built in 1897 to run with cars 21 - 32. It is turning right towards Grafton Street and Nassau Street. The nearest statue is of Henry Grattan, an 18th century politician and the statue in the background was of King William of Orange. Created by Grinling Gibbons, it was considered one of the finest equestrian statues in Dublin but regrettably it was blown from its plinth in 1929.

W Lawrence, Author's collection

question was pushed further than usual down the tracks and gradually the deliveries of hay and stacking completely surrounded the tram, losing it to view. It was not until the system's horses had eaten the load down, that the mystery was resolved and so the case of the missing tram was finally resolved by the horses themselves.

EXTENSIONS TO THE DUTC

I have now dealt with the various systems in Dublin City and those systems that ran outwards from the city to Dalkey, Blessington, Lucan and Howth. All of these lines, apart from the Dublin and Blessington route, were brought into the electrification scheme. New routes were added after the union of 1896, and the first of these was in 1901 to Ballybough. Setting off from Parkgate Street down the North Quays, it turned left into Capel Street, and down Parnell Street, past the Rotunda Hospital and across O'Connell Street, through Summerhill Road to Clonliffe Road. The line was known as the 'back street route' and served some of the poorest areas in the city around Gardiner Street.

On 7th September 1903, the Drumcondra terminus was extended to Whitehall, where the Garda Station now stands. This area was famous for the Whitehall Carnival or Festival, when the famous Directors' Car was illuminated with fairy lights. With electrification, patronage of the trams increased.

In the last year of full horse operation, 175 trams travelled 3,000,000 miles carrying 24,000,000 passengers and earned £150,000. Only six years later, 292 electric trams travelled almost 7,000,000 miles carrying almost 50,000,000 passengers and earned £240,000. So there is little doubt that the electric tram was paying its way.

Originally the destination of trams was printed in large distinctive script along the rocker panel or on the stairs, and the smaller intermediate stops were painted on the cant rail over the windows or on panels. However, in those days many people were illiterate and it was decided to introduce a series of symbols such as crescents, diamonds, circles and crosses, in various colours to help people identify their trams. These are reproduced on page 87. At night time, lights in a combination of colours, served the same purpose. The symbol system was unique in Europe, though used in Egypt. The use of lights of different colours was also found in Cork.

The symbols were superseded in the 1920s by a numbering system, based on a clockwise pattern. Routes 1 - 4 headed east towards Sandymount, 6 - 8 south towards Dalkey, etc, right up to 31 which was the Howth route. This system is still the basis for Dublin's bus routes today, though now very much modified and numerically extended.

Dublin Corporation had a right to use the tramway system for the movement of materials, and held a takeover option on the DUTC, when the leasing arrangement for the lines expired, around 1938. However, unlike Belfast, this was never taken up. The Corporation had a permit to transport street sweepings and clinker from their 'destructor's plant' at Stanley Street to the Fairview sloblands and thus Fairview Park was formed. The name is really something of a misnomer, because when the Dublin and Drogheda Railway was constructed, the so called 'fairview' (of the sea) vanished, with the appearance of the railway embankment.

By the First World War, Dublin had a fleet of 330 trams, including some bogie cars. The bulk of the fleet were vestibuled open-toppers, the exceptions being a few single deckers and several balcony-top cars. Many of the DUTC trams had been constructed at the Company's works at Spa Road, in Inchicore, not far from the terminus. In 1918, a heavy programme of tramcar construction commenced at the Spa Road Works, using a four window design, all on Peckham trucks. Some of these cars were not completely new, but retained old material, such as frames and some body parts. These were often replaced within a few years, at the next rebuilding.

This view was taken about 1905 and shows three vestibuled trams in Merrion Square. The nearest car, No 13 (Milnes 1896) is on its way to Dalkey. The central car, No 49, at first glance appears to be an open-topper, but it is actually a single deck car with advertising hoarding adorning the roof. This car was originally horse car No 99 and was converted to electric traction in 1898. It was converted to single deck in 1904 and is seen here on the Sandymount Route. It would have passed under a low bridge in Bath Avenue, hence the single deck. The furthest car, No 263 (DUTC, 1901), is returning from Dalkey to the city centre. Cars for Sandymount, Kingstown and Dalkey passed along this side of the Square, bearing route Nos 3, 7 and 8 respectively. Route No 9, which ran from Donnybrook to the Phoenix Park, also ran along this side of Merrion Square. This section was in operation on the last day of tram running on 9th July 1949.

W Lawrence, Author's collection

The new cars came in both open-top and balcony versions, and by 1924 there were 121 new open-toppers and 69 new balcony cars. Almost 60% of the fleet had been replaced in seven years. In 1924 the first fully-enclosed trams were built, to a design that came to be known as the *Dublin Standards*. These were basically modernised versions of the 1918 design and, in all, 91 were built. Some were new cars but there was considerable rebuilding of the earlier cars. Some 33 balcony cars became Standards, and 49 open-toppers in their turn were upgraded to balcony cars. Seven new Standards replaced fairly new open-top cars and it is likely that some of these were partial rebuilds. The Standard cars ran on Brill trucks. In addition, two new enclosed bogie cars were built for the Dalkey route in 1925-26 and nine more for the Lucan route in 1928.

The final development of the Dublin tram fleet was the introduction of the streamlined cars in 1931. These were a completely new design, breaking with many traditional methods of construction, and were known as the *Luxury* cars, or streamliners, because of their modern appearance and upholstered seats. In all, 57 Luxury cars were constructed between 1931 and 1936. Twenty were bogie cars, on Hurst Nelson trucks, and the balance were four-wheel cars, mostly on Maley and Taunton trucks. In contrast to Belfast, the cars constructed after 1918 were not numbered consecutively, but rather used the numbers of the cars they replaced. This left the Dublin fleet with a very haphazard numbering system, which makes it difficult to trace the origins of individual cars.

Apart from the normal trams, there were also special works cars that appear mysteriously from time to time in old photographs. There were four *water sprinklers* to cool the track in hot conditions and reduce expansion. There is a famous story about an eel that lived contentedly in the water tank of No 4 for over ten years, feeding on whatever nutrients were provided by the canal waters and on occasional titbits from the staff. Both the Corporation and the DUTC had three *locomotives*, with no passenger carrying ability. On account of the slippery nature of the cobble stones between the tracks, special *sanding cars* were used to provide a better grip for the horses during horse tram days. One old single deck tram was used as a *vacuum cleaner tram* and was fitted with a long hose for cleaning. There were *permanent way trams* to carry repair materials to where they were needed and those trams

usually hauled wagons. Several defunct trams were used as *mobile stores* and there were *sand spreaders* for frosty conditions. There were two *tower wagons* to repair overhead cable, usually operated at night time. Tower wagons could be horse drawn into position. Many systems had petrol powered cars for this purpose and at least one such existed in Dublin. On route No 31 to Howth a special adapted *fish tram* was used, up to 1925. There was a *scrubber* to clean out the grooved track and there was a *grinder* to wear away corrugations and malformations of track due to wear. All large tramway systems operated these special cars, which usually operated at night time, silently working away, so readily and easily forgotten. They were seldom recorded by the tram enthusiast.

At their zenith, the Dublin electric tramways achieved a route mileage of around $60^1/_2$ miles and had a fleet of around 330 trams. The system was efficient and comfortable and the fares very reasonable. However the versatility of the motor bus began to offer serious competition from the 1920s onwards. In some cities, the bus was only used in areas not served by trams, to the advantage of all. But in Dublin, as in most British cities, the bus and tram operators were set at each other's throats and, instead of working in unison to serve the citizens, they worked against each other.

Text continues on page 92..........

Right: **The linking of railway termini was always considered a vital role for street tramways. Throngs of people wishing to continue their journey across the city and connect with another railway system would give good patronage to such a line. The proposal of the City of Dublin Tramways Co as early as 1867 was to link the railway termini of Kingsbridge (now Heuston), Westland Row (now Pearse) and Harcourt Street. However, early attempts failed. Their successors, Dublin Tramway Co, formed in 1871, first constructed a line from College Green to Rathmines via Harcourt Street in February 1872 , and on 3rd June provided a service linking Harcourt Street to Kingsbridge Station via Hatch Street. This became known as the Hatch Street line, and soon after a link to Westland Row was added. No 82 was one of the open front electric cars operating this line, and was a conversion of horse car No 163. The photograph was taken around the turn of the century.**
Author's collection

Above: **This is the famous Directors' Car which was considered to be one of the finest cars ever built anywhere in terms of luxury, decoration and appointment. It was built as Dublin's Royal Carriage and was set aside exclusively for the directors of the DUTC. As the directors were all gentlemen, no 'decency screen' on the upper deck was necessary. It carried the Dublin City coat of arms (the three castles) on a shield where the normal company garter would be. It carried no destination or number. It was built at Spa Road Works in 1901 where most of the DUTC cars were constructed after 1896, and it sits on a Brierly truck which was assembled at Spa Road and which was unique in itself. Relations between staff and directors reached an all time low during the 'Great Lockout' (an industrial dispute) in 1913, and the car was seldom used by the directors henceforward as this might have tempted fate. In its later years it was used for promotional work and often illuminated at the erstwhile Whitehall Festival. The livery was bottle green and cream. See opposite for a more recent picture of this tram.** *RC Ludgate collection*

Left: **O'Connell Bridge circa 1930. The car to the fore, No 210 (DUTC 1920) is a vestibuled balcony car of a type introduced in 1918. It is in the new grey livery which was introduced in August 1928 and lasted only until 1935. The balcony cars in the background still retain the earlier blue and cream livery which was adopted by the DUTC in 1896 and lasted 32 years. The policeman carrying out point duty immediately behind the tram is wearing the London-style helmet which was used by the Dublin Metroplitan Police. All the trams in this view are balcony four wheelers, though 'standards' were already about, and the 'luxury' cars were on the drawing board. The monument is in commemoration of Daniel O'Connell, the 'Liberator' and the bridge and street are named after him. Try parking your car on O'Connell Bridge today!**

Thos Mason and Co collection

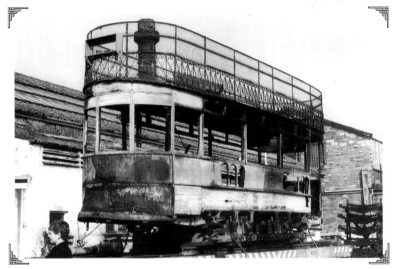

Top: This rather sad photograph shows the Director's Car some years after it was vandalised and set on fire in the mid 1980s. To appreciate the grandeur of this car, study the photograph opposite. No cost was spared. The saloon quarter lights had etched scenes of Dublin, and the intricate delicacy of the scroll work and carving was most impressive. The firm of Clery's spent £900 in richly appointing the interior, at a time when an actual tram cost much less. A smiling cherub formed part of a writing desk, and a drinks cabinet adorned one corner. The seats were of the swivel type on both decks. Although built as a Royal Carriage, no royalty ever travelled on her.

After the closure the tram was presented to a Barrister in Dalkey. Over the years it deteriorated, and after an article about the tram was published, vandals set upon it, stripping it of valuables, including crystal lamps, and brassware. The rest was set on fire. She is seen here outside Broadstone Depot on her way to the museum at Howth. Her restoration is a long term ambition.

Michael Corcoran

Centre left: This superb model, built by one of the Museum staff, is of open front electric tram No 54, a seven window car running on a Peckham truck. Any tram with more than five windows was a former horse car, and No 54 was an 1898 conversion of horse car No 158. In 1923 it was replaced by a new balcony top car, probably retaining some parts of the original.

Photo by the Author

Centre right: A 1995 built replica of Dublin Standard tram No 257. The blue and cream livery was used from 1896 to 1928. In reality no Standard car of this number ever existed. See also page 90.

Photo by the Author

Bottom: In the early decades of this century many people were illiterate and were unable to read the destinations of the various trams. The Company came up with the ingenious idea of producing symbols painted in various colours and bearing various markings. At night time a system of coloured lights was used. This was also the practice on the Cork electric trams for many years. Intending passengers could see at a glance where the approaching tram was bound. This was difficult, of course, if one was colour blind. The symbol on the open top cars was above deck level and could be clearly identified at a great distance. They would not have been so clear on a balcony car, and the practice was discontinued in favour of numbers when the standards appeared.

Michael Corcoran

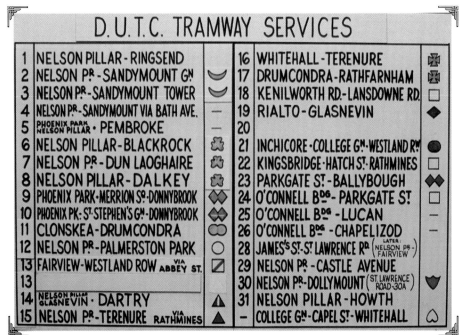

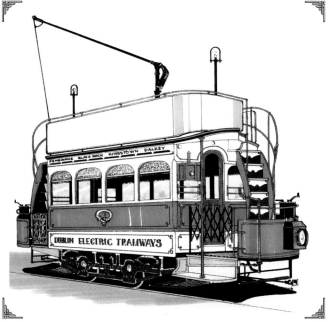

Top left: **The earliest type of electric trams were known as 'open fronts' or non-vestibuled cars and are referred to as 'first generation' trams. They could include knifeboard seating or garden seats on the upper deck, and they were prominent from 1896 to around 1910, when greater carrying capacity and economy dictated a change. They were all four wheel, as bogie cars had not as yet made their appearance in Dublin streets. The Dublin to Lucan Electric Railway did however operate some open front bogie stock. The car illustrated is No 199, converted in 1900 from a Milnes trailer and withdrawn in 1925.** *Drawing by the Author*

Top Right: **The next design progression was the 'open topper'. The upper canopy was extended to match the dash curvature in plan and wind-screens were often provided, forming a vestibule or enclosed platform. This created additional upper deck seating. The first vestibuled open topper in Europe was DUTC No 191, built in 1899 (see page 94). Not all 'second generation' trams had vestibules, those in Belfast and Cork being exceptions. Bogie open toppers operated on the Dublin to Howth route and on the Hill of Howth tramway. The car shown here, No 38, was built in 1898 at Spa Road and withdrawn in 1923.** *Drawing by the Author*

Bottom left: **As standards of comfort improved, passengers expected shelter on the upper deck. Experiments with partially enclosed cars commenced in 1904. However it was not until 1920 that a full compliment of cars with partially enclosed upper decks appeared in Dublin. These were called 'balcony cars' on account of the open section at each end. These 'third generation' cars were used latterly on most of the shorter city routes. Here we see No 128 in the blue and white livery used up to 1929. This car was built in 1919 as an open topper, rebuilt as a balcony car in 1929, and withdrawn in 1939.** *Drawing by the Author*

Bottom right: **The fourth generation of Dublin trams were the 'Standards'. Fifty eight of these cars were built between 1924 and 1929, and a further 33 converted from balcony cars in 1927-30. No 134 is shown in the CIE version of the green and cream colour scheme used for Dublin trams in 1935-49. The saloon was painted green with the windows picked out in white, and the upper deck painted green. The quarter light ventilating windows were varnished. Lining out was originally in gold leaf and quite ornate, but was simplified to pale yellow or straw. No 154 was built in 1926 and lasted until the late 1940s.** *Drawing by the Author*

Top: **In 1987 An Post produced a series of postage stamps featuring Irish trams, drawn by Charles Roycroft and John Kennedy. These illustrated the various liveries used in Dublin from the 1920s to the end. Our first picture shows Standard No 291 in the blue and white livery used up to 1929. This car was the 232rd car to be built by the DUTC at Spa Road Works. It was built as an open topper in 1902, and given an experimental top cover in 1904, though this was removed the following year.**

In 1923 a new balcony top body was fitted, and finally in 1929 it was rebuilt as an all enclosed Standard on Brill trucks. This increased upper deck seating to 38. In this form it survived until the late 1940s.

No 291 is seen here passing Kilmainham Gaol on a No 21 service (Inchicore - College Green - Westland Row). This was the type of tram recreated for use in the Michael Collins film in 1995 (see bottom left on page 90).

Reproduced by kind permission of An Post

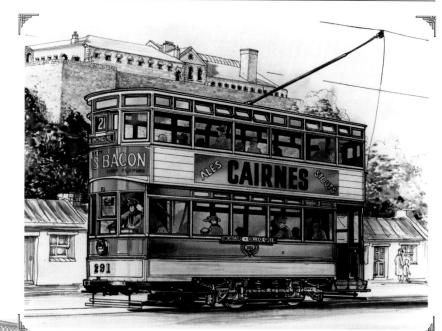

Centre: **In August 1928 the DUTC introduced a new livery of all over silver grey, as shown in this view of No 71. This livery proved to be unpopular and was superseded in 1935 by the well known green and cream scheme seen below. Bogie balcony cars of the type shown here were introduced by the DUTC on their longer routes in 1906, and No 71 was built in 1911. In windy conditions a canvas sheet was drawn across the open stairs to reduce the force of the wind striking the upper deck canopy and whirling down the stairs to cause discomfort to the motorman. The flapping of the canvas and the gleaming brasswork likened the trams to ships and the balcony cars were poetically known as 'galleons of the streets'.**

Reproduced by kind permission of An Post

Bottom: **The last designs of tramcar introduced in Dublin were the stream- lined cars known as Luxury trams. These came in two versions — 4 wheel and bogie. No 280, built in 1931, was the first of a batch of 20 bogie cars.**

The Luxury cars were built between 1931 and 1936 and initially carried the silver grey livery. In 1935 this gave way to the green and cream scheme. From 1941 the well known 'flying snail' symbol was applied to the tramcars, in place of the DUTC garter emblem. This was continued in modified form when the DUTC was absorbed by CIE and this is the version worn here by No 280.

The use of metal rather than timber in the structure of the Luxury cars made them two tons lighter than the earlier balcony trams. Some, like car No 280, even had a metal domed roof.

Reproduced by kind permission of An Post

Top: The only preserved and restored Dublin City tram is No 253, an enclosed 'Lucan bogie' built in 1928. Her sister, No 252, was the last tram to run in Dublin and is seen on page 100. Nine of these cars were built in 1928-9. They seated 75 and had Hurst Nelson bogies. On withdrawal in 1949, No 253 was bought by a convent on Tivoli Road, Blackrock. It was used as a sewing room and overflow dormitory in summer time, for orphaned girls. The nuns took good care of it. The existence of the tram was revealed to me by a window cleaner around 1982. It was donated and moved to the FAS depot (a youth employment agency) at Cabra in 1987, where it was restored by young trainees, under the supervision of John Kelleher, Michael Corcoran and myself. The work was completed in time for the St Patrick's Day parade in 1990, when the tram was displayed on a low loader, as seen here. The venture was financed from the Irish National Lottery and cost £20,000.

Michael Corcoran

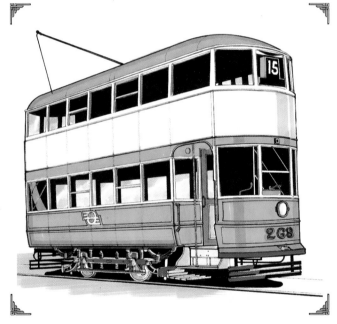

Above: The four wheel version of the Dublin Luxury tram is illustrated by this drawing of No 268, shown in its post-war CIE livery. It is based on the centre photograph on page 97, and is seen here on Route No 15, which ran from Nelson's Pillar to Terenure. Although most of the four wheel cars ran on Mountain and Gibson trucks, Nos 266 and 268 had Brill trucks, which they inherited from the 1918-built balcony cars they replaced. No 268 was one of a batch of luxury cars built in 1934 and lasted until the closure. She carried 60 passengers.

Drawing by the Author

Bottom left: In 1995 the director Neil Jordan was making a film about Michael Collins starring Liam Neeson and Julia Roberts, and set in the period around 1916-21. To recreate the centre of Dublin for the film, an elaborate set was built at Grange Gorman, in Dublin, featuring O'Connell Street, with the GPO and cobbled streets. Trams were an essential element in the set, and two replica Dublin Standards, numbered 257 and 262, were built for the film at a cost of £90,000. The replicas were operated by batteries and ran on false rails set in mock cobblestones, but nevertheless looked very convincing. However the use of Standard trams is historically inaccurate, as this type was not introduced until 1924, and never carried the route symbols used here on No 257. Michael Collins was assassinated in 1922, two years before the first Standard appeared!

Barry Carse

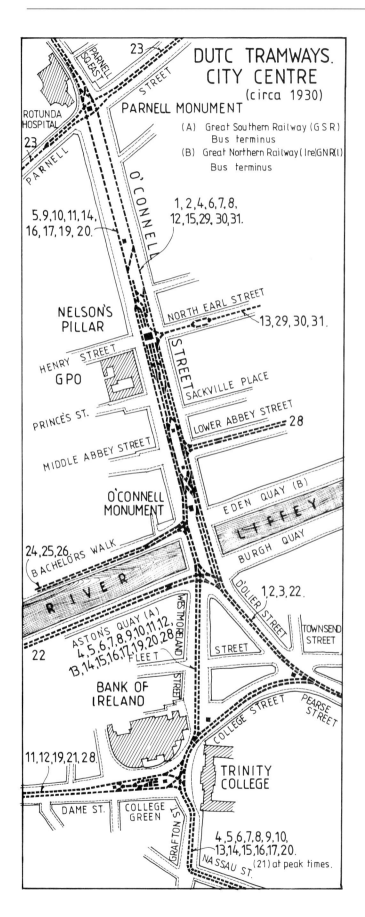

DUTC TRAMWAYS.
CITY CENTRE
(circa 1930)

PARNELL MONUMENT

(A) Great Southern Railway (GSR)
Bus terminus
(B) Great Northern Railway (Ire)GNR(I)
Bus terminus

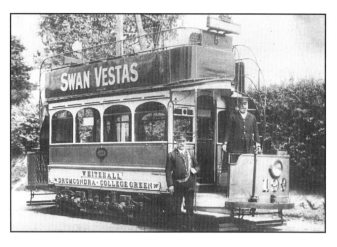

Top: The North Dublin Street Tramway introduced a route from College Green to Drumcondra in 1875, terminating at Botanic Avenue. After the electrification of the DUTC commenced in 1896, several of the original horse tram lines were extended. For instance, in 1903, the Drumcondra line was extended to Whitehall. This was as a direct result of the expansion of residential areas, and the tram in many respects helped to develop and expand the city by providing good transport from the newly developed areas.

No 199 is seen here at Whitehall and judging by the rural background, it was at the early stages of Whitehall's development. Originally No 199 was a Milnes trailer car operated by the DSDT, and was electrified in 1900, running on a Peckham truck. The platform dash has been raised, and protective caging has been provided on the upper deck. The route symbol, an inverted white heart, can be seen clearly at the rear. The motorman and conductor pose for the photographer. The dash cut-out near the motorman's right hand was to provide a grip when boarding the tram. *Author's collection*

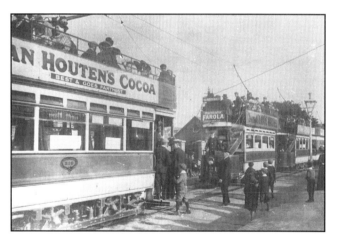

Bottom: This scene is taken at Ballsbridge around 1920. The well known brewing firm of Guinness organised an annual outing for the staff, and it was obviously a family occasion on account of so many children. The venue chosen was the Royal Dublin Society Showgrounds, presumably for the horse show or some other exhibition. There is a festive spirit as the merry makers reboard the tram after their outing. Each car would carry approximately 50, and so the four cars visible would carry as many as 200. There are possibly further cars not in the picture. The nearest car is a post-1918 open-topper with quarter lights, whereas the other cars are all of the open front variety. The second car is No 121, built by the American Car Co in 1900, on a DuPont truck. The car beyond it is No 197, a converted Milnes trailer.

Author's collection

In the early 1920s pirate bus operators scooped up passengers at tram stops and fierce competition raged throughout the city. The tramways had the serious disadvantage of having to maintain the area of road on each side of and between their track work, whereas the bus proprietors had no such burdens. Soon the mighty tram was on her knees and at their mercy. The climate was one for change and the advantages of a fumeless, reliable and safe mode of transport were not recognised.

The DUTC responded to the bus threat by introducing its own buses on selected routes from 1925 on, and then in 1933-35 bought out all the private operators. Already some minor tram routes had been abandoned — routes 5 (1928), 13 (1918), 20 (1930) and 22 (1929). The first bus substitution was Nelson's Pillar to Bath Avenue (Route 4) in 1932. In 1936 routes 16 & 17 were abandoned. After 1936 the DUTC began to construct a large fleet of double deck buses, and tram construction ceased. On 31 March 1938 the company announced its intention to replace the entire tram network over a four year period. In contrast to Belfast and many English cities, Dublin did not go down the alternative road of introducing trolley buses.

Soon the closures began, one following rapidly after the other, and over the period 1938-40 trams were abandoned on routes 1-3, 9-12, 18-19, 24-29. In 1941 the long route from Nelson's Pillar to Howth, built by the CHHT, was closed (see next chapter). The outbreak of war did not directly involve the Irish Free State, which was neutral, but the shortage of petrol and oil led to a reprieve for the remaining tram routes to Blackrock, Dun Laoghaire, and Dalkey (6-8), Dartry Road (14), Terenure (15), and Dollymount (30). In mid 1944 the fuel shortage was so intense that the remaining routes were closed for several months, and when services recommenced on 2nd October 1944, the Dollymount route remained closed.

On 1st January 1945 transport in the Irish Free State was reorganised and the DUTC became part of CIE. The famous 'flying snail' motif, introduced by the DUTC in 1941, was adopted as the emblem of CIE. The post-war years began with only three tram routes in Dublin — Dalkey (routes 6-8), Dartry Road (route 14), and Terenure (route 15). Difficulty in obtaining parts for new buses led to a stay of execution for three years, but on 31st October 1948 the Terenure and Dartry Road routes gave way to buses. It was not long before the last tram for Dalkey made its historic journey on 9th July 1949. The motorist and public opinion were as guilty as the authorities. The glorious past and excellent service of the trams were soon forgotten, and it is only now in the 1990s that their great benefits to the community are being reconsidered. With the launch of the LUAS initiative (see page 105) it won't be long before trams will once more grace the streets of Dublin.

TELL TALE SIGNS OF THE PAST

Walking around Dublin city today, it is difficult to believe that so extensive a network of electric tramways once existed. At one time, there were $61\frac{1}{2}$ miles of route and over 300 trams. On a busy route, a five minute service was provided and on long stretches of road, when standing at a tram stop, one could see the tram just missed vanishing in the distance, as your own arrived. To the rear you could see the following car approaching. A similar procession would be visible going in the opposite direction. This does not seem to happen with the buses. On the less frequented routes the trams would arrive at greater intervals but never more than twenty minutes or so.

For the more observant, relics of this extensive network can still be seen, standing silently over the years in some quiet corner, a testimony to the tramways' extensive past. There was once a time when many of the fine trams themselves could be seen at seaside resorts and as house extensions or garden sheds.

Mrs Carmel Houlihan told me that it was on account of such trams that the family entered the hotel business. They originally started off with one tram in north Co Dublin which served as a holiday home and it was rented out during periods of non-use. A second tram body was purchased and placed beside the former. Gradually, one merged into the other and extensions were added. Eventually, the extensions grew and trams diminished until finally a fine guest house emerged. Carmel and her husband Gerry are now the proprietors of Clontarf Castle Hotel and she thanks the trams.

If one drives along the old road from Phoenix Park to Lucan one can still see many of the

This is one of Dublin's most famous trams, known as *The Submarine*. Originally, No 80 was a horse car and was converted to electric traction in 1900. The nickname derived from the fact that the tram was designed to pass through occasional deep flood water at Clontarf and No 80 was officially known as the 'Stormcar'.The trucks were Peckham four wheel, and it was the only car with the suspension bars above axle level as shown by two black squares in the heavy body frame. As a result, the motors were well above flood level. Three platform steps can be seen with a fourth leading into the saloon. The photograph was taken in 1937 or 1938 outside what is now Clontarf bus depot. The tram was withdrawn in 1938.   *H Fayle, courtesy IRRS*

old tram poles along the roadway, sometimes on the left and sometimes on the right. Originally, they were set into earthen mounds and concrete packing surrounded the base of the poles. Now that the mounds have been removed, strange concreted amorphous forms envelope the base of the pole with a splayed top, the reasons for their origin now obscure.

The route out to Dalkey served by the tram is still rich in tram memorabilia as a great many of the tram- poles survive, with finial and bracket parts. Recently, many of the tram poles within the town itself were replaced, but evidence of the trams' past is still strong. Tram-poles with fluted bases can also be seen along Amiens Street, and plainer poles along the roadside perimeter of Fairview Park.

Until recently, as one drives to Howth along the Howth Road, where this road joins James Larkin Road, or the Coast Road, one could have seen a small junction box on the right hand side, just before the open space, still bearing the DUTC crest. This junction box can now be seen at the National Transport Museum in Howth.

Along the coast road the sea wall to the right was built by the tramways and opposite Kilbarrack cemetery the wall sweeps outward to allow for the laying of a passing loop. Again, at Baldoyle Road the wall sweeps out to form what was the largest loop on the system to serve the throngs who once arrived there to visit the now sadly defunct Baldoyle racecourse, for a day's outing.

The old tram depots still survive at Sandymount, Dartry, Clonskea, Terenure, Blackrock, and in part at Phibsborough and Clontarf and some have been converted to bus depots.

Sadly, the tram depot at Dalkey was destroyed in a recent fire. At Clontarf bus depot the corner 'draw off' tram pole, which took the full weight of the overhead power network of cables over the original marshalling yard, is still as impressive as the day it was erected in 1898. At Donnybrook bus depot the new buildings are built over a genuine tram graveyard where the truck and body parts of trams were crushed into the rubble to make way for progress. The name of the Dublin United Tramways is still just detectable on the old sheds at Conyngham Road. However these were actual bus sheds built by the DUTC while the trams were still in service. The tram fanwork set in the original cobble stones still survives under the present yard surfacing at the former tram depot in Dalkey. There is still much for the enthusiast to see.

Every so often the strongest evidence of all — the tracks themselves — emerge from the years of silence, awaiting their rediscovery, when the road is broken up to give access to services or to lay new mains. When the tramways were abandoned, many of the tracks were also abandoned in situ on the roadways and simply covered over for reasons of economy. At the time of writing, such trackwork made its reappearance along Howth promenade during the construction of new apartments. Recently, when the laying of the gas mains proceeded along Palmerston Road, lengths of track were removed to permit the work to proceed. It was possibly a cause for confusion to Dublin Corporation personnel to see four rails so close together and this is because the trackwork here was interlaced on account of the narrowness of the road. In July 1993, Dublin Corporation removed sections of tram track used as bollards at the end of Dodder Walk in Dartry, which gives access to Dodder Park.

There is also still plenty of evidence along the route of the Lucan line. Incidently the welding factory at Font Hill, on the latter system supplied, free of charge, the electric cable used to re-power one of the trams restored at the National Transport Museum.

On the positive side, much of the track work which was removed in recent years has been collected by the National Transport Museum for future use. When the road surface and central island in O'Connell Street were recently upgraded, vast amounts of grooved tram rail were saved and delivered to the museum. If anyone wants to see some grooved tram rail in cobble stone, go down to Dublin Corporation's Cleansing Department in Stanley Street. But hurry, it will not be there for much longer!

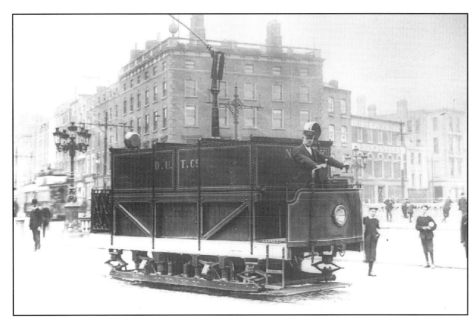

This is one of the DUTC water cars. It has a Du Pont truck and is on O'Connell Bridge. The water car has stopped and the motorman is posing for the camera, the spotlight almost mistaken for his head! The water had several functions — to reduce track expansion in continued hot weather, keep track dust from being whipped up by a passing tram, and generally keep the tracks clean.

Her sister water car, No 4, was recorded as having an eel living in the tank. The water was taken from the canals and must have been nutritious for the eel. It was fed on titbits proffered by the tramway staff and is reputed to have survived for ten years, and quite content.

Author's collection

Top: Car No 191, built in 1899, was the 202nd car built at Spa Road for the DUTC, but she was different from previous cars. During the early years of electric trams, the motor-men, on their exposed platforms, suffered greatly from the elements. Even though they were given 'great coats' — something similar to army attire — wind-driven rain penetrated, and long exposure brought about great sickness. In this respect the horse trams were not so bad, on account of the leisurely pace, but an electric tram travelling at 20 mph against a head wind or blizzard was injurious to the health of the motormen.

No 191 was the first tram in the world to sport a fully enclosed platform and, on account of the angular nature of the experimental dash, she became known as *The Coffin*. She was one of several Dublin trams to carry nicknames. No 111, was known as *The Sergeant*, on account of the three stripes, and No 80 (page 92) as *The Submarine*.

No 191 was turned out more splendidly than the ordinary cars of the day, and until the construction of the *Directors' Car* in 1901 (see page 86), was used by the Company top brass on special occasions. In this view the tram is seen festooned in flags and foilage, and its plaque proudly declares 'Built at the Company's Works, Dublin'.

TMSI collection

Centre: This is a rare internal photograph of activity in the Spa Road Works at Inchicore in West Dublin. In the left background is sprinkler car No 2, used for cooling track-work in dry hot weather conditions. In the centre, and raised from her Peckham truck, is Milnes open top car No 32, built in 1896. The vestibule was added in 1902, so this photograph was taken after that date.

On the right is No 65, a former horse car, still unvestibuled. This car was built in 1884 as No 135, and was motorised with its new number in 1898. The staff have probably been told to "Stand still" for the photographer. The gearwheel on the nearest axle indicates that it is a driving axle linked to the motor. The overhead crane bears the inscription 'T SMITH STEAM CRANE WORKS RUDLEY LEEDS'

TMSI collection

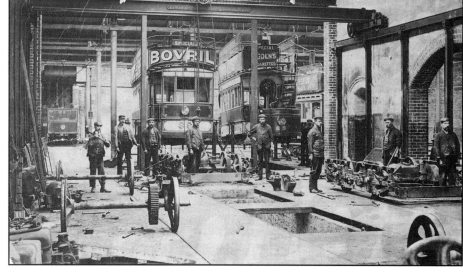

Bottom: This is a very impressive view of Castle Street, Dalkey, with one of the Preston-type bogie balcony cars central to the photograph. The clock to the right picks out the Findlater premises, owned by a well-known merchant of the day. The tracks turning to the left lead into the depot. When the Preston-types first entered service in 1906 they were much longer than the four-wheelers, and it was necessary to cut away some of the gate pillars at the depot to permit them to enter. The cuts in the pillars can still be seen, though their cause has long been forgotten

The lady in black in the left foreground is reading a panel of advertisements for the sale of household items. Many of the ornamental tram poles still survive along this street. The track-work and points are still intact in the depot forecourt, out of view.

National Library of Ireland, 3980L

Top: The next five photographs were taken in the early 1930s when the silver-grey livery was in vogue. The first shot is taken from Bachelor's Walk looking south east and the bogie car to the extreme left, on route No 24, is on its way to Lucan. A standard and a balcony car are passing one another on O'Connell Bridge.

From a photographer's point of view, the pole cuts the frame almost centrally, but gives an excellent view of the strange lantern carried by the light standard. The photograph was probably taken from the third floor of a building. The stonework of the Liffey wall appears to have been recently re-pointed, and stands out in contrast with the darker jointing. Some of the other vehicles are also of great interest, and include a ZD registered bus turning into Bachelor's Walk, and a row of taxis parked on the right hand side.

Author's collection

Centre: This view of the Liffey, looking north east, is taken from Aston's Quay, the scene of Dublin's first horse tram trial run in 1869. The type of rail used was known as the 'step rail' and was used by George Francis Train, who played a major part in introducing trams to Dublin.

Crossing O'Connell Bridge from south to north are a balcony car, a standard and one of the new luxury cars all in grey, followed by another balcony.

The bus in the foreground was operated by the DUTC and is about to pull out and set off. Today, the Quays are one way with west bound traffic using the South Quays and east bound using the North Quays. The DUTC single decker is east bound, and would now be breaking the law.

Author's collection

Bottom: No 4 waiting to be scrapped at the Donnybrook permanent way yard. The platform is sagging badly and No 4 would have been withdrawn for reasons of body rot. This car is a good example of the vestibuled open top cars introduced by the DUTC in 1918. This particular car was built in 1919 as No 124, and renumbered in 1922 to make way for a new balcony top car. She is sporting the grey livery with its elaborate lining and the year must be circa 1935. Like the advertisement for the zoo, the sign over the door is a sad reminder of busier days and reads 'Car full'. The car behind is minus its upper deck.

During the Eucharistic Congress in 1932, several open top cars like No 4 which had been withdrawn from traffic, were quickly ushered back into service to cope with the massive crowds. Some open-toppers were converted to service cars, and survived for many years in their new guise.

Author's collection

Top: The archway to the right is the Dublin Fusiliers' Arch, and is the north west corner of St Stephen's Green. The tram is No 240, built in 1927, and the year is circa 1933. The route number is 14, and the car is on its way to Dartry from either Nelson's Pillar or from Glasnevin. The livery is grey. The tram is setting down and taking passengers, and this entailed crossing the road to reach the tram. The approaching bus to the right is operated by the St Kevin Bus Company and by law must not pass until the tram is fully loaded and ready to move off. This led to a certain amount of strain between bus and tram operators.

Thos Mason and Co collection

Centre: With Nelson's Pillar in the background, O'Connell Street appears busy and the tram is not yet under threat. All cars shown are in the grey livery and the nearest car, No 148, is one of the smaller four-wheel luxury cars, built in 1933. The smart appearance and neatness of line can be appreciated from this elevated shot. No 148 is on its way to Sandymount Tower and is heading towards D'Olier Street. It has just met a standard, returning to the Pillar. Other cars, including a luxury car and two balcony cars are veering off to the left towards Westmoreland Street, or returning therefrom. Notice the horse drawn cart cutting across the line of traffic.

Bill Birney collection

Bottom: A lovely study of No 291 at College Green, with the Bank of Ireland in the background. It is on Route 21, which is the Inchicore service. A luxury car can be seen at Trinity College. The photograph is taken in 1938 and the tram is in the recently introduced livery of green and cream, which stayed with the trams until the closure. The green and cream was later adopted by the buses after the demise of the tram. No 291 is a four wheel standard, and began life as a balcony top car in 1923. It was rebuilt as a standard car with Brill trucks in 1929.

The pole base in front of the tram is painted white and this indicated that trams stopped at this pole. The angle of the trolley boom matches the angle of the stone pediment of the Bank of Ireland almost perfectly.

WA Camwell

Top: Standard tram No 24 was built new in 1926 and is arriving at Inchicore, the outer terminus of Route 21. The public house to the left of the photograph is the Black Lion and many passengers waiting for the tram had a refreshment while doing so. The conductor will shortly dismount and turn the trolley and soon No 24 will return to College Green.

When old Dubliners think of trams, it is usually one of these standards. They were more prolific than any of the other cars, and first made their appearance in 1924. They were in four and eight wheel versions, there being 91 of the former and 12 of the latter. During their history they sported all three liveries of the Company.

WA Camwell

Centre: Car No 268 at the Terenure terminus. This is one of the four wheel luxury cars and ran from Nelson's Pillar to Terenure via Rathmines. No 268 ran on a Brill truck, and was one of 37 to this design built in 1931-36.

Note the dip of the domed roof. This was to accommodate the pulling of the trolley tie rope and movement of the boom. This became a design feature, reduced wind pressure, and was a form of streamlining. The waist panel is carrying the CIE 'winged wheel' logo, known to all as the 'flying snail'.

The man and woman pushing the pram, and leading their dog, form a nicely composed picture in themselves. The year is 1947 or 1948, shortly before the closure.

TMSI collection

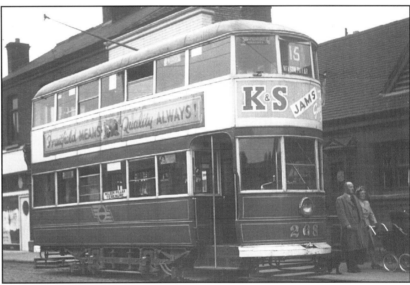

Bottom: This shot of No 326 makes an interesting comparison with the previous photograph. The angle is not too different and it allows comparison between a four wheel and eight wheel version of the luxury car. The four wheeler had five saloon windows and one platform window along each side, whereas the eight wheeler had a total of seven side windows. There were 20 eight-wheel cars and they ran on Hurst Nelson or Mountain and Gibson bogies.

The 'winged wheel' logo is an interesting study in itself. Originally the top wings faced the same way on each side of the tram, but eventually the same transfer was used on both sides and the top wing was always to the left with the lower wing to the right, as seen on car 268 above. This only occurred towards the closure when such attention to detail mattered less, and can indicate the year to some degree. The buses always had the top wing to the left.

The tram is in Blackrock depot.

TMSI collection

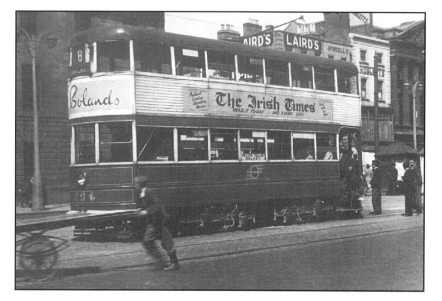

Top: Another bogie luxury car, No 294, built in 1933, is seen at the Pillar terminus on the No 8 Dalkey service. She is on Hurst Nelson bogies. Notice the very rounded dome to the front of the car. Later, these were modified by reducing the angle, and giving a flatter appearance, as seen on the previous page. Notice also the narrow strip sheeting along the upper deck side panel, and compare this with the luxury car on the previous page.

Design changes like this indicate that No 294 was in its experimental stages, and smaller differences were always found exciting to the tram enthusiast, as they learned to identify trams by their departure from the design norm. In March 1941 No 294 was the last 'Howth Tram', bringing that line to a closure. The Howth trams should not to be confused with the GNR Hill of Howth trams which survived until the end of May 1959. The luxury bogie cars which ran on the Pillar to Howth service were transferred to the Dalkey route, just as the Lucan bogie cars had been earlier.   *Author's collection*

Centre: Bogie standard car No 314 at Blackrock depot. This photograph and the one above give a good opportunity to study the differences between the standard (or fourth generation), and the luxury car. The main difference is the more rounded appearance of the luxury car, particularly the ends. The flat felted roof of the standard gave way to the domed roof of the luxury tram. The arch over the platform softens the lines of the luxury car, and the absence of cant rail louvres and upper deck quarter lights all contribute to a more pleasing effect. The lining out was simpler on the luxury cars and was two-tone. In contrast, the standards had some varnished external parts.

No 314 was constructed in 1928, especially for the Lucan route, and was one of a class of nine. At 16' 11" high they were the tallest Dublin trams, and seated 29/46 on transverse seating. The almost identical Dalkey cars had longitudinal seating in the saloon. The latter seating was more popular with conductors who found it easier to collect fares, as they had a wider central aisle. The inset destination box on the luxury car also added a touch of elegance.

TMSI collection

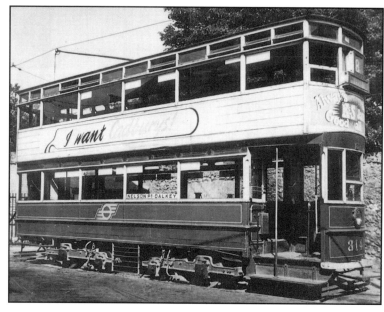

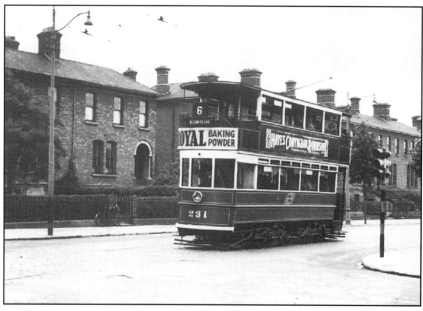

Bottom: The oldest bogie cars still running in the late 1940s were these balcony cars dating from 1910. No 231 is bearing route No 6 on the Nelson's Pillar to Blackrock line. It is running along Northumberland Road where it passes the junction with Haddington Road. The first electric trams of the Dublin Southern Districts in 1896 operated its fleet of open front powered cars with trailers, from Haddington Road to Dalkey, and No 6 is passing over venerable ground where electric traction is concerned, only a few years from closure.

In terms of streamlining, the balcony cars were not well designed. The speeds would never reach more than 40 mph, though the luxury cars were capable of much more than this, and buses of the day could hardly keep up with them. The balcony cars survived to the closure and, in summer conditions, the balcony was eagerly sought. The dark panel on the upper deck was a short-lived variation of livery.

Author's collection

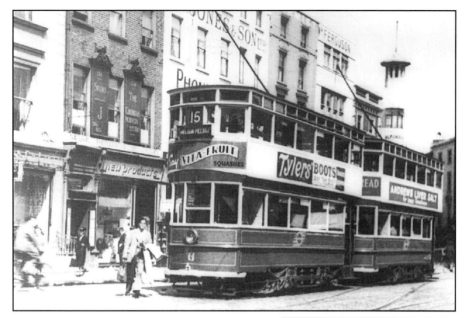

Top: Two 4-wheel standards at the north-west corner of St Stephen's Green, with the commencement of Grafton Street directly ahead. The Art Deco tower of the corner building can be seen over the roof of the second car and still exists.

No 6, the nearer car, is on the No 15 route from Nelson's Pillar to Terenure via Rathmines, which ceased operations in 1948 and this photograph was taken close to closure. The car in front may have been No 246, judging by the advertisements carried.

The numbering system of the Dublin fleet was haphazard and confusing, as numbers did not run in sequence. New cars simply took the numbers of withdrawn cars, so the numbers were no guide to the type of car, and could give the impression that all cars between 6 and 246 were the same. In the early years when a large addition to the fleet ran in series, it was easier for the tram enthusiast to identify the year of introduction.   *Author's collection*

Centre: No 224 was one of the Dalkey bogie standard cars mentioned on the previous page. It is seen here in CIE days near the closure. She is passing St Michael's Church in George's Street, Dun Laoghaire, in the direction of Dalkey. No 224 was specifically built for the Dalkey route and had longitudinal seats in the lower saloon, seating 29/44. There were only two cars of this type — Nos 218 and 224 — built in 1926 and 1925 respectively.

This type of car was called an 'Enclosed Dalkey Car'. In 1928-9 a fleet of almost identical cars was built for the Lucan line to replace the earlier narrow gauge service. After the closure of the Lucan service, the fleet of 'Lucan bogies' was transferred to the Dalkey route and No 224's true identity was lost. The chimney stack directly above the front end of the tram looks as if it is sitting on the roof of No 224 — if it were, I suppose No 224 could be described as a *steam* tram!

John Kennedy

Bottom: Four wheel luxury car No 245 passing through Rathmines, on the No 15 route to Terenure. The photographer has obviously specifically selected this position to frame his shot carefully so that the clock tower of the fire station would appear in the background, and yet the tram is the obvious subject.

This photograph was taken in CIE days and No 245, built in 1932, is in the green and cream livery used in the last days of service on this route. Perhaps the photographer knew this and was on a nostalgic mission as he waited for a tram to approach. The tram poles are all on the left hand side as one faces the clock tower. Many tram poles were converted to lighting standards after the closure, when the outreach bracket and electric traction paraphernalia were removed. and many still serve as street lights to this day.

Author's collection

Top: A striking shot of luxury bogie car No 297, taken around 1946 outside Dublin's most famous shop, Clery's. Nearly every Dubliner in their courting days arranged to meet under Clery's Clock and many a blind date blossomed into romance under it. Perhaps some still do!

We can tell that the Terenure route was still in operation, because the Dalkey-bound cars were moved onto the nearer tracks in this photograph when the tramway system retracted.

Notice how empty the street appears, despite the throngs of people filling the footpath. Not many people were car owners in those days, but I suspect that the photographer waited until there was a clearing in the traffic to optimise his study of one of Dublin's finest trams, the pride of the electric fleet, the magnificant bogie streamliners.

No 297 was built at Spa Road in 1932, and survived at Courtown Co Wexford, until early 1996, when it was tragically destroyed in a fire caused by vandals.   *V Goldberg*

Centre: This night scene is of ex-Lucan standard bogie car No 252 on her historic last journey into transport history, surrounded by crowds of well wishers. The tram was full to capacity with well over 100 passengers clinging to every conceivable part. Those who couldn't board the tram walked alongside it as if in a procession, and further crowds joined the throngs along the way. The night was the 9th July 1949, and No 252 was to be Dublin's last tram. There was an air of festivity as the crowds were jovial and boisterous. However, as the last mile approached the mood changed and the crowds became silent witnesses to the demise of Dublin's most loved system of transport. In a desperate bid to hang on to some memory, souvenir hunters stripped the tram of anything that could be taken, including the seats. Her sister car, the restored No 253, can be seen today at the Transport Museum in Howth.
Author's collection

Bottom: After the closure, the tram bodies were removed from their trucks, and were stripped of seating and brassware down to the bare shell. They were offered to the public for around £30 each, and were eagerly bought up for sheds, chicken coops and holiday homes. One served as a hairdressing salon in Galway, another a football pavilion. It was sad to see them slowly rot through neglect and decay. However they became a rich source of parts and indeed full tram bodies, to museums such as the Transport Museum at Howth.

No 197 was a four wheel luxury car, built in 1932, and is seen here derelict years after the trams were withdrawn. To preserve a tram such as this, it would be necessary to raise the frame at least 300 mm from the ground, locate it in a sheltered area, and ensure that the windows are sealed to keep out the weather. The fact that many are still capable of being saved is testimony to their excellence of construction.

The Transport Museum Society of Ireland has six trams rescued from the brink of oblivion, and hope soon to acquire a seventh. It will then have a full range of all five generations of tramcar design, as well as a pioneer design from the Giant's Causeway.   *Author's collection*

CLONTARF and HILL of HOWTH TRAMWAY (DUTC)

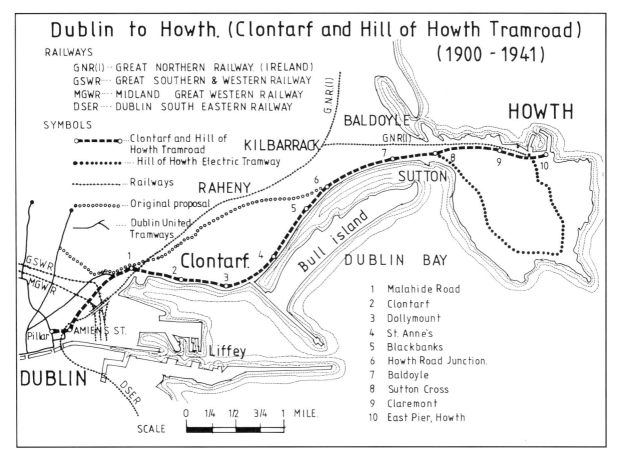

Dublin to Howth. (Clontarf and Hill of Howth Tramroad) (1900 - 1941)

RAILWAYS
GNR(I)··· GREAT NORTHERN RAILWAY. (IRELAND)
GSWR···· GREAT SOUTHERN & WESTERN RAILWAY
MGWR···· MIDLAND GREAT WESTERN RAILWAY
DSER ··· DUBLIN SOUTH EASTERN RAILWAY

SYMBOLS
o━ ━ ━ ━o···Clontarf and Hill of Howth Tramroad
•••••••••••···Hill of Howth Electric Tramway
·········· ···Railways
oooooooooo···Original proposal
⌃⌃⌃···Dublin United Tramways

1 Malahide Road
2 Clontarf
3 Dollymount
4 St. Anne's
5 Blackbanks
6 Howth Road Junction.
7 Baldoyle
8 Sutton Cross
9 Claremont
10 East Pier, Howth

SCALE   0 1/4 1/2 3/4 1 MILE.

If one studies the map of Dublin at the turn of the century it is strikingly like a giant lobster (see below). A study of the basic layout is helpful for understanding how the city developed and its transport needs evolved. This is even more helpful when discussing the peripheral lines such as Dublin to Howth and Dublin to Dun Laoghaire. The body of the lobster is contained by the Grand and Royal Canals. The spine is represented by the River Liffey and its segmented back by the many bridges. The mouth is where the Liffey flows into the sea and the North and South Bulls correspond to the tentacles. The Dodder and Tolka are the fore limbs. The sweep of the bay out to Howth and Dun Laoghaire are the massive claws and Howth and Dun Laoghaire (Kingstown) harbours are the nippers.

Originally the mail boat berthed in the new harbour constructed in Howth. However, by the time the Dublin and Kingstown Railway was constructed in 1834 the mail boat had already changed allegiance to Kingstown (in 1822), and has remained there ever since. In an effort to regain the lucrative traffic generated by the mail boat, the Dublin and Drogheda Railway sent a branch line, from what became known as Howth Junction to the recently constructed harbour of Howth, arriving on 30th May 1847. But it was too late. The mail boat was never to return.

Throughout the millennia, Howth had always been a jewel in the Dublin crown and was invaded by every passing marauder from Milesian, Celt and Viking, to Norman and English.

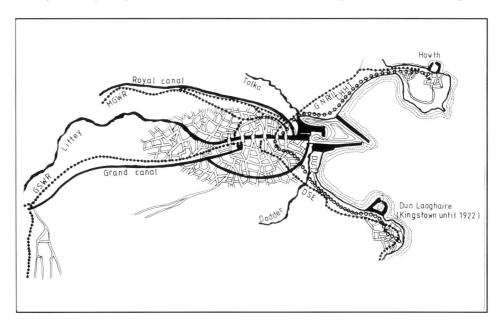

With the advent of the railway and better roads, the new invader was the well-to-do Dublin merchant and business man seeking refuge from the pressures of city life. Howth itself was inhabited by a sturdy race of fishermen and the fine castle provided work in abundance. However, despite this, the peninsula and lands between were sparsely populated and little revenue was drawn by the railway. The circumstances were very different on the south side, from Dublin to Kingstown. This area developed quickly and was a rich source of revenue for the railway.

The horse trams had spread outwards from the city centre, spider like, in all directions and, on the north side, as far as Clontarf (Dollymount). The tramway entrepreneurs of the day felt that a line to serve Howth would help develop this area. The first plans for a tramway, in 1890, were for a 3'0" gauge line from the fish markets to Howth harbour, via Raheny, with a branch along West Pier to pick up the fish. This line would have commenced in Mary's Lane, opposite the North City Markets, passing Halston Street, Little Brittan Street to Capel Street, down Parnell Street and eastwards to Fairview via Summerhill and Ballybough. The line would then have followed the inland Howth Road to reach the Coast Road at Kilbarrack, continuing to Howth via Claremont Gates.

In 1894, the Clontarf and Hill of Howth Tramway made a new proposal, this time for a line of 5'3" gauge. This was to commence at the DUTC terminus in Dollymount and follow the coast road via the small cluster of old houses at Raheny-on-Strand, later known as Blackbanks on account of the colour of the soil. The Company also applied for powers to construct a line to the Hill of Howth which rise from Claremont Gates, pass Howth station at high level, and ascend more or less directly to the summit. The concept was ill-considered as the gradients along the route suggested were in the region of 1 in 8, which was too dangerous for horse traction and impossible for steam. A cable tramway with a power station at the Summit would have succeeded, but

the cost was prohibitive.

The GNRI (the successors of the DDR) viewed the intrusion of this newcomer with concern, as they also had plans to provide a service around the Hill to pick up passengers and deliver them to their stations at either Howth or Sutton (see page 66). When the CHHT applied to lay a second line from Sutton Cross to link with their proposed summit line, the GNRI could no longer remain inactive and the matter was challenged in the courts. The GNRI maintained that for another company to link two stations on their existing railway line was not only duplication, leading to loss of revenue, but was also legally unacceptable. The GNRI immediately applied for powers to electrify their line from Howth Station to Amiens Street and run a fleet of single deck trams into the city. This would have been in direct competition with the CHHT proposals to run from Howth to the city.

A compromise was reached. The Clontarf company agreed to restrict itself to a line from Dollymount to the East Pier of Howth harbour. The GNRI was, therefore, left alone to operate their fleet of 'Hill' trams. The branch along the West Pier

The Clontarf and Hill of Howth Tramway purchased its tram fleet from the Electric Railway and Tramway Carriage Works at Preston in 1900. These fine bogie open-toppers were known as 'Preston cars', and when taken into DUTC stock in 1907 they were renumbered 301-312. There is no record of their CHHT numbers, but presumably they were 1 - 12. They seated 30/45 and ran on Peckham maximum traction bogies with the pony wheels leading. This view shows No 304 in early DUTC condition, in the blue and white livery used by the DUTC until 1928. The destination board on the rocker panel was deep turkey red with white lettering. The cars were unusual in that the lower saloon was vestibuled internally into first and second class, and third class was located on top. The provision of a sheltered vestibule for the motorman was a welcome improvement. When built, they were the largest trams that had yet appeared in the Dublin area and were so successful that the DUTC built nine almost identical cars with balcony tops (294-300, 316, 317) in 1906-1907. These were often referred to as 'Preston type' cars. However, balcony cars could not run on the Howth route, on account of bridge height restrictions, so in 1932 the DUTC altered Nos 320, 321, and 324 to open-top condition, to increase the fleet.

TMSI collection

was never constructed and, instead, the fish were brought to the early morning tram by the Howth fishermen and, in Dublin, were brought to the markets by a fleet of hand pushed carts. This practice gave rise to the affectionate name 'fish trams'. which survived long after the practice had ceased.

There is a moving anecdote associated with the line concerning the death of a young English track layer, in 1900. Known only by his Christian name, his family could not be contacted and his work mates laid his remains in the Stranger's Bank, opposite the terminus, at St Mary's Abbey. They created an appropriate monument consisting of grooved tram rail, which is still in place and is known as the 'Unknown Tram Man's Grave'.

The operation of the line was unusual in many ways. Although trams ran right through from Nelson's Pillar, there was (in the early days) a change of crew from DUTC personnel to CHHT at the beginning of St Anne's Estate, where the present Coast Road follows the line of the original tram road.

Baron Ardilaun, the owner of St Anne's Estate, required that a special wire fence be erected along the foreshore with gates to provide access to his private rifle range. He also stipulated that the tram poles, along the boundaries of his lands, be more ornate than elsewhere. He did not permit cars to stop other than for the setting down and collection of passengers. It was also a requirement that the two rivers running through his estate, the Naniken and the Santry, should not be impeded in any way on their arrival at the foreshore. Two passing loops were provided, on this otherwise single track section, at Heronstown and Bettyville townlands. A brisk run could be expected along this stretch of relatively straight track.

The CHHT could never stray too far from their great rival, the GNRI. They passed its station at Amiens Street, under its skew bridge at Clontarf, over its tram line at Sutton Cross and finally under the GNRI Howth Station viaduct. The largest passing loop on the line was at Baldoyle Road, which served the Baldoyle race course. Instead of commencing at the reverse side of Nelson's Pillar, 'Race cars', to cater for the heavy traffic to the race course, started from Lower Abbey Street, using the relief lines along Beresford Place. This special line reunited with the main Clontarf line at the end of Talbot Street and the convoy of full cars proceeded in ceremonial procession to Baldoyle.

Past Sutton Cross the tram kept to the right hand side of the road, stopping at Saxe Lane (now Church Road) the other end

of which was served by the Hill cars, and continued past the quarries at Corr Castle with a loop at Corr Bridge. At Claremont gates the track crossed over to the left hand side but soon changed sides once more to serve Howth Castle gates, with its rhododendron gardens and prehistoric dolmen. A waiting room and parcel office was provided at the East Pier terminus where the present day public toilets are sited.

From the 1930s the line never managed to operate at a profit and the aspirations that residential development should materialise along the route never happened. If the inland route via Raheny had been chosen, the line might have survived to the end of electric trams in Dublin. As it was, the traffic on the line was highly seasonal, with four trams sufficing in the winter, but anything up to thirty needed in the summer. In the late 1930s Luxury bogie cars were put into service on the Howth route. These were fully enclosed trams, but were lower in height than the balcony trams. Towards the end the Howth cars operated from Conyngham Road depot, which entailed a very early start for the tram crews.

The last tram from Howth, 'luxury' car No. 294, with motor man Mr Dick Ward at the controls, left at 11.45pm on 29th March 1941 to the cheers and tears of spectators. So concluded the service on a line which, to the end, was still referred to by many as the 'Clontarf Company', even though it was worked by the DUTC. After the closure the new DUTC luxury bogie cars were transferred to the Dalkey route. Although the older cars 301-312 had been overhauled in 1940 with the intention of a similar transfer, they were withdrawn and stored at Conyngham Road depot, from where they were later removed in two convoys of six to Donnybrook depot and scrapped.

The track from Howth Station to the East Pier remains intact under the road, complete with granite sets and tie bars, and any road works along this stretch will reveal the old line with memories of a bygone age of transport.

This rather sad shot shows the remains of Preston car No 308 after it was destroyed in North Earl Street in Easter Week, 1916. It was said that it took a direct hit from the gun boat HMS *Helga* which pounded O'Connell Street during the Rising. The insurgents formed a barricade from the remains of No 308. The destruction of the buildings in the background reveal the extent of the bombardment. The innocence of the milk advertisement carried on the upper deck panel strikes a discordant note with the dismembered remnants of No 308.

Author's collection

Top: The main reason for not fully enclosing the Howth cars was the need to negotiate low bridges en route. Here we see a CHHT car posed underneath the viaduct that carried the GNRI 'Hill' trams over the route of the DUTC. The GNRI tram is perched up on the viaduct, with the staff of both cars posing for the photograph. No 301 of the CHHC fleet is city bound, and the 'Hill' car is bound for Sutton Station.

Although there were poor relations between the two companies, the staff grew to know each other quite well from their many crossings at bridges and on the level. At the Sutton level crossing the rule was that the car 'setting off' from its terminus had the right of way. Thus a CHHT car 'setting off' from its Howth terminus had priority over a GNRI car returning to Sutton, and a GNRI car 'setting off' from the Sutton terminus took precedence over a CHHT Howth-bound car. Over the forty years that the two systems ran alongside, there is no recorded instance of a collision.   *Author's collection*

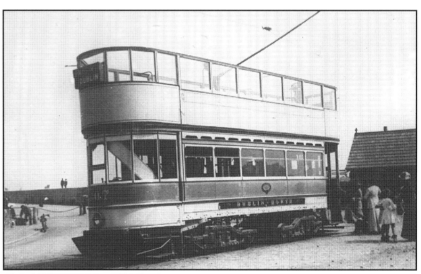

Centre: In 1913 No 307 was experimentally fitted with a glass screen surround on the upper deck and the bogies reversed. It is seen here in this condition at Howth Harbour terminus. The experiment was unsuccessful and the screen was removed in 1916.
RC Ludgate collection

Bottom: Between 1918 and 1926 the Preston bogie cars were completely rebuilt with new DUTC four-windowed bodies as seen here in this view of No 307, also at Howth terminus. The rebuilds were fitted with either Hurst Nelson or Mountain and Gibson maximum traction bogies.

No 307 bears the route No 31 which is still used by the buses of today, and is in the green and cream livery introduced in 1935. The rebuilds remained open top to negotiate the low bridges en route, and it wasn't until the arrival of the more compact luxury cars of the 1930s that the system was operated by all enclosed cars. The benefits were shortlived, however, as the route ceased operations in 1941.
H Fayle, courtesy IRRS

LUAS - Dublin's new light rail transit system

Dublin City lost its electric tramway system in 1949. At the time it was considered one of the most efficient and advanced in Europe, providing an excellent service for the public. It is now becoming more and more recognised that electric trams are still the most efficient means of transporting large numbers of people in an environmentally friendly way, both in terms of noise and pollution.

BRITISH AND EUROPEAN TRAMWAYS SINCE 1949

It might be of interest to readers to know something of the history of tramways between the closure of the Dublin trams in 1949 and the announcement of the Luas proposals in 1995. The last Irish city to lose its tramways was Belfast in 1954, with the Fintona and Hill of Howth trams (which were rural) lingering on to 1957 and 1959 respectively.

In Britain the pattern was broadly similar. Some cities tried to retain trams and continued modernisation after 1945, introducing designs of streamlined trams that were even more advanced than the Dublin 'Luxury' cars or the Belfast 'McCrearys'. Other cities hastened to get rid of their tram systems altogether. Glasgow and Sheffield remained enthusiastic for trams right through the 1950s.

However, even Sheffield and Glasgow succumbed in the end, as trams came to be regarded as old-fashioned and a nuisance. In 1962 even Glasgow gave up its trams, leaving Blackpool to carry on as the only major urban centre with an electric tram system. This stampede to dump the tram led to considerable wastage of excellent cars. Possibly the most attractive trams of all, in Sheffield, had just been introduced when abandonment of the system took place. Several of these fine specimens still survive in various museums throughout Britain and are a testimony to their advanced design and smart appearance.

Between 1962 and 1992 the urban electric tramway survived in the British Isles only at Blackpool and, in an enduringly attractive form, at Douglas, Isle of Man. However, in certain parts of continental Europe a completely different attitude was taken to trams. Our continental cousins always favoured the single deck car, chiefly on account of its faster loading and unloading abilities. The British Isles favoured double-deck trams because they took up less road space, though as against that they retained road space for longer when filling and emptying. Single deck trams also lent themselves to trailer haulage and articulation, which was rarely attempted in the British Isles

The major European cities, by and large, retained their tram systems, particularly in Belgium, Holland, Germany and in Eastern Europe. Over the years since 1962 tramcar design continued to evolve and develop. The first development was to segregate the driver from the passenger saloon, and to build sliding or folding doors giving quick access directly from the street. In long vehicles there were several doors and, as many passengers are content to stand for short journeys, movement on and off the tram was greatly increased and the stopping time reduced. To facilitate slow moving elderly folk, a central section of the vehicle is now often dropped towards street level, and this also benefits wheelchair-bound travellers. It also makes it easier for even able-bodied passengers to step on and off. To further enhance ease and speed of access, low street platforms have been created so that wheelchair and pram users can have readier access. These changes draw even greater numbers back to the tram.

The most modern concept is a totally low floored vehicle throughout, and this will be a feature of the *Luas* system. A low floor can only be achieved by great advances in truck or bogie design. The principle is to eliminate the 'wheel axle' as we now know it and substitute individually powered wheels of smaller diameter, carried on a stub axle. These wheel sets are capable of slight side to side movement to facilitate cornering and this in turn reduces track wear and screech.

In the interests of weight reduction, stretched aluminium panelling and lighter alloys are making an appearance. The acceptance by the public of standing for short journeys has allowed a reduction in seating and thus weight. Modern trams are lighter, swifter, safer and more people friendly than the massive 'Dalkey bogies' of yesteryear. Even the metal clad 'Luxury' car would be considered heavy and cumbersome by today's standards.

Perhaps the most important aspect of a modern tramway is not so much the cars themselves, but the methods of operation. Ticket dispensing machines, swipe cards, etc, have replaced the ticket office or on-car purchase, and these machines can be located anywhere en-route. The main objective of a modern tramway is not only to win passengers from other forms of public transport, but to convince drivers to abandon their cars and use the tram instead. This is not as easy as it might seem, as a car is not only an extremely comfortable machine, but is also a status symbol, and one not willingly forfeited without good reason. In a car, one is free to choose one's own music on best quality stereo, and enjoy a relaxing cigarette. Not so on the tram, where smoking would be forbidden. What, therefore, is the lure and the attraction? The answer is the time taken to reach one's destination — in other words speed, or *Luas* in Irish.

Crowded streets, cluttered traffic, and obnoxious fumes undo the benefits of personalised transport and create stress and anxiety and an appalling waste of time and energy. People arrive at their places of work often exasperated and drained, having spent perhaps more than an hour travelling a relatively short distance. This is neither good for the economy nor the spirit. Imagine a stressless, swift, frequent and comfortable means of transport,. A modern tramway or light railway vehicle (LRV) can offer this — but not without careful planning and forethought.

First of all, car drivers must have good parking facilities en-route to entice them to leave their cars. Cars must be forbidden in many central parts of the city accessible only to the trams. Rights-of-way and reserves must be established for the trams, to give them preference over other road vehicles. This will ensure a swift and reliable service.

In the past the trams were given no such rights, and their paths were clogged persistently. The chaos that ensued was unfairly blamed on the trams. The shoe is now firmly on the other foot. If the tram is given a free rein, the results will transform our city centres. City after city is coming to realise that the old solution was in fact the right one. Anyone who has recently travelled in cities where the tram has survived will recognise its benefits. Other cities, also long suffering the ill effects of traffic jams, are now considering the same solution, and are turning again to the electric tram for salvation.

All over Europe, the tram is making a return. New systems have recently been introduced in Utrecht, Nantes, Grenoble, and Lausanne. Nearer to home, in Britain, Manchester re-introduced trams in 1992 and Sheffield in 1995. Several more cities, such as Leeds, are planning to do the same.

The demise of the electric tramcar was particularly lacking in vision. In Dublin it will cost £200 million to provide three simple routes, whereas if the trams had been retained and upgraded gradually as technology evolved, Dublin might still have one of the finest public transport systems in Europe. Instead it has what is possibly one of the most chaotic, with sluggish traffic and constant jams. It is possibly only a matter of time before Belfast, and possibly other Irish cities, follow the lead of Dublin and consider the re-introduction of electric trams.

THE LUAS PROPOSALS

Dublin is now to construct *Luas*. It should be in operation for the first year of the new millennium. Extensions are already planned to follow. Perhaps the new tram system will never be as extensive as the old tramway, and will look very different, but in essence it is a true successor of the once glorious tram. In December 1995, the plans for Dublin's proposed new light rail transit system were launched by the Minister of Transport, Energy and Communications, Mr Michael Lowry. He stressed the advantages of, and indeed the necessity for, such a system.

The new rail system will provide a clean and swift service, substantially reducing the time of travel by up to 50%. The service will begin with 30 modern trams, each capable of carrying 200 passengers. This is the equivalent of removing 125 cars from our streets. The service will have a six minute frequency at peak times (not unlike the old trams), reducing to a fifteen minute frequency at other times. This gives an hourly capacity per direction on each line of 2400 passengers.

The introduction of the new light rail system will be carried out in two phases:

Phase 1 City centre to Tallaght
        City centre to Dundrum

Phase 2 City centre to Ballymun
        Extension from Dundrum to Sandyford

However, at the time of going to press, the phasing of the project has been questioned, and a strong case made for placing the Ballymun line in the first phase. It had also been planned to terminate a phase one line at Dundrum but, at a public meeting held in March 1996, residents of Dundrum argued for an extension to Sandyford Industrial Estate, as Dundrum was too built up to allow a 'park and ride' facility.

The announcement of the *Luas* proposals has led to considerable debate in Dublin. Several city venues are running exhibitions highlighting the advantages of the proposed system. Schools are being targeted and questionnaires are circulating. A recent opinion poll showed that 95% of the population was in favour of the scheme.

Not everyone is happy. A similar scheme in Sheffield caused considerable disruption to business and commerce during the construction phase, and some prominent businessmen fear a repeat of this in Dublin. There is no doubt that the inconvenience will be great. The choice is basically between a long drawn out scheme stretching over several years, with limited disruption at any one time, — or a sudden blitz, involving the complete closure of several thoroughfares for a limited period of months. In this respect, the example of Belfast's conversion from horse to electric trams in 1905 in seven months might be worth studying.

Some members of the public have asked the authorities to look at the alternative of an underground system, such as that of London or Paris. However, this too would present major problems. Tunnelling would make it a lot more expensive that a street system, and elevators or stairs would make it slow for crowds to gain access to the system. This would defeat the purpose of light rail transit and ease of street access. Another expense that such an alternative would incur would relate to rolling stock — underground trains move at greater speeds and would need to be of heavier, and therefore more expensive, construction.

The *Luas* system will operate on 750 volts DC with supply from overhead cables 6 metres above the ground. These will be fed from approximately 12 sub-stations. The total length of the system will be 21 kilometres of double track with up to eight new bridge structures. About half of the track will be flush paved with grooved rail and the remainder ballasted with flat bottomed railway track.

There will be 32 stations with low level platforms, 300mm above street level (see opposite). Each platform will be 40 metres long and 3.5 metres wide, with stations, on average, 650 metres apart. Each station will be equipped with a shelter, seating, ticket machine, information panel, public address system, and close circuit cameras where appropriate.

Trams will travel at a maximum speed of 70 km/h. The journey from the City centre to Tallaght will take 38 minutes and that to Dundrum, 22 minutes. City centre stops will be 40 seconds on average, and at main suburban stops, 20 seconds.

It is expected that *Luas* will create up to 600 jobs during the construction phase and, in the long run, 200 full-time jobs. It is hoped to commence construction in the near future, and it is envisaged that the programme will take five or six years to complete.

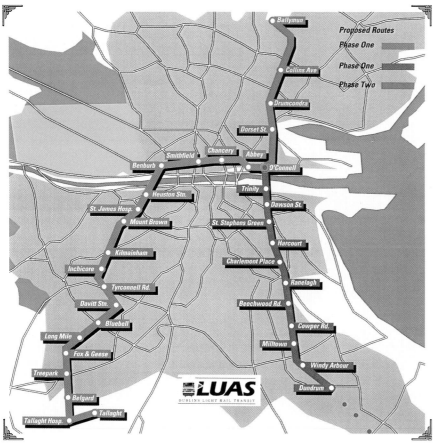

Top: **The Luas system is designed basically to serve the major conurbation of Dublin, north to Ballymun, south to Dundrum and west to Tallaght. The construction of the lines will be phased, mainly for financial reasons and to reduce disruption.**

Phase 1 will see the construction of the Dundrum and Tallaght routes. The Dundrum line will start off at street level but, after crossing the Grand Canal, it will follow the trackbed of the old Harcourt Street to Bray line which closed in 1958. The Tallaght route will follow streets and roads for its entire length, though some stretches will be on a central reserve.

Phase 2 will be the Line to Ballymun in North Dublin, which will also be at street level. In addition, it is planned to extend the Dundrum line to Sandyford Industrial Estate in this phase.

These are the immediate plans for the Luas system but, over the years ahead, extra routes and extensions may be considered. Much depends on the success of the system and the acceptance, on the part of Dubliners, of the return of the tram.

Official map, courtesy Eamon Brady,
LRT Information Officer

Centre: **This is an artist's impression of what Westmoreland Street will look like after the re-introduction of the tram. Note how there will be a special tram reserve in this section, with small elevated platforms for picking up and setting down passengers. The high standard of the street finish and tram environment should encourage a positive attitude towards the new form of transport.**

Courtesy Eamon Brady,
LRT Information Officer

Bottom: **An artist's impression of what the new Light Rail Transit (LRT) vehicles might look like. The trams will be articulated and run on bogies. They will be 30 metres long and weigh 35 tonnes. There will be seats for 60 passengers, with standing room for a further 140.**

For ease of access, at least 60% of the floor area will be only 350mm above street level. One surprise is that the gauge will have to be the standard European 4'8½" instead of the Irish 5'3" gauge of the old Dublin trams. This is because the trams will have no axle to adjust the gauge, if an existing design is bought 'off the shelf'.

It should be stressed that the tram depicted, and its livery, are conjectural, based on contemporary European practice.

Courtesy Eamon Brady,
LRT Information Officer

Top: **Our study of Belfast trams starts with this view of the two types of car common at the time of the closure. McCreary car No 423 and Chamberlain No 359 show some interesting contrasts in livery and design. For one thing the small chrome numbers carried by the McCreary cars were always much less readable than the larger gold numbers carried by the other trams.**

The Chamberlain has just emerged from Queen's Quay railway station, and is clearing the single road loading bay. No 423 is about to enter the terminus. Although it was rare in the British Isles for a tram to enter a station building, there were two instances of it in Belfast, the other being at York Road, the LMS terminus.

WG Robertson, ColourRail

Centre: **Chamberlain No 354 is at Wellington Place, near the city centre and is probably heading empty for Donegall Square. The large building towering over the tram is Belfast Technical College, whilst in the background is the Belfast Royal Academical Institution, built in 1805. This part of Belfast is known as *The Black Man*, a reference to the statue of the Rev Cooke, visible above the tram.**

WG Robertson, ColourRail

Bottom: **Another Chamberlain, this time No 359, is seen here at Castle Junction, the hub of the Belfast tram system. The term 'Castle Junction' was a tramway term and referred to the junction of Donegal Place, Castle Place and Royal Avenue. All fares ended here. The tall building behind the tram is the Bank Buildings and behind the trolley bus is the Provincial Bank of Ireland. The trolley bus is entering Castle Place from Royal Avenue and is passing the famous Fifty Shilling Tailors, a well known shop of the 1950s. Note the tar boiler at work outside and the sign 'Keep left except for trams'.**

WG Robertson, ColourRail

BELFAST ELECTRIC TRAMS

The introduction of the Belfast horse trams has already been dealt with in an earlier chapter (see page 30). As with Dublin, where horse traction gave way logically to electrification, the reader is recommended to refer back to this earlier chapter before reading on.

Given that Belfast was the technological capital of the country, with firms like Sirocco, Mackies, Harland and Wolff, etc, and in view of the fact that Ulster had pioneered electric traction on the Giant's Causeway, and Bessbrook and Newry tramways, it is a source of great surprise to me that Belfast was the last city in Ireland to electrify its horse tramways.

The first discussions about the possibility of a change over occurred in the early 1890s and the postponement of further extensions to the expanding horse tram network were most likely due to the pending arrival of electricity as a transport motive force. Apart from the Cavehill and Whitewell Tramway, the control of the horse tramways was almost exclusively with the Belfast Street Tramways Co. The BST also worked the nominally independent lines owned by the BCDR, the Sydenham District, Belfast Tramway Co, and the Belfast and Ligoniel Tramway Co.

In 1896 the BST obtained powers to electrify the system, but could not reach agreement with the Corporation, who in 1893 had agreed to let the Company operate the tramway for another 14 years. On the other hand, in Dublin, the DUTC had the Southern Districts Tramway, known as the 'English company', snapping at their heels to accelerate electrification of the horse tramway network. Like the DUTC, the horse tramways in Belfast were profitable and there were no predators to seriously threaten their control. There was no economic pressure for change, simply a social need.

Following negotiations with the BST, Belfast Corporation was rapidly taking a personal interest in the success of the horse tramways and entered the scene themselves. An 1899 Act gave them powers to construct lines along the following roads, radiating outwards from the city:

1   Springfield Road (constructed in 1900)
2   Newtownards Road   "   "
3   Cliftonville Road   "   "
4   Stranmillis Road   "   "
5   Malone Road   "   "
6   Ravenhill Road   "   "
7   Shore Road   (constructed in 1904)

It was the Corporation which was now making the expansionist moves, although the above lines were operated by the BST on a rental basis. In 1904, Belfast Corporation exercised its options and took over the BST in its entirety, including the three small independent companies. The Corporation immediately sought to electrify their lines, even before the date of the formal takeover, in an effort to make up for lost time. Further extensions, approved by the 1904 Act, would now be laid for the electrification of the existing network, erection of overhead cable, constructing a generating station,

conversion of existing depots, etc. The tender was awarded to the company of JG White for all the work associated with the changeover, apart from building the generating station which was constructed by the local firm of McLaughlin and Harvey. The total cost of the changeover was just under £563,500.

The plan of action was carefully drawn up. Work commenced at the outer termini moving inwards, ever converging on the city centre. To speed matters up, the services within the city centre were abandoned to facilitate an early target for completion. The work commenced on 1st February 1905 and was completed in seven months. This was considered a record in these islands and, whilst the city centre disruption was total for almost three weeks, the protracted interruptions over many months, if not years, common to such work, was eliminated. It was agreed that this procedure was for the better public good and perhaps it was. However, at the time there were constant protests about the inconvenience and nuisance. The Corporation turned a deaf ear and simply worked all the harder to complete the task.

Although the system was completed, it was not until 29th November 1905 that the official opening took place. On that day, six specially decorated cars set off from the City Hall at noon carrying the Lord Mayor and many dignitaries and prominent citizens. Sir Daniel Dixon was heard to remark "This is as good as hunting" as the convoy glided through the streets, cheered on by a jubilant crowd. Later that evening the trams delivered the guests to the Ulster Hall where the Lord Mayor held a banquet in their honour.

The newly appointed General Manager of the Corporation Tramways, Mr Andrew Nance, proved his worth over the formative years of the new undertaking. He decided that the entire horse tram fleet of 171 cars should be replaced by 170 new electric cars and that perhaps 5 or 6 of the horse cars could be converted. During their conversion, their condition proved so sound that it was decided to convert the best 50 horse cars, bringing the strength of the fleet up to 220 in total.

The new cars were built by the Brush Electrical Co of Loughborough and the electrical work was undertaken by Westinghouse. The total cost per car was £586. They seated 54 (22L/32U) which was considered quite large at the time, and were unvestibuled open toppers. Each car had Brill 21E trucks, Westinghouse No 200 motors and 90M controllers. Unladen, the cars weighed around 8 tons each.

Anyone who has visited an airline company, which trains its pilots in simulators, will be impressed by the lengths to which Belfast Corporation went to afford the best possible training for their staff. Many of the original horse drivers were seeking a similar role with the 'horseless wagons', and it must have felt very strange for them to stand on the platform of a moving vehicle not propelled by the heaving haunches of an equine quadruped. Instead of the steady clipity clop of steel clad hooves, they heard the heavy drone of powerful motors. Gone was the strong smell of horse sweat. The trainee driver stood on a mock platform with all the electrical paraphernalia and gadgetry in place. The equipment was electrically connected

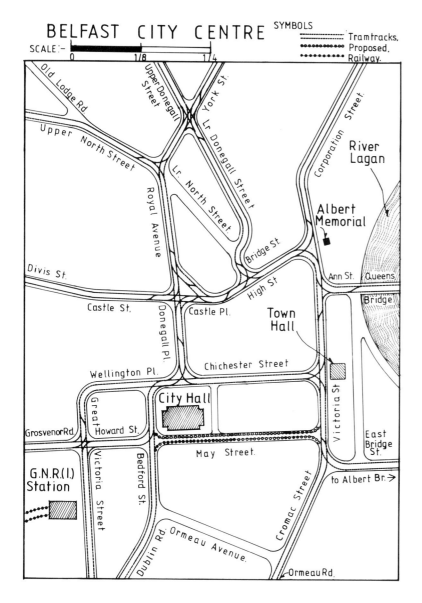

BELFAST CITY CENTRE

only $\frac{1}{4}$" to spare between tram and gates. A slightly off vertical tram, or one weighted to one side, would simply not make it and great care was required not to lurch the tram when entering. The usual caustic remark of motormen taking these sharp corners was "another coat of paint and she wouldn't fit", and they were not far wrong.

The livery of the trams was a vibrant red with heavy gold lining and a white rocker panel and decency screen. An elaborate Corporation coat of arms adorned the waist panels. Longitudinal slatted seats were used in the lower saloon with the usual reversible garden seats on the outside. The lower saloon had a clock in a prominent position. The service could also be described as first class, with a five minute service for most routes throughout the day, or a car every two minutes where the routes were shared and a headway of ten minutes outside the city centre. Castle Junction was to Belfast as Piccadilly Circus was to London and at peak hours, cars would pass every four or five seconds.

In the layout of the system the line on all sides of the city boundary or built up areas continued on, often for a mile or so into the country. This was to promote development along the course of the track work but, surprisingly, the population of Belfast changed little over the years. Around the time of the opening, a special highly illuminated tram passed through the streets after dark. It was reputed to have 1650 electric light bulbs and in the dim gas lit streets of the day would have glowed brilliantly as it passed like a ghostly apparition floating down streets of virtual darkness.

The separate Cavehill and Whitewell Tramway Company (page 54) that ran along the Antrim Road to Glengormley went electric the following year, in 1906, and acquired ten trams very similar to those operated by the Corporation. They provided a 15 minute service and retained the earlier green and cream livery. Little co-ordination between the systems was practiced and passengers often saw the 'connecting tram' just setting off shortly before their own conveyance arrived at the terminus. Mr Nance was anxious to acquire the asset of the CWT. The latter company was financially sound and had no desire to be absorbed by their larger neighbours and this was the cause of much frustration, as Bellevue Park and the amusements were a great attraction to inner city families. However five years later Mr Nance had his way and took control of the CWT in 1911. At last the Corporation could run continuously to Glengormley. The 40 acre park previously mentioned in the ownership of CWT was developed as the Belfast Zoological Gardens and this ensured good patronage of the line, particularly during the summer months.

so that the motormen-to-be would get the real feel of handling an electric motor, controller, circuit breaker, etc. He would spend 30 minutes per day for his first week and then progress on to a real, but passengerless tram with an instructor for a further week. When at last he entered his tram into full service, he was again accompanied by an instructor and only when the motor superintendent was satisfied did he receive his 'certificate of competency' and was permitted to handle a tram in public alone. Accordingly, the record of the Belfast motorman in tram safety was second to none.

Most of the horse tram depots were converted for the new system and a new depot was constructed at Shore Road, but Sandy Row became the main works. It is interesting to note that the full capacity of all depots packed to the brim was 550 cars in all, so expansionary plans were allowed for from the outset. The Falls Park depot alone had a capacity of 210 cars, and was the largest. On account of the many narrow streets, access to several of the depots was extremely tight, often with

Left: **High Street, Belfast in the early years of this century, shortly after electrification of the trams. High Street runs from Castle Place towards Victoria Street and the view is facing east towards the Albert Memorial. Note the fascinating array of horse drawn vehicles, including the coach on the right.**

At this time the Belfast cars were all open toppers with direct stairs and extended roof. Tram No 65 is heading for the Ormeau Road and car No 9 is following behind. Note the traffic policeman in the foreground.

Many of the buildings in this view were to be destroyed in the German air raids of 1941.

RC Ludgate collection

Below: **The interior of Sandy Row workshops in 1905, during the changeover to electric operation. In the foreground are newly constructed Standard Reds Nos 2 and 3 in 'as built' condition, with two more in the background.**

The tram on the right is one of the 50 horse cars converted at Sandy Row for electric operation (Nos 201-250).

RC Ludgate collection

When electrification of the trams took place, further extensions were proposed as follows: -

1 Queen's Road Tramway, opened 1908, from the Belfast and County Down Railway terminus to Queen's Road past its junction with Harland Road to serve the ship-building industry. This was opened by the Belfast Harbour Commission and taken over by the Corporation.

2 Donegall Road Tramway, opened 1913, to run from Shaftesbury Square and terminate at the junction of Donegall Road with the Falls Road.

3 Botanic Avenue Tramway, opened in 1913, to run from Shaftesbury Square and terminate at the junction of University Avenue and the Ormeau Road.

4 Stranmillis Road Tramway, opened in 1913, to run along Stranmillis Road and Lockview Road and terminate at the first lock on the River Lagan.

5 Ligoniel Tramway, opened in 1913, to begin at St Mark's Church and terminate at Mill Avenue.

6 McArt's Fort Tramway (never constructed), to have run from the Antrim Road along the Cavehill Road and terminate at McArt's Fort.

7 Castlereagh Road Tramway, opened in 1913, to begin at Mountpottinger Junction and run via Castlereagh St and Castlereagh Road to terminate at Houston Park.

8 Bloomfield Road Tramway, opened in 1913, to commence at the junction of the Woodstock Road and Beersbridge Road and terminate at the junction between Bloomfield Road and North Road.

9 Oldpark Road Tramway, opened 1913, to run from the Crumlin Road to the Cliftonville Road.

10 Holywood Tramway, (never constructed), to have run from the Old Holywood Road via Demesne Road, and Church Road to its junction with High Street.

The First World War provided a period of stability for tramways in general on account of fuel shortages. The threat of bus competition, which had not yet really presented itself, was curtailed for many years. Inflation, however, which had been almost static for years, rose rapidly and to remedy this it was necessary to increase fares. Also to effect savings resulting from increased costs, it was necessary to curtail non profitable runnings, decrease headways between cars from 10 to 20 minutes and to reduce staff.

Mr Nance's contribution to the Belfast Corporation Tramways was enormous and it is worth saying a few words about the man himself. He was born in Portsmouth in 1847 during the Irish Famine years, and at a young age got a job on the railways. He joined the Belfast Street Tramways when he was 34 years old, taking the position of manager and engineer. He was regarded as an exacting manager, demanding absolute obedience, but was very fair to his staff and was given respect and loyalty throughout his long service. When he took over in Belfast, there were only 8 miles of tramway and under his guidance and control it increased to 50 miles. He was involved with every decision and knew precisely everything that mattered about the company. When the Corporation took over the BST, Nance came with the job. He dealt personally with all issues concerning any large or minor extension or withdrawal of any service. He was noted for his elegance of speech and his concern for the welfare of elderly people.

On one occasion, in 1912, when the Company had made a healthy profit, he rewarded the loyalty of his faithful staff by dividing 10% of the profits equally amongst the 700 staff, so that everyone from the lowliest apprentice to the General Manager received the sum of £4 15s 2d, which was a huge sum in those days. This procedure was found by the auditors of the Company to be illegal and in spite of Mr Nance's best efforts, was never repeated. The staff, however, never forgot his kindness and it strengthened their loyalty to him. When, after 35 years of service, he retired from the Company in 1916, at the age of 69, there was a genuine feeling of loss. He was described as the 'Clifton Robinson' of the Belfast Tramways.

Belfast followed the same evolution in tramcar design as most British cities, but never used bogie trams on account of the physical restrictions en route. The first electric cars were almost identical to the final designs of three-windowed horse cars, with open vestibules and roofless upper decks. As early as 1907, the first experimental top cover was provided with large arched openings and it gave the tram, No 107, the appearance of a floating pavilion. Between 1908 and 1910 the Corporation built 22 new cars to the original Brush design taking the numbers 171 to 192. The CWT cars taken over in

1911 became 193-200, and a further 41 standard cars (251-291) were built from 1913 onwards, these being top covered from new. From 1908 onwards, the earlier open-top cars were gradually rebuilt with top covers, but there was no attempt to vestibule the lower deck, leaving the Belfast motorman very exposed to the wet Ulster weather. The Belfast top covers were of an unusual design. The length of the upper saloon was considerably less than that of the lower saloon and had very deep windows, amost down to floor level. As rebuilt the Belfast cars seated 58 (ex-horse cars, 50). Some remained open-top until scrapped.

When Mr James S D Moffett became the General Manager in 1919, he introduced an all-enclosed type of car, giving full protection to driver and passenger alike. These cars seated 26 in the lower saloon and 42 on the upper, a total of 68, which was not far short of the Dublin bogie car capacity.

In Belfast there was a policy that all new tramcar designs were named after the General Manager responsible for their introduction and this new batch were known as 'Moffetts'. They could be easily recognised by the four large windows in the lower saloon (the standard cars had three), even though they bore the usual livery of red and white with gold lining. From the 1930s all balcony and open top cars were know as 'reds' to distinguish them from later designs which opted for blue. A unique feature of the 'Moffetts' was that the platform had a second opening under the stairs, the purpose of which was to accelerate evacuation of cars at Castle Junction. They proved unsuccessful and were eventually sealed off by continuing the dash panel across the opening.

Between 1920 and 1923 Ireland was embroiled in political conflict that was sometimes violent. In 1921 six of the Ulster counties became Northern Ireland, and the following year the rest of Ireland achieved independence from Britain as the Irish Free State. There was civil strife in both parts of Ireland, with a civil war in the Free State in 1922-23 and inter-community violence in the North, known as 'the Troubles', in the years 1921-1922. The tramway system of Belfast became a target in itself and the object of direct attack.

The Government of the day introduced a curfew in April 1921, and the tram services ceased to operate after 10.00pm. The last homeward bound cars were scheduled to leave around 9.45pm and the last cars from Castle Junction operated to about 10 minutes after 10.00pm. Those who broke the curfew were treated very harshly and were at every risk of being shot. The curfew had severe repercussions for the economy and the social life of the city, but it was a necessary prerequisite for law and order. During these circumstances the trams continued operating, often in the most dangerous of situations, and there were cases of crew being injured and, in one incident, Conductor Mansfield of Ardoyne depot was killed removing a bomb from a tram.

Trams were shot at, set on fire and their passengers attacked and, in some instances, killed. In spite of this, the Corporation continued to provide what could only

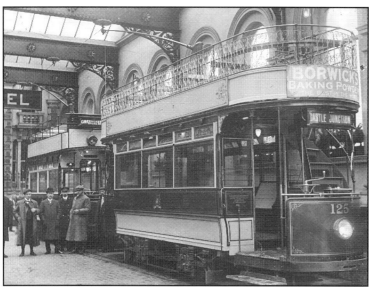

As mentioned on page 108, Belfast trams not only came inside Queens Quay station, but also York Road. This is probably an official photograph taken in 1905 to mark the introduction of the electric service. Note how all the lights are on, reflecting the new-fangledness of electricity! This view is inside the tram bay at York Road. Car No 125 is one of the 170 standard Brush cars which launched electrification. The third railway terminus in Belfast — Great Victoria Street (GNRI) — never had a tram-bay as it was near the city centre with a frequent service passing the front entrance.

RC Ludgate collection

be described as an efficient service under the circumstances. This took a lot of courage on the part of the tramway staff. These attacks on public transport in Belfast were also a feature of the more recent troubles, all adding to the difficulties of providing a good public service.

In the early 1920s, private operators began to run buses in competition with the trams. Belfast Corporation, in the face of bus competition introduced a bus service of their own in 1926, running between the City Hall and the Cavehill Road. It proved very popular and a cross-town service between the Gas Works (Ormeau Road) and Agnes Street (Crumlin Road) quickly followed. In those years a bus proprietor could set up overnight, and should it prove unprofitable, simply move to a different route, abandoning whatever patronage he had developed. These 'pirate' bus companies abided by no schedule and adhered to no fixed stops. They usually set off some minutes before the tram was scheduled to arrive and scooped up the passengers waiting for the tram. They often blocked the tram's approach while they stole their clientele.

In the face of competition, the tramways reduced their fares. The city streets were chaotic without controls and the streets became a veritable battleground between bus and tram. The citizens at first enjoyed being wooed by both concerns and the cheaper fares proved popular, but the chaos and traffic jams soon cancelled the benefit. New byelaws were introduced and basically Belfast Corporation was given a monopoly within the city centre. Private buses could run routes which *commenced* within the City boundary, but only to destinations *outside* it. This decision was a recognition of the basic efficiency of the tramway system, which was considered to be worth protecting.

One of the constraints that affected the tramways was known as the 'Aberdeen clause', or Section 68 of the 1904 Tramways Act. This basically required the tramway to attract sufficient revenue to balance expenditure so that the rate payers were protected. This discouraged tramways from utilising revenue as capital to modernise, or to extend a profitable route and to a degree tied their hands in the face of bus competition. This law also applied in Dundee.

During this bus war episode, Samuel Carlisle was the general manager and, as often happens, if a team does not do well, the manager is sacked. In 1929 Carlisle was replaced by Mr William Chamberlain. He had been previously General Manager in Leeds and the Corporation felt that they needed his expertise to help the tramway. Many of the trams dated from the 1905 electrification, so, starting in 1929, Chamberlain took 50 of the older pre-Moffett 'Standard Red' balcony cars and completely rebuilt them. He vestibuled them top and bottom, providing brown leather upholstered sprung seats and turned them out in a splendid livery of princess blue and white, a colour scheme which was to be extended to other modern cars and remain until the tramway's final years. These trams were initially known as the 'Rebuilds' and were unique in the British Isles for their unusual top covers, which had windows of different heights (see page 122).

Maintaining the now established tradition of buying or

rebuilding 50 trams at a time, in 1930 Mr Chamberlain purchased 50 new cars which resembled the 'Rebuilds' and were known as 'Chamberlains'. At 33 feet long these were the largest trams in the Belfast fleet, with a capacity of 66 passengers. They also had brown leather upholstery and were blue and white in colour. They were equipped with Westinghouse air brakes, Metrovick 50hp motors and Maley and Taunton trucks.

The 50 'Moffetts' were also upgraded with similar equipment and received the blue and white livery. Their redundant Dick Kerr motors were in turn fitted to the 'Rebuilds', which became officially classified as 'DK1s'

By 1929, most of the pirate bus companies had disappeared and slowly passengers began to return to the tramways as the novelty of the motor bus wore off. This brought valuable revenue back to the tramways. The Corporation themselves continued to introduce buses, at first to supplement the tramway system and, by 1935, the overall bus route mileage had risen to 46$\frac{1}{2}$, which was not far behind the total tram mileage of 51$\frac{1}{2}$. Even as the mileage gap narrowed, the trams still served the citizens of Belfast more efficiently and in 1935, for example, carried 111 million passengers as against the buses' 11 million—ten times more.

The Corporation naturally found it cheaper to introduce bus routes than to extend the tramways and continued with this policy. In 1935 Mr Chamberlain was replaced by Col Robert McCreary who was also an engineer. He was responsible for the introduction of fine streamlined modern trams, called 'McCrearys', and again 50 were built. Twenty of the 'McCrearys' were built by the English Electric Co of Preston and the balance were built to their own specification at the Service Motor Works (Albert Bridge Road). In many ways the 'McCrearys' were more advanced than their Dublin counterparts, in that they had folding platform doors and had a more modern livery.

Although modern trams in terms of equipment, the 'Chamberlains', built only five years earlier, had been traditional tramcars in terms of bodywork. Alongside them the 'McCrearys' looked much more modern.

McCreary had sought to emulate the features of 1930s bus design in an attempt to modernise the traditional tram concept. The sides or skirtings descended lower to almost camouflage the tram trucks. The more rounded appearance conveyed a sense of streamlining, and the livery was now mostly blue with some white relief, again a style more typical of buses. Although all the windows could be raised or lowered, there were raised vents built into the panel work over the window. The roof was domed, typical of bus design of the day.

The new image was mainly a repackaging of an old concept, in the face of the massive onslaught of motor bus competition. More comfort and greater speed were provided. It appeared to be too late, however, as the general view was that trams and tracks were outdated. Hardly had the 'McCreary' cars appeared when the decision to abandon tramcar operations became the accepted stance.

This, in many respects, was a backward step, for which many cities paid dearly, as improvements in the tramcar put them on an equal status with any bus competition in terms of efficiency and viability. No bus system could compete with them, where mass movement of crowds was concerned. But the motor bus had now entered centre stage. The curtain was dropped to hide the advantages of the new tram design. The city fathers failed or refused to notice their great advances, and the scene was set for their untimely extinction.

In the mass destruction of city tramways that ensued, Belfast could not hold back the onslaught and soon the closures began. In some cities, such as Edinburgh, Liverpool, Sheffield, and Glasgow, it looked as if the tram might survive as technological advances in tram design made them in many respects superior to the motor bus, but the die was cast and to retain the tram was considered retrograde. Instead of tram and bus working together to best serve the community in their own appropriate ways, one system was set against the other, to the ultimate loss of the community they served.

In October 1936, the section of track along the outer portion on the Cregagh Road was abandoned on account of the poor state of the permanent way. This decision was the beginning of the abandonment. The following year, the service to Mountpottinger was also abandoned for the same reasons. The policy was now to abandon rather than replace.

The Belfast Corporation Act of 1930 permitted the use of trolley buses on any route operated by trams. However, it was not until 1938 that the Corporation chose to exercise this option. The tram track along the Falls Road was in a poor state of repair and the Corporation chose this opportunity to introduce the first trolley bus, on 28th March of that year. The advantage of using the trolley bus was that it availed of the overhead cabling system which was already in place. It was necessary to provide two overhead cables instead of the usual one, to carry the return current which, in the case of trams, was carried by the track.

The Falls Road conversion was a trial and 14 prototype trolley buses were built to eight different designs. All were large six wheeled vehicles capable of carrying 68 passengers, equal to the trams. After one year of operation, the new mode of transport had proven itself both popular and economic and in 1939 it was decided that tramcar operation would formally be abandoned in favour of the electric trolley bus. Belfast was the only city in Ireland to introduce the trolley bus system and eventually had the largest fleet of trolley buses outside London.

It was planned to fully phase out the trams over a period of five years, by 1944. However, the intervention of the Second World War and shortage of fuel, etc, gave the tramways a reprieve. During the war every available tramcar was rapidly ushered back into service to cope with the shortage of motor buses and it was almost impossible to acquire further trolley buses. So the tram came back and carried out sterling work for the duration of the war.

When it was possible, the conversion to both motor bus and trolley bus quietly continued in piecemeal fashion. The Cregagh route was converted to trolley bus in February 1941 and the Castlereagh tram service was replaced in June the same year. In March 1942 the Stormont route was converted and extended. Later, that year the Dundonald via Queens

Bridge service was next to go, but it was not until after the war that serious changeover took place.

With the abandonment of the Bloomfield route in May 1946 the East Belfast trolley bus scheme was completed and the Corporation could now turn its attention elsewhere. By 1948, after further tram route abandonments over 250 million passengers were carried by Belfast Corporation with the trams carrying half this figure and equal to both motor bus and trolley bus combined. It should have been very obvious that the tram's superior crowd moving ability could not be surpassed, even considering their weakened state. In 1949, the longest route (to Glengormley), operated at various times by steam, horse and electric tram, was now to experience a new system, the trolley bus. In August 1950, the LMS Station tram service (via Corporation Street) was abandoned. The Greencastle tram services were abandoned in October 1950 and were converted to trolley bus operation. In April 1951 the Oldpark and Malone Road tram routes were closed, followed by the Stranmillis Road and Queen's Road services in July.

It was quickly realised that more buses were required to replace trams, not only on account of the greater carrying capacity of the trams, but also because the trams unique ability to move crowds was hard to emulate. Procuring more trolley and motor buses took longer than expected and it was not until November 1952 that the Balmoral, Ballygomartin and Springfield routes ceased operation. By October 1953, the trams were reduced to peak periods only on the Queen's Road and Ligoniel routes. A quantity of ex-London double deck buses were brought in to complete the conversions and trams were withdrawn on a daily basis as they were replaced.

The final day of tram operation came on 28th February 1954. By this date only ten McCreary cars remained in service, corrosion having led to the withdrawal of the others. It is very sad that no representatives of these fine cars survived and it is testimony to the reliability and durability of the traditional tramcar design that on the final day of operation twelve Chamberlains had the honour of terminating tramcar services.

These cars made their way, setting off at short intervals from Queen's Road, via High Street and Shankill Road to Ardoyne Depot. The trams were packed with well wishers who came to see them off and young people stood on the fenders clinging on to any part that afforded a finger grip. The last tram was No 389 and the motorman was Joseph Weir, with forty years of service, and his conductor was Alexander Mackle. Col McCreary and Samuel Carlisle were there, with the General Manager of the day, Mr J Mackle. They were accompanied by the Lord Mayor of Belfast, Sir Percival Brown, and other dignitaries. Thus ended 82 years of tram transport in Belfast, almost 50 of which were with the electric trams.

I could not end this chapter more appropriately than by using the title of the lovely booklet published in 1979 on Belfast trams — *Gone, but not forgotten.*

Top left: **A group of workmen posed in front of three open-top trams at Mountpottinger Depot in East Belfast. The photograph was probably taken at the opening of the depot and is interesting for showing the original spelling on the destination blinds. It was soon abbreviated to 'M Pottinger'.** *RC Ludgate collection*

Top right: **This unidentified open-topper is a former horse car and has been decorated for a visit of the Prince of Wales, possibly to open the new Stormont Parliament in 1932. It is seen here leaving Sandy Row depot to tour the system. Behind is No 213, another former horse tram, now with its top deck covered.**

RC Ludgate collection

Centre: **The standard open top Belfast trams were rebuilt with balcony ends between 1907 and 1920. Note the very short upper deck saloon on these cars. In later years they became known as 'Standard Reds'. The photograph clearly dates from World War One.**

RC Ludgate collection

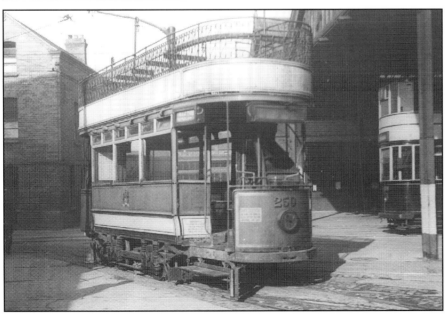

Bottom: **Another ex-horse car, but this time still running as an open-top car. No 250 was one of seven cars (244-250) which never received top deck covering, and were retained for traffic to football matches and excursion work in the summer. The ex-horse cars differed from the Standard Reds in some respects, most noticeably in being fitted with 5'6" truck wheel spacing instead of the standard 6'6".**

These cars were very popular with visiting enthusiasts, as open toppers had long disappeared in most British cities. Nos 244, 249 and 250 survived after 1948 on snow plough duties at Ardoyne, Sandy Row and Mountpottinger Depots, and No 250 is so fitted in this view at Mountpottinger. Nos 244 and 250 were scrapped in 1951, leaving No 249 to survive into preservation.

RC Ludgate

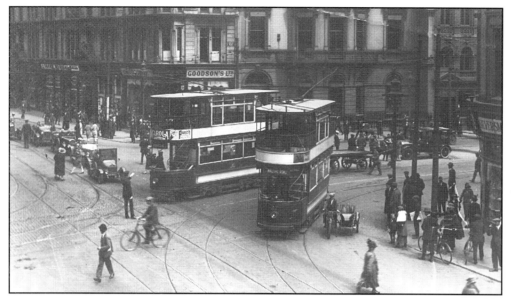

Top: **Castle Junction around 1930, showing a variety of transport including cars, trams, bicycles, a motor cycle with side car, a taxi, and a dray wagon. The presence of no fewer than five open touring cars in Royal Avenue suggests that some sort of rally is on. Perhaps it is Ards TT week.**

The two trams are of course Standard Reds. No 27 is on a Malone Road service and will be passing the City Hall. No 115 has just crossed Castle Junction from Castle Street and the Falls Road. The Falls route went over to trolley bus operation in 1938 and at that date the track layout at Castle Junction was simplified.

JR Bainbridge
RC Ludgate collection

Centre left: **Top covered former horse car No 227 is seen here at Knock Road depot in East Belfast. This depot remained in use until 1946, although the main Dundonald route was abandoned several years earlier. Like the Standard Reds, a number of ex-horse cars survived the Second World War and No 227 is a good example.** *RC Ludgate*

Centre right: **Serious damage is evident in this view of Salisbury Avenue depot in North Belfast, just after the German air-raid of 15th/16th April 1941. This was the only depot to sustain a direct hit. The two standard red trams in the foreground, Nos 112 and 104 were both scrapped a month later. Notice that the balcony roof on No 112 has collapsed.** *RC Ludgate collection*

Bottom: **Standard Red No 2, built in 1905, is about to enter Sandy Row depot after a morning working. Entry to the depot was by Gaffikin Street and the track swung to the left, as shown here, to allow the trams to swing round the sharp curve into the depot, which was behind the photographer.**

Sandy Row did not appear on destination blinds, and for some unknown reason Donegall Pass was used, even though Donegall Pass, on the east side of Shaftesbury Square, did not even have tram tracks.

Like most Standard Reds, No 2 was rebuilt as a balcony tram before the First World War. The tram is in a rather run-down state with the front headlamp broken. *RC Ludgate*

Top: **Chamberlain No 351 running along Station Street on a No 51 working to Queen's Road, 1¹/₂ miles further on. Queen's Quay terminus is just round the corner to the right. At this time the docks in Belfast were working at full capacity and there is plenty of evidence of this in the background. Note how the road is still completely cobbled. The Ford coal lorry in the foreground was registered around 1944. The construction of the cross harbour bridges in 1995 has completely obliterated this area.**

WG Robertson, ColourRail

Centre: **Chamberlain No 350 emerging from Ardoyne depot through the impressive entrance arch. Another tram is visible in the background inside the shed. After leaving the depot the track swung sharply to the right and then left again before dividing into double track. Ardoyne depot was built in 1913 and in 1954 was the last depot to close. It had 12 tracks into the extensive shed and was capable of holding 84 trams.**

WG Robertson, ColourRail

Bottom: **Another Chamberlain, this time No 349, is seen here on the Woodvale Road with a Ligoniel-bound tram. Woodvale Road was about half way along this route and was really an extension of the Shankill Road, carrying it over to the Crumlin Road. The tram is quite clearly climbing in this view. The Chamberlain fleet consisted of 50 cars numbered 342-391, built in 1930. They had Maley and Thornton 8'0" swing link trucks, two 50hp Metrovick motors and Brush bodies. At 33'0" they were the largest cars in the Belfast fleet.**

WG Robertson, ColourRail

This superb photograph, from the top deck of a Ligoniel-bound tram, gives a grandstand view of Royal Avenue on a Saturday afternoon in 1953. The view includes 3 trams, 6 trolley buses, 3 petrol buses and a gaggle of bikes, vans and cars including some with operating semaphore signals. The nearest tram is No 438, a streamlined McCreary car. It was one of the 20 McCreary cars built in England by English Electric in 1935-6, the other 30 being built in Belfast. The McCreary cars were 32'0" long and seated 64 passengers (24/40).   *WG Robertson, ColourRail*

This scene is on the Ligoniel Road, and is particularly interesting because of the road works going on in the foreground. The tar boiler on the left was a common sight in the 1950s, before asphalt was introduced as a road surface. Chamberlain No 350 is about half a mile from the terminus, on its way back to the City Hall. Another Chamberlain is a short distance behind. To the right of the tram is the rectory and church of St Mark's (Church of Ireland). The early Belfast trams had a red and white livery, and the blue and white scheme shown here was introduced in 1929. It was similar to the livery Chamberlain had earlier introduced in Leeds. Any cream evident was due to weathering.   *WG Robertson, ColourRail*

McCreary car No 430 is approaching College Square East from Wellington Place and is being overtaken by an OZ registered Commer van, virtually brand new in this 1953 view. The tram appears to be empty and is probably coming from the City Hall to turn in College Square" (see page 108, centre). The well-known gents outfitting firm of Parsons and Parsons can be seen on the left. Nowadays the site of the jewellers on the right is occupied by the local history bookshop *Familia*.   *WG Robertson, ColourRail*

This is Donegall Square North with the City Hall out of sight behind the photographer. The large building on the left is the Water Commissioners' Office and is now part of Marks and Spencer. At this time Chichester Street, in the background, was bi-directional. An Austin taxi, followed by a Vauxhall await their fares. Note the shiny-top caps worn by the taxi drivers — now a thing of the past. Three trolley buses, in Chichester Street, and an Austin car complete the scene. Tram 364 is probably heading off to go round Donegal Place.   *WG Robertson, ColourRail*

Top: **This view shows one of the McCreary cars built at the Service Motor Works, Belfast (393-422). These cars were distinguishable from the English Electric-built version by the lower position of the headlamp.**

No 397 is emerging from the turn round loop at Ligoniel terminus, which is just out of sight down the steep incline to the left. The procedure was for the tram to arrive here, switch tracks, reverse the trolley pole, and then come back onto the Ligoniel Road, where the tram waited for passengers to board. The tram destination blind reads 'City Hall', a route indication which only came into us towards the end to replace 'Castle Junction'.

The Ligoniel Road itself continues up the hill in the background. The small structure to the right of the stone wall behind the tram is a gents toilet primarily intended for platform staff. The mill houses on the left have since been demolished.   *WG Robertson, ColourRail*

Centre: **The Fifty Shilling Tailors is prominent in this scene, as McCreary car No 438 turns the corner from Royal Avenue into Castle Place on a summer Saturday in 1953. This picture was almost certainly taken a few seconds after the one at the top of page 118. The livery of No 438 in this near broadside view makes interesting comparison with the black and white shot of No 392 opposite. Note how the lining has gone from the doors and the upper deck panelling.**

The McCreary cars had 50hp motors, some by Metrovick and some by Crompton Parkinson. The class had air brakes and folding entrance doors. The bodies largely used metal components, rather than timber and this feature created problems with corosion so that at closure only 10 remained in service out of the original 50. No 438 was an English Electric car and the Belfast built cars (393-422) carried their headlamps lower (see above).

WG Robertson, ColourRail

Bottom: **This view of No 427 was taken just after the tram had emerged onto the Crumlin Road from the Ardoyne Road, seen on the right. Ardoyne tram depot is to the right behind the corrugated iron fence. The absence of buildings is evidence of bomb damage during the 1941 blitz. To the right of the tram is a cast iron tram stage post. Note the lovely Riley car parked at the pavement.**

WG Robertson, ColourRail

Top left: McCreary tram No 392 brand new in 1935. There were fifty of these cars, numbered 392 - 441. The first two (392/393) were non-standard in having separate driver's cabs. The livery of the McCreary cars was very elaborate with gold lining in abundance. Comparison with the colour photograph opposite will show how the livery was simplified later. In particular the white roof gave way to a more practical blue. Whilst Nos 392 and 423 - 441 were built by English Electric, Nos 393 - 422 were built at the Service Motor Works in Belfast, on frames supplied by Hurst Nelson.

RC Ludgate collection

Top right: One unusual vehicle in the Belfast fleet was stores car No 8. Although sometimes described as having been built in 1931 by HMS Catherwood Ltd on the chassis of a standard car, an ex-employee claimed to have been involved in its construction at Sandy Row depot. Its 5' 6" wheelbase truck came from a converted horse car (the original No 8 would have had a 6' 6" wheelbase truck). This view shows No 8 proceeding along East Bridge Street in 1945, probably towards Mountpottinger depot. The background includes a McCreary tram, a trolley bus and an NIRTB low bridge double deck bus.

RC Ludgate

Centre: Water car B in action on the Falls Road, near its junction with the Donegall Road. On the left are the grounds of Our Lady's Hospital, and on the right is the site of the present De La Salle Estate. Two watering cars (A and B) were built by Mountain and Gibson Ltd of Bury, Lancs in 1905-6, and they lasted until 1932 and 1942 respectively. The improvement in road surfaces in the 1930s made them redundant. I am sure that the watering cars were given a wide berth by pedestrians and cyclists alike.

RC Ludgate collection

Bottom: After the Second World War the steady closure of tram routes saw an equally steady withdrawal of the older trams, particularly the Standard Reds. This scene is at the permanent way yard in Mountpottinger depot in April 1951, where Standard Reds Nos 88 and 14 await scrapping. Someone is posing at the controls of No 88, even though the trolley pole suggests it is going in the opposite direction! The yard contains an interesting assortment of tramway material. Judging by the similar position of the trolley pole on the car in the background, the trams were driven under power to their final resting place.

RC Ludgate

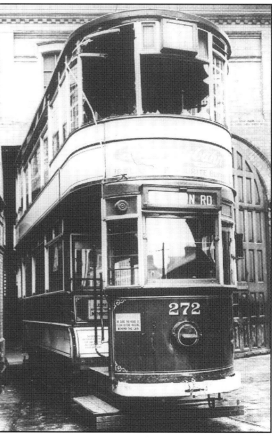

Top left: **No 164 was an extremely significant tram in the Belfast fleet, which explains her choice for a tram enthusiasts' special in this May 1952 scene. The tram is rounding the little used sharp curve which connects the Albert Bridge Road with the Newtownards Road. Behind it is the now demolished wall of what was then the largest ropeworks in the world.**

No 164 had the distinction of being the first Belfast car to be painted in the new blue and cream livery in 1929, when it was rebuilt from a balcony car to the DK1 class. Fifty were so treated, the others being 21, 22, 31, 35, 78, 123, 159, 186 and 251-291. The Rebuilds utilised the redundant 40hp Dick Kerr motors and Brush trucks from the rebuilt Moffett trams (see below). The upper deck arrangement on the Rebuilds was unusual and arose from the fact that they retained the windows of the original, smaller, upper deck saloon. *RC Ludgate*

Top right: **The Belfast tramway suffered considerable damage in the German air raids of April and May 1941. Here No 272 is seen outside the main works entrance in Napier Street (Sandy Row) with superficial damage to the upper deck. Note the tape on the windows and the blackout covers on the head-lamps. No 272 was a DK1 rebuild of a Standard Red built in 1913.** *RC Ludgate*

Bottom: **Moffett car No 311, on Greencastle service No 7 is seen here waiting outside the old main post office in Royal Avenue on a summer morning in 1946. Comparison with the view of No 292 opposite will show how the original door under the stairs has been sheeted over. The Moffett cars were built by Brush Electrical, and cost £2500 each. The cars were originally mounted on Brush Brill-type trucks of 7'6" wheelbase and were fitted with two Dick Kerr DK30 motors and DB1 K4 controllers. They seated 26 downstairs on longitudinal wooden seating and 42 upstairs.** *RC Ludgate*

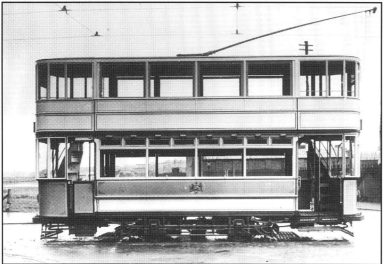

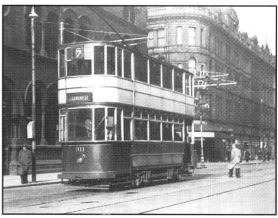

Above: **In 1920 James Moffett, the new General Manager, began modernising the Belfast trams with the introduction of the first all-enclosed cars in Ireland. No 292 was the first of these 50 cars, which were numbered 292-341. It is seen here, as built, in red and white livery. Notice the unusual feature of the extra exit door under the stairs, intended to speed loading at Castle Junction. These doors were unsuccessful because passengers ignored them, and they created a draught which was unpleasant for the drivers. They were removed when these cars were rebuilt in 1929-32. The car is seen here with its original Brill type trucks and Dick Kerr motors.**

RC Ludgate collection

Top: A long-vanished land-mark in Belfast — the old gate lodge at Botanic Gardens, at the junction of the Malone, Stranmillis and University Roads. In this view Moffett car No 315, looking in good condition, has just turned into the Stranmillis Road on a route No 52 working. Behind is Moffett No 304 on the Malone Road Route.

The Stranmillis route went over to buses in July 1951, and the Malone Road route the following November.

RC Ludgate

Centre: On a wet April day in 1950, Moffett No 295 is city bound on the Oldpark Road. It bears the pre-1951 Route number 21. William Chamberlain rebuilt and modernised the Moffett trams in 1929-32, remounting the whole class on Maley and Taunton swing link trucks of 8'0" wheelbase, with 50hp Metrovick motors (10 had Crompton Parkinson motors). The cars also received the new blue and white livery and were given upholstered seats.

RC Ludgate

Bottom: The last day of tram operation in Belfast was Saturday 28th February 1954. Since the previous October, trams had been used for rush-hour services only.

This is the scene at Queen's Road terminus as a procession of 12 Chamberlain cars, led by No 347, waited to depart for a final run via Station Road, Queen's Bridge, Ann Street, Victoria Street, High Street, Castle Street, Royal Avenue, North Street, Peter's Hill, Shankill Road and Woodvale Road to Ardoyne depot. Ironically, due to corrosion, only ten of the modern McCreary trams survived to the closure.

This procession marked the end of tram operation in Ireland's cities, leaving only the Fintona horse tram and the Hill of Howth trams to carry the banner for another few years.

RC Ludgate

Preservation

The preservation of our heritage, whether it be transport, architecture or prehistory, is very important as it reflects part of what we are. As with other forms of transport, from early horse drawn vehicles to jet propelled aircraft, trams were conceived by man to serve his needs. In some strange way the circle has turned fully and the community now serves the vehicles themselves by rescuing them from destruction, providing covered accommodation and eventually restoring them and putting them on display. Such exhibitions not only evoke happy memories and nostalgia but are also links in the chain of progress and have an important educational value. They are historical stepping stones over which our technological feet have passed and stepping stones show us from whence we came.

NORTHERN IRELAND

Recognition of the importance of preserving our transport heritage is far more advanced in Northern Ireland than in the Irish Republic. There is a very deliberate policy of preserving the past and transport falls into this category. In 1954 the Museum and Art Gallery at Stranmillis, Belfast set up the nucleus of a transport collection, at a time when trams and steam trains were fast disappearing. Mr Eric Montgomery and Sir John Harcourt (then Belfast's Lord Mayor) were prime movers in this.

The collection was initially located in the old rail-motor shed at Queen's Quay station but, in 1961, it was moved to more spacious accommodation at Witham Street. In 1962 the Transport Museum was separated from the Museum and Art Gallery and came under the direct control of Belfast Corporation. Over the years the Museum had actively searched out and collected vehicles which were considered worthy of preserving. When the famous Fintona Horse Tram came out of service in 1957, there was a home ready to receive it.

Trams were not only sought out as they were withdrawn from service, but items long thought lost were discovered. For example, in 1961, the body of an old Belfast horse tram was located at Coolshanagh, Co Monaghan, and it is difficult to see how this and other items would have survived without the swift action of the Belfast Transport Museum authorities.

As the museum structure developed in Northern Ireland, the Belfast Transport Museum was amalgamated, around 1970, with the Ulster Folk Museum at Cultra near Belfast, to become the Ulster Folk and Transport Museum. In 1995 the tram collection was moved to a new purpose-built road transport gallery at Cultra. With eight restored trams on display, the Transport Museum is certainly well worth a visit.

I understand that support in the region of £6,000,000 has been given in recent years, to provide the new galleries for road and rail transport, in recognition of the importance of transport memorabilia in our social heritage. Part of the new display is featured on the rear cover.

REPUBLIC OF IRELAND

In the Republic of Ireland matters are very different. Recognition of the need for a museum to preserve transport goes back to 1942, when a society was formed by the forerunners of the present National Transport Museum, to rescue and preserve Dublin City trams, complete with bogies and trucks, in running order. In many cases, the purchase costs were paid by the members themselves, while an attempt was made to awaken public interest in the construction of covered accommodation. However, the Society met with indifference and lack of support, and several of the early acquisitions sadly perished.

When the Dublin tram system closed in 1949, three trams — Nos 129 (Standard), 132 (Luxury), and 328 (Balcony) — were purchased and brought out to Howth, where they were located adjacent to the Hill of Howth tram depot. The Society knew that it was only a matter of time before the Hill of Howth tramway would be closed, and anticipated that the Dublin trams could be brought into the defunct depot. It was hoped to keep a small section of track for running, perhaps as far as Sutton Cross. However this enterprising plan received no support from the authorities.

In 1959, three Hill of Howth trams — Nos 3, 9 and 11 (the Works Car) — were purchased for a small sum, on condition that they were removed from the premises. Accommodation was kindly made available at Guinness' Brewery, though the Dublin trams still lay at Howth. Endless efforts were made to create public interest, but in the meantime the exposed Dublin trams deteriorated due to the attentions of vandals, souvenir hunters and the weather. In the end, the authorities regarded them as a danger and ordered their destruction.

Even the Hill of Howth trams, which had been offered accommodation at Guinness' Brewery, suffered from souvenir hunters, to the extent that the Brewery asked for them to be removed. Premier Dairies at Monkstown agreed to take No 9, but no home could be found for the other two and they were scrapped around 1965. Even No 9, in the years that followed, lost so many fittings that she finally arrived at the TMSI premises, in 1974, as a decaying shell.

The loss of five of the first six trams acquired by the Museum was very disheartening to the founding members. Despite this they have, in the last twenty years, searched out and found replacement examples of the Dublin trams. The first was 'Lucan bogie' No 284, which arrived at the Castleruddery depot of the TMSI about 1974. More acquisitions arrived in the 1980s — Giant's Causeway No 9 from Youghal, Co Cork; former London Transport trailer tram No T24 (which turned up in Abbeyleix!); and DUTC No 253, another 'Lucan bogie'. A grant of £20,000 from the National Lottery enabled the almost immediate restoration of No 253.

The Museum hopes to restore No 284 as a Balcony car, and aims to acquire one of the two extant Luxury cars. This will be expensive (in the region of £30,000) and sponsorship would be essential for the project.

List of Preserved Irish Trams

ULSTER FOLK AND TRANSPORT MUSEUM, Cultra, Co Down, N Ireland
All trams in this museum are fully restored but none are in working order.

Horse Trams
GNRI Fintona horse tram No 381. Built 1883, by Metropolitan Carriage and Wagon Co. Double-deck open-top and open front car.

Belfast Street Tramways car No 118, built by the BST in 1885 and withdrawn 1905. Double-deck open-top and open front car.

Steam Trams
Portstewart Tramway No 2, built by Kitson and Co Ltd of Leeds in 1883. 0-4-0T enclosed tramway locomotive.

Castlederg and Victoria Bridge 4 wheel carriage No 3. A recent acquisition rescued from a farm.

Electric Trams
Giant's Causeway No 2 on a 4 wheel truck. Non-motorised saloon car, built in 1883 by the Midland Carriage and Wagon Co.

Giant's Causeway No 5 on a 4 wheel truck. Non-motorised 5 bench open toast rack, built in 1885.

Bessbrook and Newry No 2. Bogie electric single-deck saloon car, with original 1885 motors. The saloon body came from Dublin and Lucan trailer No 24.

GNRI Hill of Howth open-top double-deck vestibuled bogie car No 4. Built by Brush Electric of Loughborough in 1901. Brill 22E bogies with two 30hp motors. Blue and cream livery.

Belfast Corporation open-top double-deck vestibuled 4-wheel car No 249, converted from an earlier horse tram in 1905. On Brill 21E 5'6" truck with two 35hp motors. Red and White livery.

Belfast Corporation Chamberlain car No 357. Fully enclosed 4-wheel car, built in 1930 by Brush Electric. Maley and Taunton 8'0" swing-link truck with two 50hp motors. Blue and white livery

NATIONAL TRAMWAY MUSEUM, Crich, Derbyshire

GNRI Hill of Howth vestibuled open-top bogie car No 10, built by GF Milnes in 1902 on Peckham 14D-5bogies. This car is in full working order, but is running on 4'8½" bogies. It is identical to No 9 at the Howth Museum. At present it is on static display only and is in GNRI grained mahogany livery.

ORANGE TROLLEY MUSEUM, Perris, California, USA

GNRI Hill of Howth open-top bogie electric car No 2, built by Brush Electric in 1901, on Brill 22E bogies. In full running order. Identical to No 4 in Cultra. Blue and cream livery.

NATIONAL TRANSPORT MUSEUM, Howth Castle Demesne, Howth, Co Dublin
The trams at this museum are at various stages of restoration as indicated beside each item.

Electric Trams
Giant's Causeway electric car No 9. Built by the Midland Carriage and Wagon Co, probably in 1883, in which case it is the oldest surviving electric tramcar in the world. Body only, no undercarriage. (Partly restored)

Dublin United Tramways Directors' Car, built at Spa Road Works, Dublin in 1901. Dupont Lorain Brierly truck. (Rescued after severe fire damage in 1980s. Restoration is a long term project)

GNRI Hill of Howth vestibuled open-top bogie car No 9, built by Milnes of Shropshire in 1902 on Peckham bogies. (Restored to GNRI grained mahogany livery, no motors or running gear)

London Transport trailer tram No T24, built by Brush in 1914. No undercarriage. It is to be converted to run as DUTC open-front electric car No 224. (Under restoration)

Dublin United Tramways fully enclosed Lucan bogie car No 253, built at Spa Road Works, Dublin in 1928. No undercarriage or seating. (Body fully restored to DUTC green and white livery)

Dublin United Tramways fully enclosed Lucan bogie car No 284, built at Spa Road Works, Dublin in 1928. No undercarriage or seating. This car is to be converted to a bogie balcony car. (Awaiting restoration)

HULL MUSEUM OF TRANSPORT

Portstewart Tramway steam tram locomotive No 1, built by Kitson of Leeds in 1882. 0-4-0T similar to No 2 at Cultra.

Trams in existence but not preserved

Cork City Tramways body of an open-top electric car, one of the 1901 batch (29-35). Parts of upper deck railings extant. In use as a clothes drying shed.

Dublin United Tramways enclosed 4-wheel standard cars Nos 279 (1924) and 291 (1923).

Dublin United Tramways Luxury 4-wheel car No 22, built at Spa Road Works, Dublin in 1935.

Dublin United Tramways Luxury bogie cars Nos 300 (1933) and 317 (1934), both built at Spa Road Works, Dublin.

STATISTICAL INFORMATION

SYSTEM	Gauge	Opened	Mileage	Trams
Dublin Tramways Co	5'3"	1872-75	16	c76
North Dublin Street Trams	5'3"	1875	8 $^1/_2$	c36
Dublin Central Tramways	5'3"	1878-79	7 $^1/_2$	c30
Blackrock and Kingstown	5'3"	1883	2	c 6
Dublin Southern Districts	5'3"/4'0"	1879-96	6	c24

DUBLIN AREA HORSE TRAM COMPANIES
The first three joined to form the Dublin United Tramways in 1881. The other two companies were taken over by the DUTC in 1896.

HORSE TRAM SYSTEMS

SYSTEM	Gauge	Opened	Mileage	Trams	Electrified	Closed	Survivors	Comments
Belfast	4'8$^1/_2$"	1872-92	33	171	1905	—	118	Initially 5'3" gauge
Cork	5'3"	1872	2	6	never	1875	none	see bottom table for later Cork electric system
Derry	4'8$^1/_2$"	1897	2	9	never	1919	none	Some purchased second hand from Belfast
Dublin	5'3"	1872-79	32	181*	1896-1901	—	none	*Plus those inherited from constituents (see above)
Fintona	5'3"	1854	0 $^3/_4$	2*	never	1957	381	*First car 1854-83, second 1883-1957
Galway	3'0"	1879	2 $^1/_4$	12	never	1919	none	
Loughgilly	1'10"	1897	2 $^1/_2$	1	never	1919	none	
Rostrevor	2'10"	1877	3	13	never	1915	none	

STEAM TRAM SYSTEMS

SYSTEM	Gauge	Opened	Locos	Trailers	Mileage	Electrified	Closed	Survivors	Comments
Castlederg	3'0"	1884	6	5	7	never	1933	No 3 trailer	Three of the locos are railway type
Cavehill	4'8"	1882	3	6	3 $^1/_2$	1906	—	none	See next table
Clogher Valley	3'0"	1887	9	13	37	never	1942	none	Two of the locos were railway type
D & Blessington	5'3"	1888	12	10	21	never	1932	one railcar	Two petrol-electric cars and two diesel railcars ran on this line
Dublin & Lucan	3'0"	1881	7	11	9 $^1/_2$	1900	—	part of No 24	(On Bessbrook & Newry No 2)
Dublin S Districts	5'3"	1879	4	see electric section				none	Used experimentally 1882-4
Giant's Causeway	3'0"	1883	4	see electric section				none	Used in town of Portrush due to third rail
Portstewart	3'0"	1882	3	4	1 $^3/_4$	never	1926	Nos 1&2	(Steam locomotives)

ELECTRIC TRAM SYSTEMS

SYSTEM	Gauge	Opened	Electrified	Mileage	Cars built	Fleet size	Highest No	Last tram	Survivors	Comments
Belfast	4'9"	—	1905	51 $^1/_2$	441	c340	441	1954	249, 357	
Bessbrook/ Newry	3'0"	1885	—	3	4*	9	7	1948	2 and 6	*Plus 5 trailer cars
Cavehill	4'8$^1/_2$"	—	1906	3 $^1/_2$	10	10	10	(1911)	none	Absorbed by BCT
Clontarf/H Howth	5'3"	1900	—	9 $^1/_4$	12	12	312	1941	none	Operated by DUTC
Cork	2'11$^1/_2$"	1898	—	10	35	35	35	1931	one car*	*used as a shed
Dublin & Lucan	3'6"	—	1900	8	9	15	19	1925	none	Reopened by DUTC in 1928
Dublin S Districts	5'3"	—	1896	8	32*	32*	62	(1896)	none	*Plus 30 trailers All to DUTC 1896
Dublin United T	5'3"	—	1897-1901	61	608**	331	330	1949	see page 125	** See footnote
Giant's Causeway	3'0"	1883	—	8	9*	24	24	1949	2, 5, 9	*Plus 15 trailers
Hill of Howth	5'3"	1901	—	5 $^1/_4$	10	10	11*	1959	2, 4, 9, 10	*Tower wagon

**This figure includes 30 DSDT trailers, and 86 former horse cars, converted to electric operation. It does not include the 32 DSDT powered cars, and regards all trams added after 1918 as new rather than rebuilds.

BIBLIOGRAPHY

GENERAL BOOKS

The Golden Age of Tramways, Charles Clapper, David and Charles, 1961.
Tramcars, JH Price, Ian Allan 1963.
Trams in Colour, J Joyce, Blandford, 1970.
The Critch Mineral Railways, 'Dowie', Tramway Publications, 1971.
History of Tramcars, RJ Buckley, David and Charles, 1975.
British Trams — a Pictorial Survey, LF Folkard, Bradford Barton, 1978 (Belfast, Fintona, Hill of Howth).
British Tramway Guide, PH Abell, privately published, 1984 (Hill of Howth).
100 Years of British Electric Tramways, E Jackson-Stevens, David and Charles, 1985.
Classic Tramcars, RJS Wiseman, Ian Allan, 1986.
Trams on the Road, David Gladwin, Batsford, 1990.
Heritage Trams, Dennis Gill, Trambooks, 1991.
Through the Cities, the Revolution in Light Rail, Michael Barry, Frankfurt Press, 1991.
British and Irish Tramway Systems Since 1945, MH Waller and P Waller, Ian Allan, 1992 (Belfast, Bessbrook and Newry, Dublin, Fintona, Giant's Causeway, Hill of Howth).
The Classic Trams, P Waller, Ian Allan, 1993.

BOOKS ON IRISH TRAMS
General
The Great Northern Railway of Ireland - Past Present and Future, K Murray, Dundalk, 1944.
The Narrow Gauge Railways of Ireland, H Fayle, Greenlake, 1946.
Ulster Tramways and Light Railways, DG McNeill, Belfast Transport Museum, 1956.
Some Industrial Railways of Ireland, Walter McGrath, Cork 1959.
Transport in Ireland 1880-1910, P Flanagan, Transport Research Associates, 1969.
Railway History in Pictures, Ireland Vol 1 & 2, A McCutcheon, David and Charles, 1969, 1970.
The Irish Narrow Gauge Railway, JDCA Prideaux, David and Charles, 1981.
The Trams of Ireland in Old Picture Postcards, Ian F Finlay, European Library, Netherlands, 1984.
A Tour of the Causeway Coast, C Dallat, Friars Bush Press, 1990.

Belfast
Belfast Corporation Tramways 1905-1954, JM Maybin, Light Rail Transit Association.
Gone But Not Forgotten, Belfast Trams 1872-1954, RA Hunter, RC Ludgate, J Richardson, RPSI and Irish Transport Trust 1979.
A Nostalgic Look at Belfast Trams Since 1945, Mike Maybin, Silver Link 1994.

Hill of Howth
The Hill of Howth Electric Tramway, RC Flewitt, Transport Research Associates, 1968.
Howth and Her Trams, Jim Kilroy, Fingal Books, 1986.

Other Systems
Tram Tracks Through Cork, Walter McGrath, Tower Books, 1981.
The Giant's Causeway Tramway, JH McGuigan, Oakwood Press 1964
Giant's Causeway, Portrush and Bush Valley Railway and Tramway Company, JH McGuigan, Ulster Folk and Transport Museum. 1983.
The Dublin and Blessington Tramway, H Fayle and AT Newman, Oakwood Press, 1963 (reprinted 1980).
The Dublin and Lucan Tramway, AT Newman, Oakwood Press 1964.
The Portstewart Tramway, JRL Currie, Oakwood Press, 1968.
The Bessbrook and Newry Tramway, AT Newman, Oakwood Press, 1979.
The Clogher Valley Railway, EM Patterson, David and Charles, 1972.
The Fintona Horse Tram, Norman Johnston, WTHS, 1992.

ARTICLES
Tramway Review (Issue numbers in brackets)
The Galway and Salthill Tramway Co, W Mc Grath. (No 12)
City of Derry Tramways, AT Newman. (Nos 70-71*)*
Warrenpoint and Rostrevor Tramways Co Ltd, W McGrath. (No 12)
Glenanne - Loughgilly, Co Armagh, W McGrath. (Nos 13-14)
The Clontarf and Hill of Howth Tramroad, AT Newman. (No 37)
The Cavehill and Whitewell Tramway, AT Newman, (Nos 61-63)
Belfast Horse Tramways 1872-1904, AT Newman, (Nos 78-80)
Belfast Corporation Tramways 1905-1954, JM Maybin, (Nos 97-102)
Dublin's Electric Trams, JWP Rowledge.

Other Publications
The Story of Dublin's Tramways 1872-1949, AR Butler, **Naucht**, 1972.
Dublin Tramways, Parts 1 & 2, RC Flewitt, **Journal of the IRRS**, *(Nos 26-27)*, 1960.
Ah, I remember it well (Belfast), CJ Slator, **Ulster Tatler**, 1987.

INDEX